Tragedy... or Blessing?

Tragedy...
or Blessing?

A life altering true COVID story.

STEVE BUSCHE

XULON ELITE

Xulon Press Elite
555 Winderley Pl, Suite 225
Maitland, FL 32751
407.339.4217
www.xulonpress.com

© 2024 by Steve Busche

Illustrations created by: Joshua Busche

All photographs by: Doreen and Steve Busche

The names of the Hospitals, Rehab Centers and other health care companies, as well as all the names of the Doctors and some health care professionals have been changed for privacy purposes.

All rights reserved solely by the author. The author guarantees all contents are original and do not infringe upon the legal rights of any other person or work. No part of this book may be reproduced in any form without the permission of the author.

Due to the changing nature of the Internet, if there are any web addresses, links, or URLs included in this manuscript, these may have been altered and may no longer be accessible. The views and opinions shared in this book belong solely to the author and do not necessarily reflect those of the publisher. The publisher therefore disclaims responsibility for the views or opinions expressed within the work.

Unless otherwise indicated, Scripture quotations taken from the Holy Bible, New International Version (NIV). Copyright © 1973, 1978, 1984, 2011 by Biblica, Inc.™. Used by permission. All rights reserved.

Paperback ISBN-13: 979-8-86850-525-6
Hardcover ISBN-13: 979-8-86850-526-3
eBook ISBN-13: 979-8-86850-527-0

> "And now these three remain: faith, hope and love. But the greatest of these is *love*."
>
> 1 Corinthians 13:13 (NIV)

* Endorsements *

"Steve, I am sorry for the late text, and I hope your phone is back on the counter. I just need to let you know that I just finished your book. I picked it up around 7:30 for what I planned to be an hour until I put the kids to bed. I put them to bed and couldn't wait to get back and finish. Your writing is absolutely beautiful. Thank you for making the time to share your beautiful story – I find myself with a similar feeling as I would after a Christmas Mass or after a Holy Week service with a very full heart tonight. To feel the presence of Jesus like this is such a wonderful gift. Thank you!"

— **Jeff,** Good Friend

"Dear Steve, I can't begin to tell you what a beautiful story you wrote and what a meaningful read it was. I'm so moved by your ability to not only give such a detailed account of those long months, but also by your candor and emotional ability to write with so much passion. We all know our friends, but never "know" their inner spirit until a reason is given to share their faith, and you did amazingly well. You are truly a faith filled and spiritual person and an example to all who will read "Tragedy…or Blessing?"."

— **Mary Pat Esposito**
Former Co-Worker and Family Friend

"Before I read Steve's book, I thought that I had a good idea of what Doreen had gone through as she battled COVID and its aftermath. I talked to Steve on several occasions during the months that Doreen was hospitalized. Our church had been praying for her every week. We had received numerous updates about her condition. So as I began to read, I was simply expecting to gain a little more insight into a story that I already knew pretty well. Boy was I wrong!

What I got instead was a riveting description of Doreen's epic struggle against a virus that seemed determined to take her life. I read about a woman whose will was so strong that she fought back even when she was unconscious. I read about a husband who loved his wife so much that he spent nearly every day by her side. There were close calls, and emergency ambulance rides, and encouraging steps forward, followed by heartbreaking steps back. And through it all, two themes emerged.

The first theme was of a close, loving family who supported each other and lifted each other up during the most difficult of times. And the second theme was of God's incredible blessings and provision through it all. It is truly a miracle that Doreen survived her ordeal. And God used that miracle to strengthen the faith of the entire Busche family and draw them closer to His Son Jesus Christ. Steve's title asks whether Doreen's journey was a "Tragedy...or Blessing?" I think it was both. I think it was an earthly tragedy that God turned into a heavenly blessing. And the greatest blessing of all is that we get to have Doreen with us here on earth for many more years to come!"

- Pastor Bill Shields
First Lutheran Church, Princeton, Illinois

Endorsements

"God is Good!

I've known Steve all his life. Then I read his book and realized he was so much more than I ever knew. I never saw such a strong man, who was also fighting COVID, and the amazing love he had for Doreen. His trust in God was truly a gift from God and a gift to me. I have always declared myself a Christian, but reading this book and seeing Steve's strong faith made me a better Christian. "Tragedy…or Blessing?" is a must-read book. It was impossible to put down. Steve is an amazing author."

Grace & Peace

- **Aunt Sandy**

* Table of Contents *

Endorsements:. vii
The Preface: **My Opening Thoughts**. xii
Introduction: **Pre-COVID 19**
   - In the beginning… - xv

Chapter One: **August 2021**
   - Ready, Set, Go…**Brick Wall!** - 1
Chapter Two: **September 2021**
   - Crash & Burn - 23
Chapter Three: **October 2021**
   - Whiplash -. 65
Chapter Four: **November 2021**
   - Uphill, but Forward -. 125
Chapter Five: **December 2021**
   - Slow & Steady…Almost There - 161
Chapter Six: **Welcome Home to Our New Path**
   - Ready or not…Life changes - 219
Chapter Seven: **Blessings Found**
   - Don't Look Too Far -. 265

The Closing: **My humble prayer…** 291

* The Preface *

- My Opening Thoughts -

- This is our story as seen through *my* eyes, with *my* thoughts, with *my* beliefs and *my* opinions, through *my* experience with our Savior.

- I have written what I have written. My intentions were to reach down deep and touch the hearts and souls of as many people as I could. But my words do not have the strength to do that, only God has that kind of power…and I believe if it is *His* will, He will use it for His purpose.… *Thy will be done…*

- Everyone has their own "free will" to read this or not, to agree with it or not, to believe it or not…that's *your* opinion, *your* choice.

- I'm sure there will be many who find this story hard to believe, and some who will out-right refuse to believe it at all. That's okay. They don't have to. It won't affect their lives, and they can move on untouched.

- In the beginning… "The Big Bang" or "God created the…", you decide. But before you do, here's an analogy I heard several years ago which I believe puts into perspective the monumental difference between

- My Opening Thoughts -

complete chaos and orchestrated precision. To say the world we live in, and the universe around us, which functions with such precise timed movements, from the stars and planets above down to the tiniest molecule that has yet to be seen, stems from an explosive eruption which put everything in its proper place and function. That scenario would be like saying the Webster's Dictionary is the <u>exact</u> result of an explosion in a print factory, with all the letters, punctuation's, fonts and spacing falling on the correct page and in the precise order to form the words and descriptions we can read and understand. And, on top of that, all the words are in the correct alphabetical order. That's unbelievable! Between the two "beginning's", I pick God's majestic power and orchestrated precision. But it's still *your* choice.

- In today's material world, anyone could offer me a billion dollars to say this wasn't true and that God did not have His hand in it every step of the way. I'm not only talking about The Creation, but *our* story as well. My answer to them will simply be "No, keep it. I lived this truth."

- Throughout this journey, as my faith grew and expanded, my awareness of God's presence gave me hope, comfort and peace, and His astonishing mercy and grace has blessed me far beyond my comprehension.

- For sixty plus years I have withheld real expression of my faith to those around me. It took a tragic event to make a change. Writing this story, *our* story, has opened my eyes and my heart and has allowed me to truly express my faith in God…as you will see.

* Introduction *

Pre-COVID 19

- In the Beginning... -

Back then, I was cool...*really cool*. How could she possibly say "No?" I talked with her numerous times while she pumped gas in my pickup truck. I bought it brand new, and it was only a year old. It was pretty cool, just like me. I worked full time at the local lumberyard in town for over a year since I graduated high school, and she worked for her dad at the full-service gas station across the street. I always made sure to stop there when I was running low on fuel because she was one of the prettiest girls I ever saw. She wasn't always there though because she was still in high school, so I tried to time my petro needs on when I thought she'd be working.

We were already in mid summer of 1980 and my oldest brother Don was getting married in the beginning of September. I needed a date, and I *really* wanted her to be mine. She was way out of my league, which I totally admit, but what was the worst thing that could happen if I asked her to go with me? She would say "No", right? So, I did ask. And, she did say no...each time I asked her. Three times I asked, and she turned me down every time. She was already going "steady" with someone so she couldn't go with me. Well, at least I tried. Guess what? I didn't have a date for my brother's wedding. End of story, right? Nope, that was just the beginning.

I was bummed of course, but life moves on. At that point, all I could do was daydream of what "might have been" if she had said yes. It's funny how God has a way of intervening when you least expect it.

A little over a month later after my brother's wedding, I was at home with my folks one night after work, and the phone rang. It was in the kitchen with a fifteen-foot cord. Yep, a "landline." There were no cell phones back then, or e-mails, or social media. If the phone rang, you had to get up and go get it.

That night my mom answered and said it was for me. I took the phone and walked into my bedroom because it was right off the kitchen. I said hello, and the voice on the other end said "Hi, this is Doreen." I was caught off guard and it took me a moment to figure out who Doreen even was. I never expected her to call me because I never even gave her my phone number. I asked how she got my number, and she said she called over to the lumberyard and one of the guys gave it to her. I'm so glad he did!

After my initial awkwardness wore off, it was so easy to talk to her, like we had been friends for a long time. After a little while of talking, she said she liked to play racquetball. She then proceeded to ask me if I would like to go and play sometime. I took a deep breath in and said I would love to go and play even though I had only played it once or twice before.

So, it was set. That was to be our first "official" date. By the time we were finished and I hung up the phone, I was floating on cloud nine. Did that really just happen? How

- In the Beginning… -

did I manage to pull that one off? Looking back at it now, there's only one possible answer I can come up with: Divine Intervention. That was *our* beginning.

As it turned out, our first date wasn't the racquetball match we talked about, but a birthday party for my very close friend's grandpa. They owned a bus company, and it would be a huge birthday bash. I wasn't sure if she would be comfortable going, but she was good with it. When we went, we stayed for several hours. I don't know how to explain it, but I instantly loved to be around her. We just seemed to click.

When I dropped her off at home that night, I even kissed her goodbye. Fireworks in my world! I left to go home, and, on the way, I had a feeling like I never had before. I had several girlfriends before and kissed each one of them, but none of those were like that last kiss. I can't explain it. What my heart felt triggered many thoughts in my mind, but I kept those thoughts to myself. Besides, those few hours were only our "first" date.

We talked on the phone every day until our second date. It was the following weekend, and we spent most of the day and night together and those precious hours cemented the deal. Even though she was only a senior in high school, we got engaged a month and a half after our first date. It was December 5th, 1980.

We talked a lot about our future in that short time, and we were ready to get married right away. But (there's always a "but"), we knew our parents, and others, would freak out because we were too young, and it was *so* quick. She was still in high school after all, but only for another month or so. She would graduate early. So, to keep the peace, we decided ahead of time to get married a year and a half after we got engaged.

Problem solved…now we just had to get there. We still had to maneuver through the wedding planning stage. I have to say, that was a challenge. It didn't get between us, but it was, let's say "interesting" keeping the peace among everyone else. We managed okay, but I just wanted to get my new life started with my best friend.

Our wedding was great, like something out of the "Hallmark Channel." There was only one problem. That day flew by way too fast. Remember those thoughts I talked about when I dropped her off after our first date? Well, after we got to the hotel room for the night and we got settled in bed, I told her since it was too late to change her mind because we were already married, I had a confession to make. That probably wasn't the best way to say that, because the look on her face was a cross between startled and fear.

I continued by explaining: "I know this is going to sound corny or crazy, but when I dropped you off at home after our first date, *I knew* I was going to marry you that night. Sounds silly, right?"

I expected her to laugh or make some kind of comment, but to my surprise, she just smiled.

She looked me straight in the eyes and said, "I *knew* I was going to marry you after you left that night."

We never mentioned that to each other before our wedding night. If that's not a *true love* match made in heaven, I'm not sure what would be. Some people have said over the years that we were so "lucky" to have found our *soulmates* so early in our lives. Back then, I would have agreed with them. But, especially now, looking back at our "Love Story", I know God had **everything** to do with it.

Like every young married couple, we had the rest of our lives all planned out. We were going to have kids while we were still young so we could enjoy our later years together while we would be physically able to. We had plenty of time to save and work out the details for that later.

- In the Beginning... -

We had just started our new life together and "fell" into a deal on a house that wasn't finished. We were able to buy it about six months after we were married. That wasn't the only thing that started quickly for us at that time. Doreen was pregnant with our first child as well. That wasn't exactly as planned, but we were thrilled with our new life.

It was moving along great, and our first baby was born just three weeks after our first anniversary. It was a healthy baby boy, Joshua. Life was perfect! I had an awesome wife, a new son, and a new house that we could make into our home. I had called home from work a few short months later to check on Doreen and Josh and was surprised by the news that Doreen was pregnant again. Wow, I didn't see that one coming. It only took a split-second to feel my heart jump with joy! Our second baby would be born just four days before Joshua's first birthday. Our first baby girl, Kirstyn. Life couldn't get any better than that!

Our family was healthy and growing, but maybe a little faster than what we anticipated. We needed to slow down a little. We were still living with plywood floors and still had the second-floor bedrooms to finish. It was okay though because Doreen not only was a GREAT mom, she also was doing a phenomenal job making that house into our home. I was working full time, with as much over-time as possible, and then coming home to work on getting the house finished. Little did I realize at the time; it would actually take a few years to complete.

Several months after Kirstyn was born, I called Doreen from work to check in to see how she was doing with the kids. She surprised me once again and told me she was pregnant. This time though, we were back on our "year and a half" theme. Our new little baby girl, Heather, was born a little over nineteen months after Kirstyn. Our amazing little family was still growing and doing well. I couldn't have asked God for anything better. But He wasn't done with my family yet.

A few more months passed by, and I called home to check in. You guessed it, Doreen surprised me once again with the phenomenal news of another child on the way! A little over nineteen months later (there's our "theme" again), we were blessed with another healthy son, Bryan. Doreen and I had planned all along to have four kids, and here we were just after five years of marriage with "our perfect family" that we wanted. But we still had a long life ahead of us and I didn't think we could handle this pace anymore. I finally figured it out; I stopped calling Doreen from work. Just kidding, I called her all the time.

Then our family grew up as the years passed by, often without notice. And before we even realized it, our children were grown and starting out on their own unique journeys as we stood back and wondered where the time went. Fortunately for us, we have many cherished memories which are ingrained in our hearts and minds for the rest of our lives.

As you can see, God has blessed Doreen and I from our very beginning with an abundance of His love and grace. We certainly, of course, have had our share of ups and downs, and many trials and tribulations like most family's encounter. But, by God's will and His plan, He guided our path without us even realizing it, and unfortunately, many times without us even acknowledging His presence. Rest assured though, God's will and His plan have a very distinct direction and purpose, which will unfold as you read on…

> [11] "For I know the plans I have for you", declares the Lord, "plans to prosper you and not to harm you, plans to give you hope and a future."
>
> Jeremiah 29:11 (NIV)
>
> ———
>
> [19] Many are the plans in a man's heart, but it is the Lord's purpose that prevails.
>
> Proverbs 19:21 (NIV)

Chapter One: August 2021

- Ready, Set, Go... Brick Wall! -

"The Happiest Place on Earth." That's where we were heading. We were originally supposed to go back in August of 2020, which we obviously couldn't because of all the lockdowns, shutdowns and uncertainty coming from every direction; all because of the pandemic. You literally couldn't plan on anything at that time. Depending on what day of the week, and what channel you watched, and which experts and doctors you heard speak, and then the ever-changing guidelines from the officials in charge and add all that up with the politicizing of just about everything, and it was all as clear as mud.

How could there be so many contradictions of information when there was only one virus? In my opinion, the lack of information about the virus and the pandemic was not the real problem. On the contrary, there was an over-load of information from every direction. But how do you determine what *the truth* really is? Who do *you* believe? Who do *you* trust?

We had a decision to make about our own health and safety, and how we wanted to live our lives. So, what do we do? Many months before that planned trip, Doreen and I finally decided after watching what had happened over the last four plus years in this country, *we* simply didn't trust any of them. The politicians, the government officials, the health care officials, and majority of the media. There were so many opposing views and opinions, with each one claiming their stance was the correct one.

No matter how hard we tried to figure it all out, none of it made any sense to us. With all of that said, I couldn't help but come down to this one conclusion about what the *real* problem was: For many of those in charge and those with major influence, it was about the power, the control and of course, the money. Unfortunately, many people died. So, you ask, why won't *I* trust them? Hmmm.

Enter: The magic bullet…the vaccine. Clearly that was the answer. That was the solution to counter the evil that had entered and took control of our lives in such a short period of time. That microscopic evil creature had altered the course of human history, and despite all our science and technology and wisdom, we don't even know where or how it even got here, officially anyway. But don't worry, the people in charge figured out in "warp speed" how to hit it head on.

It only took seven to eight months to come up with a cocktail of chemicals that would combat it, or at least get it under control, or maybe even eliminate it. Well, maybe. Just get the shot they said, and you will help save the world. It doesn't matter how quickly they came up with it, just take it, no questions asked. I'm no scientist, but it didn't make any sense to me how they could have possibly tested all the long-term (key word there) effects the vaccine would have on all the vital organs and have all the answers to those questions. Common sense tells me it should take at least a few years, not a few months, to see those kinds of results.

Coming from the building material industry, I've seen products over the years where they used accelerated climate labs to see how a product would hold up in the elements over time. The lab man-made weather generally works well enough for building materials, but still, the true test is in Mother Nature's elements and time itself. There are too many variables and types of conditions in nature that you couldn't possibly test them all. So accelerated testing is fine when it comes to building materials, but I felt extremely uncomfortable in this case when it came to sticking chemicals in my body. I don't even take aspirin unless I really need to.

The other big issue that really bothered me was no one would talk about what the side-affects were or what they potentially could have been. When I watch TV and see all the drug commercials that are on, they always seem to end with a rather lengthy list of side effects, which usually seems worse to me than the problem that they are trying to fix in the first place. Yet, when it came to *this* vaccine, apparently there were no concerning side effects.

How could that be? I was so confused. And, once again, who do you believe? Who do you trust? It's not like the pandemic, which had killed tens of thousands, would become such a political hot-potato that it would hinder anyone from making such an important personal decision. Oh, wait a second, yes it did.

So, what should *we* do? Should we get the shot or not? We tried to do our own research but to no avail. The more info we looked at and listened to, the more we felt like we were going in circles. We knew we had to either decide to bite the bullet and trust our caring leaders and get the vaccine, or just ride it out and take our chances.

So, after many, many hours of going back and forth, *we* decided to wait for the FDA to fully approve it. We were hoping the FDA had not become another political arm like every other department of the government had. We thought surely they wouldn't because their decisions really could make the difference between life and potential death. I found out much later that the FDA had fully approved the vaccine on August 23, 2021. That date is important to remember.

So, it took several changes in plans because of the pandemic, but we finally decided that this time, August 5th – August 11th, we weren't going to change the date again no matter what. For two plus years Doreen and I made plans for a Disney vacation with Heather's family, only to have it disrupted because of some foreign virus. Okay, Doreen and Heather did all the planning, but I was there for moral support.

But now, enough was enough. We decided we couldn't stop living our lives and constantly be in fear from that invisible creature, so it was time to boldly move forward. Don't get me wrong, it was very stressful and very scary because of all the unknowns. Decisions were made. The plans were all in place. A good chunk of money spent. We had our tickets in hand, and it was time to head to the airport.

The day had finally arrived. It had been two years in the making, but we were on our way to Disney World. We knew it wasn't going to be like all the other trips we had gone on before, but we were prepared to deal with whatever types of new protocols and requirements that Disney had in place to keep everyone safe, and more importantly, happy. We had our face masks (lots of them), our hand sanitizers, and even our own bacterial wipes just in case we needed to do our own cleaning when we got there. The only thing we didn't bring with us was a hazardous material safety suit.

Because of the way everything was for the past year and a half, we didn't get out in public very much, so it was very strange when we got to the airport. To only see half of people's faces was very weird. It felt like we were in some kind of apocalyptic movie, and that was just the beginning. When we arrived at Disney, it was even more bizarre to me. It has been billed as the happiest place on earth, but you couldn't even see anybody smile.

Well, that's not completely true; there were many people who were wearing their face masks to protect their chins, so you really could see their mouths. And, of course, it was hot and crowded there. People, people everywhere. That part of Disney didn't change. Surprisingly though, most of the people were genuinely courteous as not to crowd each other too closely as best they could.

On our past trips, people would literally push and shove just to get in front of you. Don't get me wrong, we still encountered the teenagers that would scold people for not wearing their face masks properly (even though they weren't wearing theirs) or the occasional foreigner group (not sure what language it was) that thought the shade in the long lines only belonged to them and would hold everyone up until the next shaded area was available…for them. Overall, the crowds and their actions were far better than I expected.

And then, of course, and most importantly, we were there with the kids. We were there to have fun and enjoy being together with them. And we had an **absolutely great** time! The fun we had and the memories we made will last the rest of our lives. The rides, the shows, the eating, the swimming, and every moment in between were worth every ounce of effort and energy (and patience) that went into putting the trip together. Little did Doreen and I know at the time, all our lives were about to take a drastic turn when we got back.

We landed at Midway Airport on Wednesday, August 11, 2021. We were back. Vacation time was up. How could it be over already? It took forever to get there, and now it was all done. So, it was time to get back to reality. I can't say "normal" because nothing was like it used to be. I do have to admit though, it was also nice to be home. Now back to work and I don't just mean our jobs. There was all the work that needed to be done around the house and the care for all the animals, as well as all the other activities and events that filled the rest of our time.

One of those activities was going to be the following weekend. Harvesting the honey. That's one of Doreen's biggest passions; her bees. And that's Bryan's fault. He started with them a few years ago and then got mom involved. Then unfortunately, he got stung and found out that he was allergic to them. It didn't make any sense because he had been stung numerous times before that last critical one. So, he had to stop his love of those little creatures because it could be potentially deadly for him. I understand why they both got into that hobby; the bees are very fascinating creatures, even if you get stung every now and then. But now that we were back from vacation, we had a week and a half to get ready for the harvest on Saturday, August 21st. There was plenty of time.

That week was the usual routine; get up, go to work, come home. The only other stops were the gas station or the grocery store, and occasionally a visit with the kids. I guess you could call it our pandemic routine. The Disney trip was our only other public gathering for the past year and a half.

On Wednesday before the harvest, I stopped for gas on my way home from work. I couldn't see inside because of the semi truck parked in front of the store unloading their stock. When I went in to pay (still using cash at that point), I didn't realize I was walking into a three-ring circus. They were unloading stock and had several people in line paying for whatever.

Also, there was the Veterans group selling fifty-fifty raffle tickets, which I bought and filled out while I was standing there at the counter. That was the most people I had ever encountered there. It's usually very quiet. Oh, and nobody was wearing a face mask, including me. I was planning on my usual in and out like every other time there. I don't know if that stop made a difference or not, but that's what happened.

It was the Friday before harvest. Doreen was busy doing what she needed to get ready for the next day. We also were having Bryan and Ashley (our daughter-in-law) and the grand kids coming up from Tennessee to spend the night because they were going over to her sister's house on Saturday for a family party. They would be back on Saturday night to visit a little and then head home on Sunday. It was just a quick trip that time.

I decided I needed to spray for the thistle that was taking over in the front pasture before they got there. So, I mixed up the chemicals and strapped on my backpack sprayer and got started. I was wearing a face mask because the smell of the chemicals was very strong. I had even held my breath a few times as I sprayed because of the smell. I don't know how much time it took or how many trips back to the barn to re-load, but I kept going until it started to get dark. Later on that night, I started to get a little headache, but obviously it was from breathing in those chemicals.

The next morning when I woke up, I had a splitting headache. I must have inhaled more of those chemicals then I thought, so I took a couple of aspirins and helped Doreen get the tables and equipment set up. Kirstyn and Jason (our son-in-law) were also there to help since part of that "hobby" belonged to Kirstyn as well. They had pulled the frames out of the hives earlier in the week, so they only needed to spin the frames of honey on Saturday. Once everything was set and they started the long process, I was starting to feel a little worse, so I disappeared back into the house. They thought I went out to work in the barn.

Tragedy...or Blessing?

Nobody knew that I was on the couch in the living room until they finally took a break for a late lunch. Doreen was irritated with me for not helping, but my head was pounding so bad that I could hardly open my eyes. I was really feeling horrible. They went to town to get lunch, and when they came back, I thought if I ate a little, maybe I would feel better. In the back of my mind though, I had a feeling it could possibly be COVID. I tried to keep my distance as best I could without alarming anyone, just in case. Lunch didn't help. I was feeling worse as the day went on. I thought fortunately though, everyone was out in the garage and away from me.

Then Heather called and told me there was a giant wagon load of small bales of hay coming to our house. They were running behind, so could I meet them part way and swap vehicles and bring the wagon to our house. You never pass up a load of hay. Kirstyn had jumped in the car with me just in case we needed another driver. It wasn't that many miles, but it seemed to take a long time to get back. I didn't feel that well, but I figured it would be gone in a few days like I heard it had done for a lot of other people. Besides, I didn't even know for sure that it was COVID. Whatever it was, I just wanted to get back on the couch and didn't want to move.

They finally finished in the garage with the honey for the day, which was a lot of work. By then, I had lost track of time, and apparently, awareness. I'm sure there was supper, and that Kirstyn, Jason and their boys were there. Also at some point, Bryan and Ashley and the kids came back from her sister's and visited for awhile before going to bed. I just needed to sleep this off.

Sunday Morning, August 22nd

It was time to get up out of bed. I wanted to visit a little before Bryan and Ashley and the kids had to get going home. I felt a little better than I did the night before. Maybe it was just the spray from the pasture. We had breakfast and visited for a little while before it was time for them to leave. I didn't give any hugs or kisses though, just to be on the safe side. Saying goodbye is always tough, but not even a hug that time, now that was hard to do. Either way though, there were still a lot of tears.

Now I'm not sure what time Kirstyn and Jason and the boys had come over to help finish up with the honey clean up, but I was back on the couch and not feeling too good again. I know at some point in the conversations, COVID was brought up and Kirstyn suggested getting an at-home test.

So, they went to town to the drug store and brought one home. I was afraid of what the result might be, but I was pretty sure I already knew the answer. I was right. Positive. I had heard though it was possible that it could be a false positive. I told Doreen that I wanted to go to the Urgent Care in Dixon just to make sure.

She was hesitant at first, but I told her I wanted to be absolutely sure if it really was COVID or not. We would need to let everyone know that was around that weekend. So, she drove me there and had to wait in the car for me. On the way there, I told her I thought it would be a good idea for her to get tested as well. She didn't want to, but I convinced her that it wouldn't hurt to check, just to be on the safe side. When we got there, I went in, and of course, I tested positive. Then she went in and got tested. She tested negative. She was so relieved. So was I.

When we got home, I knew I had to call my boss Jeff to tell him the bad news. I was going to have to be off work and quarantine for fourteen days. By the time Sunday night rolled around, I was starting to really feel bad. My head was pounding again, and I just wanted to curl up in a ball and not move. I went to bed in the spare bedroom at the opposite end of the house. I wanted to stay as far away from Doreen as possible.

The next morning, Doreen got up to go to work. She said she felt fine, and she would call to check up on me. We said our goodbyes and that we loved each other, and off to work she went. I'm sure she did call to check on me, but by that time, I was getting worse. I got on the couch that reclines and didn't move. I could tell now that I had a fever.

When Doreen came home from work that afternoon, we kept our distance. Or should I say I didn't move, and she did everything. There were still all the chores to do. Cows needed water, cats needed to be fed, and the chicken's needed food, water and the eggs collected. The dogs also needed to be taken care of. She also had all that honey to bottle as well. She was like a machine until she got it all done. At that point, she was still feeling fine.

Tuesday morning, August 24th and it was time for Doreen to start another day. Same routine as yesterday, or maybe not. She got ready to go like the day before, but when she walked out the door, I stood at the other end of the kitchen and told her goodbye and that I loved her. But there was no response. She just closed the door and left. I stood in the kitchen rather dumbfounded and thought maybe she just didn't hear me. I'm sure that's what it was. At that point, all I wanted to do was to get back to bed and pull a blanket over me and hope that when I woke up, it would all be over, and I could get back to normal.

A little while later, my phone rang. Doreen was calling to tell me she had gone to the Urgent Care and that she had tested positive. She was going to come home early after she finished a few things that she knew had to be done. My worst fear had just become a reality. I didn't know she had talked with Kirstyn earlier and found out that Kirstyn had tested positive that morning as well. She also called Josh, Heather and Bryan to let them know that she tested positive with COVID and that she was going home.

I was on the couch when she got home, and she went straight to the other couch, laid down and covered up with blankets on her. It really hit her fast. We didn't speak. No television or any other electronics. Just total silence. The pups even knew something was wrong. They got up on the couch by her and laid down. All you could hear was the kitchen clock: Tick-tock…Tick-tock…Tick-tock.

At some point that day, or night (I'm not sure exactly when), she told me Kirstyn had tested positive and that Jason wasn't feeling the greatest. Their house was going to be in as bad a shape as ours. And that was just the beginning. But our two households weren't the only ones that were about to change. Heather had no idea of what was about to hit hers. Life was about to change for all of us…drastically. Now obviously Heather knew about me, but now her mom and her sister were sick as well, all within a couple days of her dad. It was all moving too fast. This newfound marathon was about to start the next day, and with no preparation.

The next couple of days would become a blur. There would be light outside when we ventured out to the living room from opposite ends of the house and went straight to the couches. When I mustered up enough energy to go outside in the morning, I went to the barn to turn the water on for the cows. It felt like had I walked for miles and used every

Tragedy...or Blessing?

ounce of energy just to lift the pump handle. I sat down and looked at the time on my phone. I waited fifteen minutes and then used the rest of my energy to push the handle back down to shut it off. I had no idea if the tank was full or not, or if it had even overflowed. I didn't care. All I could think about was that I had to walk all the way back to the house just so I could get back on the couch.

When I came back inside, Doreen never moved. She was still curled up in the fetal position just like when I went outside. We hardly spoke, and I don't recall if we even ate. If we did, it was very little. I know the most fluids we got were when we took Tylenol and Advil, otherwise the glasses of water sat there on the end tables as the ice cubes melted. Everything hurt. Light hurt, sound hurt, moving hurt, breathing hurt. There was nothing we could do about it except sleep. Other than that, we had to try and tolerate it as best we could. Neither one of us had ever experienced anything like that before, not even close.

We were physically isolated in our house, but we weren't alone. Heather had to step in and take over the situation. She had no choice. Heather and Kirstyn both live about fifteen minutes away, but Kirstyn was also down. Josh lives thirty minutes away and Bryan lives eight and a half hours away, so obviously they couldn't just run over anytime in just a few minutes if we needed help. And we needed it.

The next day after Doreen came home, Heather went to the drug store and picked up all kinds of over-the-counter medications that might help, and a pulse oximeter that measures your oxygen level and pulse. I had no idea just how important that tool would become. She also picked up Gatorade and even made some homemade soup to try and get fluids in us. When she brought everything over, she had Jarrett, Owen and Ali (our grand kids) go take care of the chores with the cows, goat, cats and chickens while she put the items she brought over on the front porch.

She then stood by the driveway so we could come out on the porch to talk with her and pick up what she had brought. She had to be extremely careful around us because of her Chronic Regional Pain Syndrome (CRPS) nerve disorder. Her doctors were not sure on how COVID would affect her system, so we had to be extremely cautious. Her visits would be short because it didn't take much for the two us to be completely wiped out. A few minutes maybe? That was now a routine that would be repeated over, and over, and over again.

It was now Friday. It seemed like we were in a bad, dark version of the movie *Groundhog Day*. Everything was the same as the previous day: light hurt, sound hurt, moving hurt, breathing hurt, everything hurt. We came out of the bedrooms and ventured to the living room to the couch that we claimed as our own dark cell; like a prison cell we couldn't manage to break out of. It held us captive, and we couldn't move.

Hour after hour we sat in silence and the only sound was the kitchen clock: Tick-tock...Tick-tock...Tick-tock. The dogs never even barked. We had the back door open so they could go in and out through the dog door because we didn't have enough energy to get up to let them out. Like the prior days, I would force myself to go out to do the morning chores for the animals. They had to have water no matter what, and we don't have an automatic water system set up to do that.

So now that the animals were being taken care of, what about food and water for the two of us? Again, I don't know if we even ate or not. I think we were both wishing as each minute passed, we would be that much closer to getting to the end of this brutal experience. Just like clockwork on this new routine, Heather and the kids would come by after she was done with work to check up on us. She came to the front of the house and the kids went to the barn and chicken coop to take care of all the chores. Doreen and I would go out on the porch just like previously, but on that particular day, I had to lean on the porch post so I could even keep my balance. I knew Heather was freaking out, but there was nothing she could do. So, back in the house we went, back to the couches. Our daily repeat was done. Or so we thought.

Call 911

After a little while, Doreen picked up her phone and made a call. The person did not answer, so she had to leave a message. As she did, I heard her leave her cell number for the person to call back, but as she was saying it, the last four numbers were wrong. I got her attention and told her that she didn't say the right number. I had to tell her twice while she was still being recorded. I knew at that point there was something terribly wrong. I got scared. What was I going to do?

I knew I had to focus on her and forget about myself. I picked up my phone and called Heather to tell her what was happening. Knowing that she couldn't come to take mom to the hospital, she called 911 to get an ambulance to take Doreen to the hospital. Since we knew the dogs would go crazy if some strangers would come in the house, we went out front to meet them. I got her a lawn chair to sit in on the sidewalk and I sat on the front porch step.

We waited over fifteen minutes. It was Amboy's big Depot Days celebration and all their emergency equipment, as well as all the other local departments around were either tied up at the event, or on other calls. Then we heard the siren and saw the flashing lights coming over the hill to our house. When they pulled in, it was the rescue squad truck from Compton.

That's another small town a few miles away. I thought they would be able to get her in the truck and get her to the hospital. One problem; they can't transport patients in a rescue truck. We had to wait for an ambulance. They were so kind and wanted to help us the best they could under the circumstances. They stayed with us and kept contacting the other municipalities to get an ambulance as quickly as possible.

As they talked with us, they suggested I should even go with Doreen and get checked out. That wasn't an option. I was afraid they would keep both of us in the hospital, so I refused to go. They finally got a confirmation that Amboy was sending their ambulance to us. Amboy is about ten miles away, so it took a little longer.

After they arrived, the paramedics checked her vitals and immediately got her ready to transport. They asked Doreen which hospital she wanted to go to, Dixon or Mendota, and she said Mendota because she hated Dixon's billing system. They closed the doors and off they went. I stood there until the lights disappeared. I went back inside. Silence again.

The decision she made to go to the hospital in Mendota would end up determining the future path for what was about to change her life; forever. It's an important decision to remember. All I knew at the time was she was going to get some help. That's all I cared about. What I didn't know though, in just a few short hours, she would be walking back in the door. They had done a CT scan of her chest and gave her fluids which helped bring her stats back up. After they monitored her for a while, she seemed to be stable enough to go home with instructions on what to do.

So, Doreen called Kirstyn to get a ride back home. Since Kirstyn was already positive with COVID and wasn't well, she made the agonizing trip to bring mom home. Crisis averted; at least temporarily. I was quite surprised when

Doreen walked back into the house. I wasn't expecting her back so soon. I'm not sure exactly what time it was, but it was very late.

We didn't say much to each other, and it was time for bed. We went to our separate rooms and crashed for the night. Well, at least I did for a while. I was completely out of it when, suddenly, I literally jumped straight up and out of bed. I grabbed my stomach with my hands. I was expecting to feel my blood pouring between my fingers. I was startled and panicked because I thought someone had broken into the house and had stabbed me. I wasn't having a dream, there were real excruciating sharp pains. The pains were so sharp and severe that I was crying.

Even after I became coherent enough and realized no one was in the room with me, I still moved my hands over my stomach expecting to feel warm blood on my shirt. The pain was real, and eventually it faded. It took awhile for the adrenaline to wear off and for my heart rate to slow down, but I finally settled down enough to go back to sleep. What the hell was that?

Friday was brutal, so Saturday had to get better. We needed to get off that hellish ride. The day started off in the same way the other mornings did. We woke up and got to the couches and closed our eyes hoping it was all just a bad dream, or should I say nightmare. Doreen appeared to be slightly better because of her visit to the hospital the night before. The IV's seemed to help her, but it turned out to be short-lived by Sunday morning.

The routine stayed the same throughout the day and early evening on Saturday, including the ever-increasing intensity of feeling like we had been run over by a Mack truck. It seemed to get worse at night. Doreen looked over at me and said she was going to call the ambulance for me if I refused to go to the hospital to at least get checked out. After what happened to me the previous night, I didn't refuse.

Since neither of us would be able get behind the wheel, Doreen called Kirstyn again to drive. At that point, she couldn't drive anymore either, so she had Jason come take me. After he picked me up and we were on our way to the hospital in Mendota, even though he didn't take a COVID test, I could tell he had it. He dropped me off and went back home. I signed in the ER, and they immediately took me to their isolation room.

After the initial exam and what I told them about what happened with the sharp pains, they ordered a CT scan to try to find out what caused it. If there would have to be any type of emergency surgery, since I had COVID, the protocols and procedures would be different than normal. The only thing they could find was I had quite a few gall stones, but the gall bladder didn't appear to be infected, so it wasn't an emergency at that point. They did a variety of other procedures and tests and gave me IV fluids.

While we were sitting there, the emergency room nurse and I talked about how much the virus had been affecting their hospital. She said prior to the last two weeks, it was rather on the quiet side. They still had cases but not as crazy as it had been earlier. But she said they had been bombarded in the last two weeks or so. She said the Delta variant had hit our local region, and people were getting hit fast and hard in just a couple of days. They were doing the best they could to try and manage the onslaught. After a few hours, and an empty IV bag, they told me I would have to "ride it out" and sent me home. The fluids seemed to help a little.

So, I called for a ride home. Poor Jason. He had to drive back to the hospital to pick me up and take me home. I don't think we spoke more than ten words total the whole way

Tragedy…or Blessing?

home. He dropped me off and left. When I came in, Doreen was still on the couch. Once again, it was late.

We talked for a few minutes, and I explained what they said about how we needed to watch our oxygen levels closely. If our levels would drop in the 80's but would go back up even into the low 90's that would be okay. But, they said, if it goes into the 80's and stays there, we were to get back to the hospital as quickly as possible. They would admit us. That's about all we said to each other that night and it was off to bed.

Sunday, August 29th

It was the day that would change our path forever. It started out the same as the days before. But I must make a slight correction on our *Groundhog Day* scenario. In our version, everything didn't happen exactly like it did the previous day. In our version, our surroundings and activities were repeating, but our sickness was getting progressively worse each day and was now accelerating.

By late morning, Doreen's oxygen levels had dropped to the low to mid 80's and stayed there. She knew she had to go. Once again, a phone call and Jason was on his way to get her. He came in the garage door and stood there waiting for her to gather her things. She picked them up and headed for the door. Not a word was spoken from any of us. We didn't say goodbye, and I didn't even tell her that I loved her. Just silence.

As I stood at the other end of the kitchen, it felt strange like I was on the outside looking in. It was like I wasn't there, but I could see what was happening. The last thing I remember that day was watching her walk out the door and thinking that she's going to get help. She was going to be okay. I turned around and went back to bed. I have no idea what transpired the rest of that day. Everything went dark.

There was no more movie plot. The next three or four days were about to become unbearable. I had no idea if it was day or night, or even at times, where I was. The pain and agony were so intense at times that I might have even lost consciousness. I don't know. I have never experienced any level of pain or illness even remotely close to that before. On the pain scale from zero to ten, it was a fifty. Everything was to the extreme: the headache, the body aches, the coughing, the shortness of breath, the chills, the low-grade fever, diarrhea, and absolutely no energy. And the worst possible symptom was gaining momentum; my will to continue.

Although most of that time remains blank, there were brief moments that I can recall. I know there were three times during that period where I prayed to God. That was the first time through our ordeal that I went to Him. I prayed, "God I can't take this anymore! Just take me and get it over with." I prayed that two more times. I think I might have even added "Please" in there. I had never been in a place in my life where I would have even considered a prayer like that before.

There was one other distinct moment I recall during that time, and that was when Heather told me the hospital in Mendota couldn't help Doreen anymore and they were transferring her to the intensive care unit at a large hospital in Rockford. I know Heather gave me all the details, but all I remember thinking – "That's good. She's being taken care of." Then the dark fog set in again. I don't know what else happened that day. That was Tuesday, August 31st.

> ⁴ **Even though I walk through the valley of the shadow of death...**
>
> Psalm 23:4 (NIV)

Chapter Two: September 2021

- Crash & Burn -

God didn't hear my prayer. Or at least He didn't grant it anyway. I don't know the time frame, but somewhere later in those few days I started to see a different picture. I kept seeing the stained-glass window at our previous little church in Dixon. It was the far front window on the right side of the sanctuary. Every time we would go to church, at some point during the service, I would stare at that window. It depicted the scene of Peter sinking in the rough sea with his hand stretched out towards Jesus who was walking on the water and had His hand reaching out. Peter's prayer in that moment was, "Lord, save me!" It was short and to the point. All those times I stared at that window; I never would have imagined that my life would encounter such a raging sea like Peter did.

From that point on, I said that prayer countless times. It brought me a sense of hope, and then I would tell myself, "Just breathe, just breathe." Gradually, that dark cloud started to lift, and I was becoming more aware of the situation I was in and what had just recently transpired. There was still a lot of fog in my brain, but I could say it wasn't quite so dark anymore; it was more of a gray. But at least things appeared to be moving in the right direction for me, slowly, but moving.

During those first few days of in-coherency, Heather and the kids kept doing what they had to because there was no other option. Jarrett and Owen even had to unload that huge wagon of hay because I couldn't even lift the bales, but it had to be done. When you have animals, you can't just take a break. Especially that year.

We had already started to feed out large bales of hay in August because there was hardly anything left in the pasture because of the lack of rain. We had five cows with seven calves. There were two sets of awesome twins that year. Add those together with the steer and heifer we kept from the previous year and one of the kid's bulls we were using for breeding, and we had a total of fifteen animals on eight acres of pasture. Oh yeah, and one goat who thought she was a cow.

Between the cows, the thirty-five chickens, the bees, the cats and dogs, there was always something that needed to be done. Now, take all of that and add two extremely sick people who lived there, and it was a recipe for a crisis. It was our family crisis. By that time, I didn't know our crisis already moved up the family tree. The numerous phone calls for support and prayers had already ramped up.

I know my brief daily visits with Heather on those first few days only made the stress level even higher on her because of the condition I was in. Now combine that with Doreen's deteriorating condition that was happening by the minute, and the level of helplessness for everyone, which was different for each person, was off the charts. The uncertainty of what would happen next was extremely stressful, except for me. I didn't comprehend yet what was happening to Doreen.

At that time, I could only concentrate on the next few minutes in front of me. I knew I had to breathe. I knew I had to get up and move. I knew I had to force myself to drink water. I knew I had force myself to eat, which started with half of a Jell-O cup per day. I knew when I had to hurry to the bathroom. I knew Doreen wasn't home. I also knew I had to get better so I would be able to go see her, and to help her. I believe when I finally stopped focusing on myself and my pain and started to focus on her, that's when I turned the corner and started to get better. I had a long way to go, but at least I was on the right path. It would just take a little time. Well, maybe a lot more time than I thought.

Over the next several days, my symptoms had started to become less severe and more tolerable compared to where I was. I still had to force myself though to eat and drink. I got up to a full Jell-O cup or a full pudding cup a day. I had no appetite, so that was progress. Even though I had very little in my system, I still would have to hurry to the bathroom to have a seat. It would end up being seventeen straight days of that exercise. That's probably why I lost seventeen pounds in a little over two weeks and why I was so weak. My energy level was almost non-existent.

When I would walk from one side of the house to the other (we have a very small house), I would have to sit down just to catch my breath. So, you can imagine what it was like in the morning for me to go out and give water to the cows. It's only around one hundred feet or so from the house to the barn. My energy level going out wasn't too bad, but coming back in from the barn was the real challenge. It looked like and felt like it was a forty-five-degree incline and 1,000 feet away.

There were numerous times when I didn't know if I was even going to make it back to the house. But I knew if I wanted to be able to go see Doreen, I was going to have to push with everything I had to get myself better, no matter what. I knew she was struggling.

Heather had caught me up on everything that mom had gone through the past week, and that Kirstyn had been admitted to the hospital for a few days in Dixon because of COVID. It didn't stop there. She then told me that both Bryan and Ashley had also caught COVID a couple of weeks after they got back to Tennessee. I had a hard time trying to keep up with everything. It sounded like everyone was doing okay, but all I could really concentrate on was Doreen.

Now that Doreen was at the large hospital in Rockford, Heather told me what the doctors were trying to do for her. They were using a BYPAP mask that was forcing oxygen into her lungs to try and keep her stats up. There were many times they even had to push the oxygen level to one hundred percent just to get her stats back on track. They were also using some kind of heated high flow oxygen machine and would switch back and forth with the BYPAP mask. They were using the two different methods to try to keep her stable.

It was a roller coaster for her. It would help a little, and then not. It would help a little, and then not. I had absolutely no idea of what she was having to go through until I got a text message from her. I think it was Friday or maybe Saturday. When she had left the house on the previous Sunday, she took her phone, her I-pad and her purse with her. She obviously had no clue of what was about to happen to her. Heather said mom was still able to communicate through text messages, but they were becoming shorter and she kept saying she just wanted to come home. She was alone and isolated.

I wasn't really prepared when I opened the text she had sent me. She had taken a selfie of herself with the BYPAP mask on. I will never forget that image. I could see the panic in her eyes and the pure terror in the expression on her face. She had typed, "Come get me, I want to go home. I love you." I burst into tears and cried like I had never done before in my life. I couldn't move. I couldn't catch my breath. It felt like I was having a panic attack on steroids.

At that moment, I completely forgot about all the pains and issues I had just experienced. The pain in my heart was overwhelming. The absolute love of my life was frantically reaching out to me for help and there was nothing I could do. I had never felt such an extreme level of helplessness like that before. Never. Not even remotely close.

Once the initial shock subsided a little, I knew I had to respond somehow. But what could I say to her that would help comfort her? I couldn't lie or deceive her by telling her something I knew I couldn't fulfill. The only thing I could say was: "I love you so much! You need to stay and let them help you get better! I love you!" I hit send. I put down the phone and cried the rest of the night.

She would continue to text everyone throughout the weekend as best she could. She had sent several of them to me, and each one was like a punch in the gut. The agony of knowing that I couldn't be there for her was immense. Each time I would tell her how much I loved her, over and over again. I tried to convince her that even though I wasn't physically there, I would always be with her in her heart. I didn't know how else to try and ease her suffering.

We had been separated and imprisoned by an invisible evil demon that took total control of our lives, and whose grasp on her was gaining strength. The darkness was overtaking the light, and we were completely powerless over it. We have always been so strong together and have tackled many obstacles in our married life over the years, but that time was different. We have never been separated from each other like that before. We had started on the same COVID journey together, but our paths were about to change drastically. In just a few hours, the life we knew and shared for so long would be altered forever.

It was now Labor Day, and I had a new visitor coming to see me. For the last couple of weeks, Heather and her kids were the only ones who had been around. Since they had been thrust into this chaotic chain of events, they needed a little break from the stressful extra curriculum. Joshua was going to come up around lunchtime to visit, and to help me with chores that day.

When he got there, we sat on some chairs on the driveway. At that point, no one had come into the house just to be on the safe side. We talked about mom mostly and what she was going through. As we were sitting there, I got another text from Doreen. When I opened it up and saw what was in the message, I said to Josh, "This ain't good." I think Josh could tell by the look on my face that something was very wrong. He was right. I handed him the phone and asked him if he could understand what mom just wrote.

There were probably thirty-five or forty letters that she typed, with some in caps. But there were no spaces and only a few of the letters had actually made a word. I didn't want to acknowledge or believe what I saw, but her coherency was obviously fading rapidly. She was getting worse by the hour. I started to freak out. My mind was going a thousand miles an hour, but my body couldn't move. It was a torture that I would have to endure, to sit there and not be able to do anything to help her. That agonizing torture would soon become my new way of life.

After we did chores, Josh left and went home, and I went back inside. Heather called a little later and told me that mom had called her and asked her for some water and for some sherbet. She was very upset because mom thought she was talking to the nurse and had no idea that she was talking to Heather. Heather also found out they had stopped feeding Doreen because it was too dangerous for her to eat in her condition. The situation wasn't looking very good and was headed in the wrong direction.

At that point, my emotions and state of mind were almost out of control, which made that night very different. From the first Saturday morning when I started to feel sick up until that night, all I wanted to do was close my eyes and go to sleep. Frankly, most of those days I barely had enough energy to keep my eyes open let alone to try and think. In the next few hours though, that would be completely flipped.

I was completely exhausted and went to bed. I put my head on the pillow and closed my eyes, but within a couple of minutes, my eyes opened, and my mind started racing. I couldn't stop thinking about the text message Doreen sent and what it meant. I tossed and turned for I don't how long until I finally got out of bed and went to the living room and sat on the couch. It was completely dark outside and silent inside, except for the kitchen clock: Tick-tock…Tick-tock… Tick-tock.

My mind kept going the entire night. I couldn't stop thinking about her and what was happening to her. It was non-stop. Every time I would hear the clock strike the top of each hour, I would close my eyes and try to talk myself into going to sleep. It was starting to get light outside, but eventually that worked, or it was enough exhaustion that finally let me sleep for a few moments.

Tuesday Morning, September 7th 2021

That would be the day that brought me to my knees. I opened my eyes when the dogs jumped down off the couch and ran to the kitchen barking like crazy. It took me a moment to realize that I had fallen asleep sitting up on the couch. I leaned forward and looked to the left and I saw Heather walking around the corner which startled me because nobody had been in the house since it all started. In an instant, I knew something very bad had happened. My first words were, "This can't be good. If you came in here, this can not be good."

There was no hiding it, she had been crying. She only said, "We need to go outside and sit. Kirstyn and Jason are on the way, too." I just followed her out the door. It felt like my heart had stopped and a thousand thoughts went through my mind during those few seconds it took to get into the garage. I thought, "God no, please no!"

Heather and I sat down on some lawn chairs waiting for Kirstyn and Jason to get there. As she started to speak, she had to fight the tears back. She told me Dr. Jake had called that morning and said they had no choice and would need to put mom on a ventilator immediately. She had to pause for a bit because I broke down and cried uncontrollably out loud like I never had done before in my life. That was supposed to be the last resort, and we had just reached it. It took me several minutes to regain some sort of composure before she could go on.

She continued with what her discussion was with Dr. Jake. She told him she needed time to talk to me first before they could do the procedure. But he told her that Doreen's stats had dropped down into the low sixties and were not going back up quick enough, so they would have to do it right then or she probably wasn't going to make it much longer. Heather had no choice; she had to make the grueling decision and give them permission to put Doreen on the vent immediately. He also told her there was a very real chance Doreen might not make it through the procedure because she was in such poor physical condition.

By now it was like an out-of-body experience. I could hear the words she was saying, but it wasn't registering in my mind that this was actually happening, or that this could even be real. But it *was* real. I cried out loud, "No! No! No!", but that wasn't going to change anything. It hurt so, so bad all the way down to my soul. I felt paralyzed, even in my mind. My world was crashing down all around me, and I couldn't even think. I couldn't even ask God, "Why?" It felt like an eternity, but I don't know how long it took before I was able to regain my senses. During that whole time, Heather had to witness my break down.

I clearly remember sitting there, completely numb, when a car pulled up and stopped. Jason got out and walked around the car to help Kirstyn get out and walk up to the garage. Up until that moment, I didn't realize how sick Kirstyn had been until Jason pulled the oxygen tank out of the car. She needed it to help keep her oxygen levels up, but at least it looked like she was able to function somewhat.

The girls and I sat, while Jason stood by their side for support. That's what I should have been doing, standing by my wife's side supporting her. But instead, I was sitting in my garage wondering if I would ever be able to see her alive again. I couldn't help it. I would just burst out crying, repeatedly. And, we had not even gotten to the worst part yet.

During one of my brief moments between tears, Heather said Dr. Jake needed one more decision to be made. They wanted it as soon as possible. She told me I needed to make the decision to allow them to do chest compression's if her heart would fail or set the order as DNR. I completely lost control of my emotions and my whole body shook uncontrollably. Never in my lifetime had I been in a position where I had to make a decision of such great magnitude. The decision *was* life or death, and it had to be for the woman that I loved more than anything else in this world. I knew that would be a decision I would have to live with for the rest of my life.

But before I would make that decision, I needed to hear from all my kids and what their opinions were about this. So, the girls pulled out their phones and called their brothers at work. Once the boys found a place they could talk, we had them on speaker phone.

Heather explained to them everything that had transpired so far that morning. Mom had been put on a ventilator and it was too early to tell how well she would tolerate it. She told them what the doctor explained to her about the chest compressions. If they had to do them, it would only cause her immense pain because of the condition her lungs were in. He said at that point, she more than likely would already be gone or at least close. They would only be causing her more unnecessary pain.

After Heather had finished, I asked each one what their opinion was, or if there was anything else they wanted to say. I told them the decision was ultimately mine to make, but I wanted to hear how they felt first. It was their mom. Everyone said in their own way that they didn't want mom to have to go through any more pain than she had already gone through. I was numb inside, but deep down in my heart I knew what the correct decision was. No matter how painful it would be, I had to tell them "Do Not Resuscitate." The decision was made. My life had just hit rock bottom and couldn't possibly get any worse.

Or could it? Having finished our family call, I thought about how difficult it was for the boys to have to go back to work knowing what had just happened. I could see the emotional toll it had on my kids who were in the garage with me. I knew how much of a wreck I was. That was the darkest moment our family had ever experienced.

While we were still sitting there in the garage, we could see how dark it was getting out to the northwest and that a storm was headed our way. As it got closer, we could hear the rumbles of thunder off in the distance. It was moving rapidly, and the thunder was getting louder.

The kids had been there for several hours already, so I suggested they get going before the storm gets here. I knew the girls didn't want to leave me alone, but Kirstyn's oxygen tank was almost empty, so they left first. Heather stuck around for a little bit longer until I finally insisted, she needed to get going before she would get caught up in the storm. It was really looking bad, and the winds were picking up when she decided to leave.

After she left, I went inside right away and closed the garage door. She wasn't gone but a few minutes when it started to rain. It had really got dark outside and within seconds, it was raining so hard that I couldn't see more than a few feet out the back patio door. I started to see some small hail bouncing off the back deck, and then it really hit. Suddenly, I heard a loud bang, and then another, and another. It sounded like there were people on the roof with baseball bats hitting it as hard as they could. I grabbed the dogs and went down in the basement not knowing if we were going to get hit again from a tornado like we did back in 2016. Just like the tornado that glanced off our house back then, the front had passed quickly, and the damage was done.

After waiting a couple of minutes, I came back upstairs and looked outside. It looked like millions of golf balls had covered our yard and the pasture. I had only seen hail that large on the news before, but never in person. By that time, the hard rain had passed, and it was just a light sprinkle. The intense storm blew through in a matter of minutes. Looking at hail that size, I knew I had to go outside to see if there was

Tragedy...or Blessing?

any damage. When I opened the garage door, I immediately saw my car. I went back inside and grabbed my phone and called Heather. She didn't even make it three quarters of the way home when I called. When I told her what happened, she turned around and came right back.

She was back in just a few minutes and was dumbfounded when she saw what my yard looked like. She was not that far away when it hit and didn't run into any hail, just rain. As we walked around, we saw the shingles on the house were damaged as well as the vinyl siding on two sides of the house. The metal roofs on the barn and chicken coop were also damaged. Then there was my car. There wasn't a single piece of sheet metal that didn't have multiple deep dents on it.

There seemed to be damage everywhere I looked. I couldn't even cry, I had no tears left. It was just six hours earlier that the love of my life had been put on a ventilator to hopefully keep her alive. And now this. I thought to myself, "How could this evil tragedy get any worse?"

Doreen was now in a drug induced coma. It was the only way to keep her body immobilized enough so it would have a chance to heal, hopefully. It would also keep her from consciously knowing what was happening to her. Thank God she didn't know. I can't imagine what it would be like to have a tube going down your throat and you can't do anything about it.

The most frightening part of all of this was all the cases we heard about since the beginning of COVID. Once people were put on a vent, there were so many casualties. It was the kiss of death. It had been in the news for well over a year now, where the vent was basically their final chance to survive. And the odds did not appear to be in Doreen's favor.

I didn't think there was any hope left, and it was crushing my heart. How was I possibly going to be able to continue with my life if half of me would be gone? I have been blessed with the perfect partner, so I didn't understand how God would want to take that away in such a tragic fashion. What could I do to change God's mind? Those were the types of questions that had consumed my mind, twenty-four/seven for the next several weeks. The outside world no longer existed. I now was living in my own tiny circle.

Fortunately for me though, I had many people around me who would help carry my burden and who I could lean on. I didn't realize just how many people there were at that point already, because I was still mainly dealing with Heather. I basically dumped everything on her because I didn't know what else to do. My body was healing, but weak, and now my mind and emotions were a moving train wreck.

I found out on that horrible day that Heather had been in contact with other people who have been helping as well. She not only was talking with the doctors and nurses' multiple times a day to get updates to share with me and her siblings, but she also had been talking with Aunt Sandy to get much needed support and advice, as well as my cousin Jim in Tennessee for medical clarifications and advise. Jim's kids were all in the medical field in some form or fashion, and his daughter in-law happened to be an infectious disease doctor.

Heather was also keeping my boss, Jeff, informed with everything that was happening as well. On top of all of that, she still had her job and her family to take care of also. I did not realize how much of my burden I gave her, but fortunately God gave her enough strength to handle it.

The next day I called Jim with questions about the vent. "Cuz, because I love you, I'm not going to lie to you. I'm going to tell it to you straight." At some point in every conversation I would have with Cousin Jim, from that point forward, he would say that exact sentence.

Since that first conversation would be about the vent itself, I was petrified about it until he explained the medical professionals had learned a lot over the past year and a half and had made huge progress on improving the odds of survival on the vent. It wasn't like when they first started anymore. They were getting better at using the vent for COVID, but there weren't any guarantees that it would work for Doreen. Up until that conversation, I had lost hope. But after we talked, at least there was a small glimmer of hope shining again.

We also talked about my having to make the DNR call and how emotional I had got over making that decision. He told me how he completely understood what I was going through because he had to make the very same decision when his wife, Sue, was going through a medical trauma with her brain tumor and had to be operated on years ago. I knew she had gone through that, but it never dawned on me before how serious and critical it was for her, and for them. Here I was asking for his help in my crisis, but I wasn't there to help them in theirs when they needed it. How sad and selfish is that?

Over the coming weeks and months, I made numerous calls to Jim day or night and asked for his help in getting some kind of clarification or explanation of what the doctors had told me. If he didn't know the answer, he would find out and call me back. I needed someone to put it in a way that I could understand. Doctors don't always explain things in layman's terms, no matter how hard they try. The help I got from my cousin Jim and his family, along with their love, prayers, support and patience was invaluable and was much needed. Jim has always had a special place in my heart ever since we were kids. But now, his whole family shares that same space as well.

So, Doreen's life was now in limbo, at least her conscience life. Her physical body on the other hand, was going to go through hell. She was quarantined in isolation in the ICU and would stay that way for another week. The only contact we had would be the few minutes Heather was able to talk with a nurse each time she would call for an update. We never knew what to expect from each call. Some calls sounded like there was some positive progress, and then the next one would be the exact opposite.

That was the beginning of the worst roller coaster ride Doreen would have to endure. She had no choice. It was like that for her hour to hour, day by day. One step forward, two steps backwards, over and over again. That was her grueling unwanted routine.

Uncharted Territory

Back at home, I had a different unwanted routine. I was no longer feeling sick, but the lingering effects were still going strong. The worst one was not being able to sleep much. I was only getting one to two hours of sleep a night. I couldn't shut my mind off no matter how hard I tried. It was the worst at night when I would sit on the couch and recline. One pup would lie on my legs and the other would lie along side of me. They would sleep. I would stare at the wolf that was painted on a "dream catcher" on the other side of the living room. Doreen loves wolves. There was a night light on in the kitchen that would cast enough light in the living room if I needed to get up. Minimal light, and only one sound, the kitchen clock: Tick-tock…Tick-tock…Tick-tock.

The only other sound I could hear was in my mind. My thoughts. There were so many, but now I also started to think about what I was going to have to do to keep things going at home. I never worried about the bills or what it took to make our household run. Doreen always took care of everything. I'm the laborer in our partnership and she's the brains.

Now, my worries weren't just singular. My only thoughts up until that point had been about Doreen and what she was going through. But now, with the reality of having to take care of the things she always handled, my mind just kicked into another gear that I didn't know I would ever have to use. There were all those financial things that were going to have to be taken care of, and now I had to think about paying bills with one less income on top of it. I called Heather the next day in a panic. What are we (notice I said we?) going to do?

Unbeknownst to me, she was one step ahead because even as Doreen was lying in a hospital bed and getting progressively worse, she had talked with Heather about our bills and what needed to be done with them. She must have known somehow that she wouldn't be coming home for a while for her to give Heather instructions on paying our bills. Fortunately, she did.

I was in new territory. I paid very little attention to our finances, including the name of our bank. Doreen always had everything under control, so I didn't have to worry about the money or our bills. But now, I had no choice. I had to learn quickly. In fact, for the first few weeks, I didn't even think about work. Up until then my boss, Jeff, had been calling Heather regularly to get the updates on us.

I finally called him myself to check in and let him know how we were doing. It was a very emotional call like so many others that would follow as time went on. His empathy and concern for us was genuine and compassionate every time. He was truly more concerned about our situation than what it was doing to the company. He made it clear that I didn't need to think about work. He said I only needed to concentrate on getting better and taking care of Doreen. Everyone there was pitching in to help cover for me, and everything was under control.

He also told me on that first call that the company had a great fiscal year end in July. He and his dad, Ron, had worked out bonuses for everyone, and they had put a nice bonus in our bank account. That news helped tremendously in lowering the stress level in my new-found financial responsibilities. We had some much-needed breathing room.

Also, out of the kindness of his heart, Jeff occasionally would send Heather a check to help cover my groceries and other necessities. His generosity, sincerity and friendship went far beyond anything I could have ever hoped for. After that first call, we would keep in touch every week after that, and I would let him know how Doreen was doing. That was all he asked of me. Just keep him posted on how everything was going with my family.

The checking account was now in much better shape, but there was a big problem. The bank's computer did not recognize Heather's computer, so she couldn't get anywhere with paying the bills. She needed Doreen's I-pad and phone, and the various passwords needed to go forward. Doreen had taken them with her and now those things were in isolation with her in the hospital.

Heather had been talking with a nurse named Jennifer, who was a very special nurse. She took whatever time needed to answer any questions Heather had for her and detailed everything they were doing for Doreen. She was genuine and sincerely cared, and she did that each time Heather called when she was Doreen's nurse. Most of the other nurses didn't go close to that extent, probably because they were so overwhelmed with patients, but Jennifer was so kind and truly compassionate. You can't fake that type of compassion. She was like one of Doreen's guardian angels.

So, Heather called and made the arrangements with Jennifer to get all of Doreen's belongings out of the hospital. We needed help getting Doreen's things home, so I asked my brother Dave if he could stop by the hospital to pick up those items since they didn't live that far away. He and my sister-in-law, Wendy, went after work to pick them up and drove them an hour down to my house. When they got there, the first thing Wendy said to me was, "You look like s**t!" It caught me a little off guard because how bad did I really look? I guess I hadn't really noticed. We stood in the garage for a while and talked until it started to get dark, and they had to get going. I was very thankful they dropped what they were doing to help us out.

As they pulled out, I closed the garage door and went inside. I walked into the bathroom and was startled. I was looking into the mirror, and I didn't recognize the person looking back at me. I thought, "Who is that?" I just stared at that image. After a few minutes of starring and asking that same question a couple of more times, I realized that person was me. It was so bizarre. What was happening to my mind?

The next day I had another strange episode. Kirstyn called and asked if I could stop by and watch our grandson Liam while she went to the doctor's office in town for a follow up. I had not driven since I got sick, so I was a little nervous about it. I don't know why I was because I've been driving for over forty-five years. So, I went. Shortly after I left, it became very strange. I looked down and saw that I was driving the speed limit of fifty-five, but it *felt* like I was going in slow motion. It was such a strange sensation. It seemed like it was taking ten times longer to get there. It was only a short fifteen-minute drive, but it seemed like it took hours to get there.

After I finally arrived, Kirstyn looked at me and asked if I was okay. I told her what happened, and she was concerned because I still had to go home. While I was there, Kirstyn helped me with my social media debut on Facebook since the word about our situation was already out there. I wanted to thank everyone for all the thoughts and prayers we had received. I also had to ask for some privacy because I (and my kids) had been getting so many calls wanting to know what was going on. I even had one as early as six in the morning.

I thought people just didn't understand that my nerves were so raw and on edge that every time my phone rang, I would jump, and then panic because I would think it was the hospital calling. By letting everyone know what our situation was, I hoped everyone would understand and give us a little space. I also promised to continue to keep everyone posted as we moved forward. Now it was time for me to go home. When I left, the drive home was close to the same sensation as the way there. I was so happy when I pulled in my driveway.

The next day I had a couple of visitors. It was Aunt Sandy and Uncle Chuck. I knew they were coming because Aunt Sandy had called and asked what kind of meals I wanted her to make. She was afraid that I wasn't eating very well. She was right, I wasn't. Anything she made was always good, so it didn't matter to me what she would bring. She, of course, went above and beyond like she always had. She made enough food to last me for a month, or longer, and there were a variety of meals that could be split up into smaller portions that could be put in the freezer. I love her cooking! She did that for me several more times throughout our ordeal. It was like having my own personal chef, but with a big perk, she loves me! We have always had a great relationship over the years, and she has always had her own special place in my heart.

Over the next few months though, the love I had for her would increase ten-fold because of everything she did for me/us. I would call her countless times, day or night, and she always had a shoulder for me to cry on. I could lean on her and tell her about anything that was happening, and she would listen and comfort me with her love and compassion. She's like having a great loving mom and a best friend all rolled into one.

That wasn't something new I had just discovered about Aunt Sandy, because she's been like that for Doreen over the years as well. They too have always had a special bond. This time was different though, I had never needed her love to this extreme before. Her unconditional love and support for Doreen and I would continue throughout our tragic nightmare without hesitation, and knowing Aunt Sandy, it will never stop. I think everyone needs an Aunt Sandy in their lives.

A couple of days later I drove again, but that time wasn't as bad as the first one. It still was in slow motion, but not quite as intense. I went to Heather's house for pizza for Ali's birthday. I had only stayed for a short time because I didn't want to take the chance driving if it got dark outside. After eating and visiting for a while, I headed back home. I made it. Driving would have to be put on hold for a while. I would not drive on my own for another few weeks after that because it made me very uncomfortable. But two days later, that was the day I had been waiting for which seemed like an eternity.

Tuesday, September 14th

Doreen would no longer be in quarantine. I would finally be able to see her for the first time since she walked out the door over two weeks earlier. I had mixed emotions. On one hand, I was so excited and anxious to see her and kiss her and tell her how much I loved her. On the other hand, I was petrified that I wouldn't even be able to recognize her, or that I wouldn't be able to handle seeing her hooked up to a machine.

I couldn't drive because I was such a mess, so Heather took me to the hospital. Since I didn't know what to expect or what kinds of policies or procedures would be in place, on Sunday at Ali's birthday, I had Heather type up and laminate a letter that I wrote to Doreen. I wrote it so Doreen could hear my words and know that I was always there with her in spirit. I had heard that even when people are unconscious, they can still hear what's going on around them. I didn't know if that was true or not, but my heart needed to let her know.

We finally got to the hospital in Rockford and walked in for the first time. The ICU department was on the second floor. My heart was pounding, and my emotions were completely raw and on edge. When we walked through the doors of the ICU, I was baffled. It looked like the department was under construction. On the left side of where we entered was the nurses' station, which was the length of the rooms directly across from it. Each room was covered with a plastic film except for where the doors would open. That portion of the ICU was where they had to create the COVID isolation rooms for quarantining patients.

There was only one nurse sitting at the station when we walked in. She looked over and said, "Heather?" It was Jennifer. She knew we were coming that day, so she asked if she could be Doreen's nurse so she could meet us. After we talked for several minutes, I asked her if it was okay that I give her a hug. She had been so kind and caring that I just wanted her to know just how grateful I was for everything she had done for Doreen and our family, and especially for this visitation exception in the isolation area. I could see she was surprised by my question, but graciously accepted my humble gratitude. I tried to hold my tears back as I thanked her for everything she had done, and for what she was continuing to do for Doreen.

She then showed me to Doreen's room. Heather went to the waiting room as I walked into her room. I stood there in fear for a moment before I walked up to her bed. I immediately burst into tears when I looked down and saw that it was my Doreen! It was the face I had desperately missed. Even though I could see through my tears the tube coming out of her mouth and the wounds on her face from the mask, those images didn't matter. It was her!

I leaned over the side of the bed and kissed her multiple times. I told her over and over how much I loved her! Time stood still again, but that time, it was good. I was with the love of my life. After I regained control of my emotions, I looked around and realized the true depth of her situation. I noticed all the IV's and wires and tubes, and the noise of the machine. It was the sound from the machine that was breathing for her.

Reality had hit hard in an instant. I held back from bursting out loud like I had done at home because I didn't want her to hear that. It took everything I had to keep my composure, so I decided to change my focus to the letter I had wrote for her. I leaned in close to her and started reading it softly out loud:

"*Doreen my Love,*

I love you so much! I love you with my whole heart. I have been praying night and day and every moment in between for God to help you get through this. You need to ask God for His help as well. There are so many others that are praying for you, that we are truly blessed to have so many people who care. I need you to stay strong and to stay focused on getting better. One step at a time. Just breathe, that's where you start. You can do this! I believe in you! I always have.

From the beginning after our first date, we both knew we would be together and that our love would be forever. Next year will be our fortieth anniversary and I love you more today than I did over forty years ago. So, I need you to continue to fight for our future. We have so many memories to make yet. I am here for you. I will always be here for you, by your side, helping you every step of the way, and so will God. We have to trust in Him that He will continue to bless us through the rest of our journey together.

Doreen, lean on your faith, be strong and determined, be comforted that so many are behind you. You are loved more than I think you will ever know. We need you to stay calm so we can get you moving in the right direction. Please let the doctors and the nurses help you get through this. They are working so hard to help you. Just focus on breathing and staying calm. We are all behind you, but you need to use your strong will to help push you through. You can do this! You are the smartest, strongest and most determined woman I have ever known. This time you will also need God's help. Use Him like I did to get through it. I used St. Peter's prayer when he stepped out of the boat to walk to Jesus. When he started to sink, he said "Lord save me."

Please ask for that same help from Him. Let Him comfort you. This is going to be a challenge, but if anyone can do it, it's you.

We have made so many beautiful memories together. You need to remember and use those memories to help you find some peace and joy to help ease this burden. I will do everything in my power to help with that as well. Please know that my heart and my love are <u>always</u> with you. Concentrate and focus on that and work on finding peace that will help you get through the tough road ahead. I know if you set your mind on it, you will make it through this. This too shall pass. Know that you are always on my mind, and that my love and devotion to you will never waiver. **I love you!**

Love, Steve"

There were many times I had to pause so I could catch my breath and calm my emotions before I could continue reading. When I finished, I laid the letter on the stand next to the bed.

Later, I asked Jennifer if she could ask whoever Doreen's nurse was each day to please read it to her. That way she would know I was with her, even if I wasn't physically there. I needed her to hear my words. Jennifer, of course, agreed to do that for me. She was truly amazing!

After I had been by Doreen for some time, I wanted to let Heather have some time with mom. When I got to the waiting room, she told me about a brawl that had broken out in the waiting room while I was with Doreen. That was the waiting room for the ICU as well as for surgeries. The group got loud and belligerent, and then there was chaos that caused injuries and security had to escort them out of the building. Fortunately, I didn't have to witness that. I was already emotionally drained.

After Heather had some time with mom, she came out and got me. Both of us ended up going back in by Doreen for a little while before Jennifer told us Dr. Jake was there and had a moment to talk with us. When we met, he said he saw me in the room but decided to stay out because, "It looked like you were having a very special private moment, and I didn't want to interrupt you." I was touched by his comment.

Then he gave us a brief synopsis of what they were doing and asked if we had any questions. I told him I had so many questions but didn't want to take up too much of his time. To my surprise, he responded by telling me to ask what I wanted, and he would take as much time as needed to answer my questions. He wanted to make sure we understood what they were doing, and to know they would do everything in their power to get Doreen better and back home.

At that moment, I knew Doreen was in the best place she possibly could be. Even though we were only there for a few hours, I was physically and mentally exhausted. I at least felt emotionally rejuvenated because I was able to see the love of my life, which my soul ached so much for. I was still having difficulty coming to grips with the reality of the situation she was in, but at least I was able to see her and touch her and talk to her. My heart needed that time with her.

The next several days would be telling. Because her oxygen levels had dropped so low for as long as it did early on, there was some concern that the lack of oxygen to her brain could possibly have caused brain damage. They said they would have to wait until the sedation goes down enough to see how much damage was done, or even if any damage had been done at all. The "wait and see" how much brain activity there would be had been extremely nerve racking and very scary to think about. You can imagine the wide range of thoughts and questions that would go through your mind with just that one uncertainty. Now add those to the very lengthy list I was already going through every waking moment that I was alone.

Also on that list were the multitude of "things" I saw which were hooked up to Doreen. It looked like miles of wires and tubes that went in every direction to different machines, plus all the IV bags of medications that were moving through all those tubes. I have no idea on how many there were, but it was overwhelming.

What stood out the most though was the distinct sound the vent itself had made. I never heard that sound before, not even on TV. The eerie thought of that machine; that machine was "breathing" for her to help keep her alive. I've watched that scene on TV before, but to see it in real life, especially when it's in your life, dwarfs any emotions or drama the directors try to create to make it believable. There's no possible way anyone could re-create the same raw intensity level that you have to go through when it's in real life, especially your life.

Even though she was technically out of isolation, I would have to wait a couple of more days before I would be able to see her again. She was still in the isolation area of the ICU. They were waiting for a bed to open in the other area of the ICU that was away from the COVID isolation rooms. During those couple of days, I began to learn about the path and the goals the doctors were going to use to wean Doreen off the vent, and hopefully get her on her way home.

The doctors and nurses continually tried to manage our expectations by telling us over and over that, "This is a marathon, not a sprint," & "No news is good news." They also made it clear that no two COVID cases were alike, so there was no distinct "road map" on how to treat each patient. I would hear that from them so many times during Doreen's stay there. Basically, it would have to be a "trial and error" approach to see what might help improve her condition.

One specific thing they were doing since she had been put on the vent was to have her on her stomach for sixteen hours and then flip her over to her back for the other eight hours each day. That was one procedure they had learned over the last year and a half which proved to help increase the success rate of survival. From the way I understood it, flipping her back and forth helped to lower the risk of phenomena which would be a potentially deadly combination with COVID.

Another important part of the vent procedure was the PEEP level they would continually monitor and adjust. I believe it was a number scale that's used to set the amount of pressure it takes to keep the lungs open, and to help push the oxygen in, and what percentage of oxygen was needed to keep the patient stabilized. It was way more complicated than that, but that was the basic idea.

When we first learned about this, Doreen was down to a fourteen on the scale. When they initially put you on a vent, they start out at a PEEP level of five and keep increasing it up until you are stable, and it could go up to eighteen or twenty. I'm not totally sure on what the maximum number could be. Regardless, Doreen had already come down some.

She would need to be down to five before they would even consider taking her off the vent. That was their goal. There were so many other steps and details they were constantly doing that I didn't know or comprehend, but that was just the beginning of my newfound education. One I didn't ask for or want.

Having skipped the multiple years of actual classroom time in health care, I learned quickly during that waiting period, there was going to be a lot more to Doreen's medical journey than I realized. I already saw the vast array of medical apparatus she was hooked up to, but I thought all those measures would just "fix her."

Come to find out, that was just the beginning stages of what would lie ahead. We were told that her case would more than likely require some type of long-term care, and she would only stay in the hospital until she became stable enough to move to the next phase. What? The next phase? I never heard anything about "phases" before. How many phases would there be?

The next phase they were talking about was a place like an acute rehabilitation hospital. Those hospitals specialize in weaning patients off ventilators. After that, it would be a long-term care facility like a nursing home or some other type of physical rehab center. What the hell? I could barely wrap my head around what was happening to Doreen at that time, let alone looking down the road, apparently way down the road, at what she would need just to come home.

Oh yeah, there was another possible outcome they discussed which totally depended on her progress. If there wasn't any improvement, or even minimal, we would have to decide on what they called "Comfort Care." That basically was just another type of Hospice care. I was spinning in every direction and didn't know which way was up. I just thought she would get over COVID in the hospital and come home. Strap in, that wild and insane emotional roller coaster had only just begun. But, they said, just take it one day at a time. That's a lot easier said than done. I was strapped onto the same roller coaster as Doreen was, but her ride would be an extreme physical torture that would dwarf my mere emotional experience.

The vent was only one small portion that her body had to tolerate. She also had to be constantly stuck with needles to check her blood gases, her glucose levels, and to check on all her other vital organs to make sure they were all functioning within the tolerable ranges allowed. Then there were all the bags of medications and solutions, including liquid nourishment which was a smaller tube also going down her throat.

Between all the IVs in her arms and all the wires that were attached in some form or fashion, they also had to physically maneuver her for x-rays, CT scans, and to flip her over regularly. Fortunately for her though, she was unconscious and had no idea of what her body was going through. There were so many things going on all at the same time, I don't know how the nurses possibly managed it all. But they did, like clockwork.

And, since her body was in such poor condition, she had a difficult time tolerating any movement they did with her. Her stats would tank, and they said she would become anxious. She obviously couldn't communicate because of the drug sedation they had her on, but they could tell by how her body was responding that her system was not tolerating it very well. Sometimes her stats would show signs of improvement and make a step forward, and then there so many times that everything took three steps backwards. That was the on-going ordeal her body would have to go through hour by hour, day by day, week by week.

Sunday September 19th

Finally, the day came that I could see her again. She was in a regular ICU room. I was still nervous and unsure of what to expect, so Heather was able to drive us there to see mom. We would both be able to visit Doreen together, and hopefully get a chance to talk with the Hospital's primary Pulmonologist, Dr. Hanson. We heard his reputation made him one of the best in northern Illinois and he was highly respected, which gave us some comfort and hope. As Heather and I found the correct area of the ICU and started to walk down to Doreen's new room, we walked past a doctor in a white coat, and I saw his name badge. It was Dr. Hanson.

We introduced ourselves, and he said he would show us to her room, and we could talk. We walked towards her room and stopped a few times as he explained her situation to us. As he went through the list of possibilities of what we might encounter throughout the process, he ended up with the possibility of Doreen needing a lung transplant.

He immediately followed that shocking information with, "But we're not to that point yet. That's way down the road. There are many other steps that would need to be done first."

He had barely finished his sentence when I responded with a few questions. "In order for a transplant, you would need a matching donor, correct?"

He answered, "Yes."

Then I asked, "If I'm a match, can I donate one of my lungs? I have two. Can I give her one of mine?"

He paused for a second and went into an explanation that it wasn't possible, and then finished with, "...but the lungs and the heart are the only two organs that cannot be transplanted from a living donor."

I understood what he had just said, but I looked directly at him and asked, "But if I *am* a match, can I give her *both* of mine?"

I could see he was totally caught off guard and looked somewhat shocked and dumbfounded that I would ask such a question. He obviously didn't understand that my love for Doreen was so strong; I would be willing to give up my life for her. I would do it in a heartbeat, with no hesitation. My love for her means more to me than life itself. I understood exactly what I was asking for. I also knew Doreen was a strong enough woman who would be able to handle living on her own without me physically there. And I know I can not do the same without her. I may be going out on a limb here, but I'm pretty sure he never had anybody ask him that question before.

It took him a moment, but he finally replied, "Let's not worry about any of that right now, we have a long way to go before we even come close to a transplant."

I was so caught up in the moment it didn't dawn on me that Heather was standing there the whole time and heard what I asked. I found out later it had really upset her because if they would do what I requested, it would be possible to still have her mother around, but she would be guaranteed to lose her dad. And she was afraid of the possibility of losing both her parents. I only hope that she and everyone else can understand my intentions and where my heart lies, then and now, and as long as I live.

We finally made it to her room. Dr. Hanson finished explaining what his plans and goals were for her and had to move on to his other patients. I felt really good that he was involved with Doreen's case. Once again, I was amazed at the level of compassion and care that we were receiving. Doreen was in the right hospital.

After he left, I noticed the room seemed different. There was a large column at the head of the bed which looked like the central command center. Everything seemed to be attached to it one way or another. There still were miles of wires and tubes like before, but the room sounded very different.

Her other room had an exterior ventilation system which pulled air to the outside. I'm not sure if that make-shift system altered the sound of the ventilator Doreen was on, but her vent in this new room barely made any noise. You could hear it, but it wasn't so pronounced. Partly because there was a TV up in the corner of the room by the doorway, and it was playing soothing tranquil music very quietly and was showing beautiful scenery that scrolled on the screen.

It was a completely different atmosphere than I had envisioned. The nurses told me the music and scenery help bring a sense of peace and calm to the room which can help the patients. I know it helped me be calmer and more relaxed.

It would stay like that until the alarm bell would go off on Doreen's vent. The first time I heard it, I was terrified. I thought it was an emergency and I expected people to come running in from every direction to help. That didn't happen. I was told it was just an alarm and not necessarily an emergency.

But every time it went off, it would startle me, and immediately my heart would start pounding at the fear of what could be wrong. It would raise my level of anxiety. Then the nurses would calmly walk in and turn the alarm off and check to see what triggered it. It was highly sensitive to any kind of change in pressure based on how Doreen's body was trying to breathe. By that time, the vent wasn't set to completely breathe for her. It was set up more as a guide to assist in helping her body start to breathe on its own again.

Up until then, the tube for the vent was still down through her throat as well as her feeding tube. Dr. Hanson had explained they would have to take the tubes out soon because they could cause permanent vocal cord damage after fourteen days. But with COVID patients, it was possible to go as long as twenty days. We would have to decide soon about changing the vent over to a trach tube and add a PEG feeding tube or pull her off the vent entirely. It was explained that the tube currently down her throat was like breathing through a long skinny straw, but a trach tube which goes directly to the lungs would be like a larger very short straw that would be more comfortable and easier for her to breathe.

We knew there was only one right option. Put the trach and PEG feeding tube in as soon as possible. Maybe that would help with the anxiety they kept talking about every time they tried to adjust her sedation meds, or when they would lower the settings on the vent. She was never an anxious person before, but if you are struggling trying to breathe through a long skinny straw, even if unconscious, wouldn't you naturally be anxious? That made sense to me anyway.

I was ready to have them do the procedure right then and there, but there were still a couple of days to go before the fourteen-day time limit. He still wanted to try and wean her off before having to do any surgical incisions that would leave a lifetime reminder on her neck. I trusted Doreen in his hands, so we waited a few more days.

Those days would not be a calm waiting period. It was like riding a wild bull in a rodeo while being on an intense roller coaster…in the dark…going backwards. Imagine what that would look like. Now keep that image in your mind because we would be on that ride for a long, long time to come. Doreen's very existence had no choice but to ride it out.

Any time they would try to lower her sedation's or change the settings on the vent, her body wouldn't tolerate it, and they would have to change it back to where it was, or even worse, they had to increase the dosage of medications to get her stable again. Anything they would try didn't seem to work, at least not very long. Back and forth we went. Back and forth again and again. The only thing we could do was to wait, to hope and to pray.

Since we felt so helpless and had no idea of what to do while we were there, we would keep track of levels of the various drugs she was on, and what her stats were while we were there. I guess it was our way of trying to see any progress forward, or backwards. We continued with that regiment for the whole time she was there, so when we would leave for the day, we could let the rest of the family know where she was at for that day. Every evening then would be spent calling my other kids to give them the details about mom. We did that every day, but at least that routine would make us feel like we were helping her in some way.

Another way we were able to help Doreen was when we brought up her favorite blanket that had a wolf on it, along with her favorite hand lotion. Another one of Doreen's special nurse's named Kayla told us it was okay to bring up something from home that could help comfort Doreen. Since her hands and skin were so dry, it would be good to use the lotion she was used to. It would not only help Doreen, but it helped us feel useful as well.

By that time, the kids had their schedules arranged so I didn't have to drive and go by myself. I would say by that point in time, I was only fifty percent at best. I was not comfortable with driving, or with having to talk to any doctors and nurses on my own. I couldn't focus on anything but Doreen just lying there motionless, let alone of trying to retain any important information that might be crucial in making any potential critical decisions for her.

I wasn't sick anymore, but I certainly wasn't anywhere even close to being back to normal. Physically, mentally or emotionally. I was really struggling with the reality of the whole situation. I needed all my kids to lean on. At that point, I was still hoping it was all just a bad dream, and I would wake up and everything would be like it was before this terrorizing nightmare.

Wednesday the 22nd

The day finally arrived when they would clear her throat and remove the tube which was so hard for me to look at because it made me anxious. I knew it was the very thing that had kept her alive, but now she would have something that would be less invasive and more comfortable for her to breathe. Since Josh didn't work on Wednesday's, he came with that day.

I got very emotional when we walked in her room. I could see her whole face for the first time since she walked out on that Sunday almost a month ago. But now I could also see all the sores on her face from the BYPAP mask, as well as the sores on her lips and even on the inside of her mouth from the tube. I was so focused on her face that it took me a few minutes before I even noticed that the vent was now attached to the trach tube in her neck. She looked more at ease breathing, which made me less anxious.

They were also supposed to put in the PEG feeding tube at the same time, but apparently like everything else, there was a shortage of parts. They said they usually do both items in one procedure so there's less movement and agitation for a critical patient. In Doreen's case though, it would have to be done in two procedures. They would put the PEG tube in the next day as soon as it got there. It would have been better for her to have them both done at the same time since her body was in such poor condition, but there was no other choice.

When the next day came, it was Heather's turn to bring me up there. We were only there for a short time when they came to get Doreen for the PEG tube procedure. The timing was perfect because we also had to meet with Carrie who was the liaison person from the Acute Rehab Hospital in Sycamore. She took us to a consultation room so we could discuss what the next steps were for Doreen. She explained that their facility was not a standard hospital because they didn't have an emergency room or an operating room. Other than those two services, they have everything else full-service hospitals do.

She said their hospital specialized in weaning people off ventilators. They have multiple locations around the country and are one of the largest transitional hospitals in the country. They also had a full line of specialized doctors that could cover everything Doreen would possibly need. It didn't even matter what kinds of medications Doreen would be on because they even had their own pharmacy.

But there was a waiting list to get in. We also had to wait for the insurance company to approve it first. The approval process from the insurance company would be a weekly routine. Their approval dictates where you can go and how long you can stay. That was nerve racking just by itself.

Carrie explained that once it would be approved, their facility would be able to tie into the current hospital's computers and monitor Doreen's case in real time. They had access to everything that was being done to Doreen as it was happening. I knew that the Rehab Hospital in Sycamore would be the perfect place for Doreen to go next. So now it was a matter of waiting for the approval and for a bed to open. Hurry up…and wait.

So far so good, it felt like we were on the right track. The next day I had to go to my doctor's office for a chest x-ray. I was still coughing quite a bit, and I was always trying to catch my breath. It had never dawned on me before how much air it takes just to complete a sentence. Kirstyn was able to take me to my doctor's appointment, but I needed a ride to Rockford to see Doreen. Fortunately, I was able to get my brother, Don, to take me up that day.

When he got our house, I was surprised to see my sister in-law, Vicki, and my niece, Brittany, had come with as well. It was nice to have the extra support. Since Doreen was in the ICU, only two people were able to go in at a time. Don and I at first, then he switched and let Vicki come in. It was a somber atmosphere in the room, and we talked quietly to Doreen and each other. I was on one side and Vicki on the other.

I was looking at Doreen when she suddenly opened her eyes for a moment and closed them again. I was startled and wasn't sure if I just saw what I thought I saw. I looked over at Vicki and she mouthed "Oh My God." It really did happen. That was the first time I saw her open her eyes. My heart jumped with joy! From that moment on, we both watched intently to try and catch another glimpse of hope, or dare I say, witness a miracle?

The clock kept moving. Then a little while later, Doreen tried to pick her arm up to move it. Once again, I looked to Vicki for confirmation, and she saw the same thing. We both cried at what we just witnessed. Doreen was fighting to come back to us, and I knew at that moment, there couldn't possibly be any major brain damage. That *was* the miracle I had been patiently waiting for. We didn't stay much longer after that because I could only handle being at the hospital for a few hours at a time. This time though, I could hardly wait to get home and tell the kids what mom just did.

It looked like she was finally moving forward. But not so fast. During the next several days we went back to the rodeo/roller coaster. The game plan was still the same, to try and lower the sedation meds and to wean her off the vent. The fentanyl was the scariest one of them all. With all the horror stories you hear about, it's hard to handle when you see an IV bag of it behind a locked case with a tube going directly into the arm of the person you love. What made it even harder was when they told me the number I saw on the machine was almost at the max dosage a person can get.

Every time they would start getting the dosages down on the different drugs, Doreen's body just wasn't tolerating it. I explained to the nurses that she always had a difficult time coming out of any kind of anesthesia, and they should try lowering the dosages in smaller increments. I'm not a doctor, but I know my wife. So, the cruel ride continued. One step forward and two steps back.

By now it was Monday, and we finally got word the insurance company had approved moving Doreen to Sycamore. But we still had to wait for a bed to open. And par for the course, Doreen had a fever and wouldn't be released by the hospital until it came down. Once again, it was good news bad news. Just to clarify, not every day necessarily was either good or bad. There were many days that were just in limbo. No movement, just flat. Those days didn't help to calm the nerves or give rest to my emotions, but at least it wasn't going backwards, right?

I believe it was the next day when Heather and I were there doing the usual routine of staring at Doreen with all her attachments. We were just hoping to see a positive sign. While writing down our daily update info, we had an unusual conversation with Doreen's nurse Kayla. She had been Doreen's nurse a few times and was a very special nurse just like Jennifer.

I need to mention two other nurses, Molly and Hailey, who were also extremely special nurses. The level of care and compassion they all showed to Doreen, and all of us, was beyond extraordinary. Not only could you see their commitment to Doreen, but you could actually *feel* their genuine concern for her. Even though the health care system had been overwhelmed by the pandemic, you could tell they gave from their hearts. They truly were Doreen's guardian angels while she was there.

Now, I thought the conversation we had with Kayla that day was unusual because of a comment she had made while we were sitting there. She told us we were not the normal family they were used to seeing. She said it was because we were there every single day to visit, and we were always friendly and kind to all of Doreen's nurses and everyone who was taking care of her. I thanked her for her compliment, but I was somewhat confused.

I asked her, "How could anybody have a loved one in the hospital, especially one in the ICU, and not go visit? On top of that, how could anybody treat or speak harshly to the people who are caring for their loved one?"

She replied, "You would be surprised!"

She went on to say the nurses and staff have way too many people who yell or cause a confrontation in some form or fashion. I was dumbfounded. That was hard for me to comprehend. I'm sure it was because of their frustrations from the situation they were in, and probably from being overwhelmed. But still, it didn't make sense to me that someone would take it out on the very people who were helping take care of their loved one. To me, kindness always goes a lot farther than anger. Our family certainly appreciated everything they had done and were continuing to do for Doreen. Their skilled high level of care and compassion continued the rest of the time we were there.

It was Thursday, September 30th. The day had finally come, and her fever was down. All the stars were aligned, and she was good to go. All the arrangements had been made, and she was on her way to the next step of her journey at the Acute Rehab Hospital in Sycamore. We made it through the agonizing month of September.

[28] "Lord, if it is you," Peter replied, "tell me to come to you on the water." [29] "Come," he said. Then Peter got down out of the boat and walked on the water to Jesus. [30] But when he saw the wind, he was afraid and, beginning to sink, cried out, "Lord, save me!"

Matthew 14:28-30 (NIV)

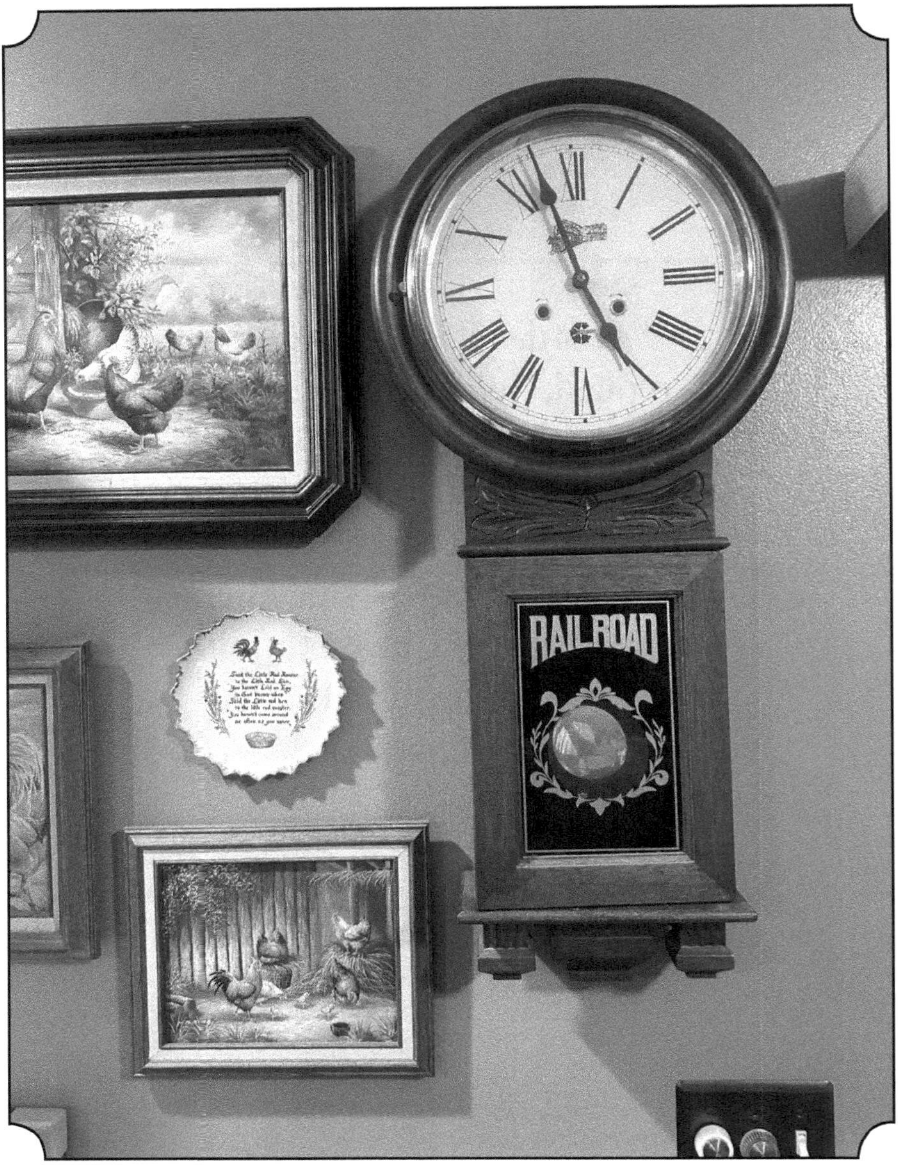
RAILROAD

Chapter Three: October 2021

- Whiplash -

She made it to the next phase in this hellish living nightmare. We were done with the hospital in Rockford because they had done everything they possibly could for her. Now it was time for the Acute Rehab Hospital in Sycamore to do their part. It was about a fifteen-minute shorter drive for us between the two, but the traffic in Sycamore was not nearly as congested or chaotic as it had been in Rockford. By now I would take less stress no matter where it came from.

Even though I wasn't feeling the ill-effects of COVID anymore, the lingering after-math still weighed heavy on me physically, mentally, and emotionally. I was lethargic and it felt like I was constantly in a fog. But it wasn't about me. I knew I needed to focus on Doreen and what she would need to come home.

The transfer to the new facility had not been an easy ride for Doreen because of her physical condition. Since she had arrived there late Thursday afternoon, we were asked to give her a full day with no visitors so she could get accustomed to her new surroundings and settle in and get some much-needed rest. They said even though she was still fully sedated, she would need some time to adjust to all the new activity and sounds around her, and especially getting acclimated to the new ventilator.

Even though it was a different vent which served the same purpose, like any machine, each can operate in its own unique way. Just like two of the same model cars can feel and drive completely different from each other. We understood what they were asking, and we certainly didn't want Doreen to have any more added stress on her system than she already had with the move. So, we waited until the next day.

Saturday, October 2nd would be dual emotion day. On one hand, I was very nervous and scared of going to see her for the first time in the new facility. There was the uncertainty of not knowing what to expect when we got there. Where do we go? Who do we talk to? What are the protocols? Are they going to be as nice as the last place? It had taken a little while, but I had finally become comfortable at the other hospital and now I had to start all over again with a different place. Obviously, I was very nervous.

Now, on the other hand, I was also excited because Bryan and Ashley and the kids were on their way up from Tennessee that day and they would be at our house later that evening. Ashley is a schoolteacher there and they were off for a week for their fall break, so they decided to come up for a few days to see mom (and me).

I still hadn't driven by myself yet at this point, so Heather went with me to Sycamore for the first time. I not only needed a chauffeur, but there also was some initial paperwork that we would have to sign. When we got there and walked up to the door, we had to wait to get buzzed in. As we walked inside, we had to stop immediately to get our temperature taken and recorded, and we had to sign in and tell them who we were visiting. They had a strict visitation policy of only two people a day and their normal visiting hours were Monday to Friday, 2 p.m. to 6 p.m. and no weekends.

We had made special arrangements ahead of time because of the timing of Doreen's move, and we also asked for special arrangements for our out-of-town kids for Sunday and Monday. They were very accommodating and understanding. They showed us to Doreen's room in their ICU department which was very different than the last place. Rockford was a very large general hospital with multiple floors and so many hallways you could get lost and easily turned around. The new hospital was a much smaller facility with just a single floor which made it very easy to figure out.

The facility was licensed to handle around one hundred beds. However, during the pandemic, they were only using around forty beds or so. The liaison, Carrie, told us they found that people were getting better faster when they didn't have another patient, along with their visitors, right next to each other in the same room. That's very unusual in today's business climate, but I'm sure the mandated COVID protocols help dictate much of those arrangements.

I felt more at ease after we were there for a little while and talked with the ICU nurse, Sarah. She took the time to explain to us on what they would be trying to do for Doreen, and what some of the different protocols they had in place because of the pandemic. She was a nice lady and was very accommodating. I knew that was going to be a great place for Doreen to be in. We only stayed for a few hours though because they had moved up the sedation meds to keep her calm and resting from the strenuous move.

Even though the transfer was almost two days before, she was still struggling a little with the third ventilator at that time. She had been on the other hospital's ventilator, transferred over to the ambulance's ventilator, and then transferred over to this new ventilator when she got there. That had been a major stress on her lungs and her system. But she was at least stable at that point. I gave her a kiss, told her I loved her, and then said I would bring a surprise for her tomorrow. Then we left and went home, and I waited for my Tennessee kids to get there.

The timing was perfect for our visit. I really needed to see them, especially Bryan. I knew it had to be hard for them to be so far away during that time, and feeling like there was nothing they could do to help. I knew that same helpless feeling they had, and I was here. Even though I would talk to Bryan every night on the phone, it was going to be nice to catch up with everything in person. There had been so many tears we shed over the phone, but at least now for a short time, we could follow them up in person with a hug.

Just like anything else, when you are waiting for something to happen, time seems to drag on. After hours of waiting, they finally got here. We stayed up and talked for hours before it was time for everyone to go to bed. Bryan and Ashley took Doreen's room, and the grand kids took my room which was the spare bedroom. Now the kids were finally settled in for the night to get some sleep after their long day of travel, and I was on my familiar couch. It had been a very long day for everyone.

The next morning after everyone was up and had breakfast, Ashley and the kids went over to her parent's house to visit with them for the day. Bryan and I went to go spend some time with mom and see where her new place was. Since I only had been there once for just a few short hours, I was still a little uncomfortable going to the new facility because I wasn't familiar with them yet. I knew it was far worse for Bryan because the last time he had seen his mom, she was just fine. That would be the first time he would see his mother on a ventilator and completely unconscious. I knew how difficult it was for me, and for his siblings to see her like that, so I knew he would have a hard time with it. It was gut-wrenching when you had to see your loved one in that condition.

When we got there and checked in, we walked a short distance to the ICU section and went into her room. I could immediately see the stunned look on his face and the tears in his eyes. I could feel the pain in his heart. That was the same heartbreaking scene I had witnessed with my other kids the first time each of them saw their mom in that same position.

It took some time for the shock to subside, but we finally were able to talk a little about what the game plan was going to be moving forward. It was very difficult for us to try and have a "normal" conversation in that setting because we never had to deal with anything like that before. Our family has been fortunate enough over the years that any hospital stays have never had any extreme measures like this before.

Most of the time while we were there, we both just looked at Doreen and stayed quiet. After a few hours of watching the machine and the non-stop care of the nurses, we left to go back home. We were both exhausted. I don't know how it's possible to have no physical activity yet be completely drained. We stayed up late again that night talking before everyone had to get to bed. I stayed on the couch like so many nights before, listening to the kitchen clock: Tick-tock…Tick-tock…Tick-tock. After several more hours, I eventually went to sleep.

Monday Morning, October 4th

Everybody took their time getting up, having breakfast, and getting ready for the day. We weren't in any big hurry because the visiting hours didn't start until 2 p.m. anyways. This time though, Ashley would go with Bryan and I to see mom. Once everyone was ready to go, we took the kids and dropped them off at Ashley's parents for the day, and then went on to Sycamore.

Since Ashley was driving and had the GPS set to go there, I was able to focus on our conversation about Doreen. We talked about how the journey for mom had been so far, the ups and downs with good days and bad days with no consistency. I knew they had already heard most of what I was telling them because I had called every night, but somehow, I thought they would be able to understand better now that they were here in person. I'm sure they already completely understood the situation with mom, but realized I just needed to talk about it.

When we got there, we went through the new regiment to get in. As we walked into her room, I glanced over at Bryan and Ashley to make sure everything was okay. No matter how much you think you're prepared to see and deal with someone you love in a situation like that, it still hits you hard like running into a brick wall. Even though Bryan had been there the day before, I could see it was really taking a toll on him. Just six weeks earlier, mom was fine, and everything was normal. Now, she was lying in front of them completely motionless and frail with so many wires and IV tubes, and a machine to help her breathe.

While we were there, one of the nurses came in and told us they had taken an X-ray that morning and had found something that didn't look right. They were waiting for a technician to come in to get a CT scan so they could get a better image of what the X-ray had showed. They were going to have to take her out of her room and didn't know how long it would take. Since we had been there for several hours by that time, we left and went home to wait it out. They told us they would call and let us know what they found. Somehow,

I knew it wasn't good. I had a bad feeling that something was very wrong.

We spent the rest of that evening at home talking and waiting to hear on what they found on the CT scan. It was getting late, so they put the grand kids to bed. Bryan, Ashley and I stayed up waiting for that call.

It was about 11:15 p.m. when my phone rang. It was Heather. She said the rehab hospital called and said they were going to send mom back to the hospital in Rockford for an emergency surgery. They found "free air" inside of her which could be lethal. They couldn't tell where it was coming from, so that's why they needed to send her back right away for the surgery.

We were supposed to wait for the surgeon in Rockford to call us after he examined her, and then he would let us know what the options, if any, would be. Heather said she would stay up and wait for the call, and so would I. I told Bryan and Ashley to go to bed, and I would let them know as soon as I would hear something.

I sat on the couch, like I had done for so many nights before, but that night, I was completely paralyzed in fear. That would be the darkest and the most excruciating night of my life. Doreen's life was literally hanging in limbo, and I didn't know what was happening to her, or even if she was still alive. I had to just sit and wait.

That damn kitchen clock: Tick-tock…Tick-tock…Tick-tock. It was torture. Between that clock and the million unanswerable questions that went through my mind, I felt like I was going to burst. I have dealt with some tough times in the past, but this was ten thousand times worse than all the others combined.

The waiting was pure torture. Every minute of every hour was driving my mind into a frenzy that wouldn't slow down. But I had to be quiet because everyone was sleeping. I grabbed a pillow and put it over my face and cried uncontrollably so many times I couldn't count. I didn't understand why it was taking so long for the surgeon to call. Did she get there, and things were so bad that they had to take her into surgery without calling? Or did the ambulance get in an accident, and she didn't even make it there yet? Or the most gut-wrenching question: Did she die? Why wasn't anybody calling?

Those were the types of never-ending questions that constantly went through my mind that night. The only thing I knew for sure was that she left Sycamore around 11:35 p.m. It should have only been a thirty-minute ride to Rockford. The clock struck 1 a.m., then 2 a.m., then 3 a.m., then 4 a.m. And still no phone call. It was like she had vanished without a trace. My head was pounding. I was absolutely going out of my mind.

Then, just before the clock struck five, I couldn't take it anymore. I completely broke down. I hit the absolute lowest, most raw emotional state that my heart and soul could possibly go. My very being was crushed and the tears streamed down my face. It felt like there was some kind of invisible g-force pushing me down into the couch, and I couldn't move a muscle. I was frozen in place. I just hit bottom.

I cried quietly out loud: "God...I got nothing left..." I was sobbing uncontrollably. "I... got... nothing... left." At that very moment, everything seemed to stop. I no longer heard the clock. I couldn't see anything through my tears. I couldn't even feel my heartbeat. My mind suddenly was completely blank, and I was no longer sobbing. It was as though time itself had suddenly stopped. I knew that I was conscious, but everything was very still, in complete silence. Then, out of the deafening silence, I heard a voice in my mind and felt it in the depth of my soul say just two words:

"Trust God"

Stunned, I just sat there in silence. Then my mind was on the move again, but I didn't know or understand what had just happened. I didn't know if I was dreaming or if it was just an illusion. Suddenly, I heard the clock strike five. I then noticed my eyes were clear and I could see, and I could feel my heart beating again, but now with less anxiety. At the same time, it felt like the intense pressure that had been pushing and holding me down had now been lifted off my shoulders and I could move again. I just sat there baffled for a while replaying in my mind what had just happened.

"Trust God." Each time I would say those two words in my mind, I would re-live that very moment. I could still *feel* it. Whatever that was, it was *real*. I will never, ever forget that exact moment. I couldn't comprehend it at the time, but I had just received a priceless reminder from my Creator, one that I should have already known. Little did I know at that moment, in just two short hours, that reminder would test my faith.

It was a little after 7 a.m. when my phone finally rang. It was Heather. The surgeon had just called. He told Heather what all the issues were, and in his opinion, Doreen needed emergency exploratory surgery to find where the "free air" was coming from. She told him she needed some time to discuss it with me first to get the okay. He told her there wasn't much time because of Doreen's condition, but he would call back by 8 a.m. to get our decision. I hung up with Heather and went to wake up Bryan and Ashley to tell them what was going on. There was now a frenzy of phone calls to the rest of my kids to alert them about what was happening.

At exactly 8 a.m., the surgeon called back and talked with me. He explained what he found with his examination and the scans. I asked if there where any options, and he said there were just two. He could operate to try and find where the air was coming from, and then try to fix it, or don't operate and see what happens. I was petrified at the term "exploratory", so I asked him if we could wait to see if the air might dissipate and repair itself on its own. He replied that was an option, but if we chose to do that, we would need to call Hospice. She wasn't going to make it because she was so weak and was barely hanging on as it was.

He followed that up with, "With the condition she is in right now, she's barely a candidate for surgery as it is. If you wait much longer, I don't know if I will even be able to take her. If she deteriorates any further, I will refuse to operate on her. She may not even make it off the table as it stands right now. So, what do you want to do?"

I was in shock. It felt like I had just been hit head-on by a runaway freight train. It took a moment to regain my composure. There was only one obvious answer: surgery. I explained we needed at least an hour to get everyone up there, and I wanted to see her before she went into surgery. He told me he couldn't promise that because he didn't know how long she could wait. If he thought it was time to go, he was going to take her whether we made it there or not. I asked him to at least try to wait but told him he could do whatever needed to be done if it was absolutely necessary.

By that time, all my kids were doing what they had to so they could get there, hopefully in time. Heather left work and was on her way to pick us up. Ashley was getting the kids ready to go to her folks, and then she would get a ride to the hospital. Josh and Natalie were leaving work and meeting at their home so they could get up there together. Jason was leaving work to drive up by himself, and Kirstyn was on her way to our house to ride up with Bryan, Heather and I. Everything was happening so fast.

As Heather drove quickly, Kirstyn sent out a cry for prayers to the rest of our family for everyone to pray right now for Doreen. She needed everyone's prayers immediately, and so did all of us. It felt like my heart was going to jump out of my chest as I called Aunt Sandy and Jeff from work to tell them what was happening with Doreen. Please, everyone, pray for Doreen!

We made it there in record time to the emergency room. They took the four of us back to the room where they were prepping her for surgery. There were multiple people there getting her ready, including the surgeon, Dr. Roswell. While he was explaining what he would be doing, he told us two more times that he didn't know if she was strong enough to handle the surgery, or even make it off the table.

It felt like my heart was being crushed and my world was collapsing all around me. I had completely forgotten all about what had happened just a few hours earlier. I could only focus on the few precious seconds in front of me. I asked Dr. Roswell if we could have a few minutes alone with Doreen. He agreed to a couple of minutes before they would come in and take her. Time was not on her side, and it was cruel to us.

I have known and been around Doreen for over forty years of my life. How could I possibly tell her everything I needed to say about how much she means to me, and how much I love her in just a few short seconds? And not just me, Kirstyn, Heather and Bryan had their love to express to mom as well. I had been standing by the head of her bed from the moment we walked into the room. As I leaned over to kiss her and tell her I loved her, my tears fell on her face. I knew I needed to step back so each of the kids could take their moment with mom also.

When I stepped back in, I did something I never had done before with my children. As I held Doreen's hand, I prayed

Tragedy...or Blessing?

out loud to God, straight from my heart like I had never done before. When I finished, I leaned in close to Doreen. My heart was breaking, but through my pain and tears, I said, "If you see Jesus and He asks you to come, you go to Him. It's okay...just go to Him. But if He says it's not time, you fight like hell to come back to us! We all need you! I need you! I will love you forever...I promise!"

I kissed her one more time before the door opened back up and Dr. Roswell said, "It's time. We can't wait any longer." We moved to the side, and they rolled her out of the room.

We followed them down a couple of hallways to an elevator and went up to the second floor. When the doors opened and we got out into the hallway, they told us we couldn't go any farther and we needed to say our goodbyes. The kids each took their turn with mom as I stood there and watched. I couldn't help but think to myself: Is this it? Will this be the last time I can tell her how much I love her? Is this the last time our hearts will beat together? How am I possibly going to live without her? I was a complete wreck.

I knew there was a strong possibility that she might not make it, but no matter how much that hurt, I knew I had to try to keep it together the best I could for my kids. This was it. My turn to say goodbye. I told her I loved her as I leaned over and gave her a kiss, hopefully not the last one. That's what I was praying in my mind at that very moment, "God, please don't let that be the last one...bring her back to me...I beg you, please!" It was time to part ways. They pushed her down the hall to the operating room and one of the surgical team members showed us to the waiting room. He told us someone would come out in a couple of hours to give us an update on how the surgery was going and how well Doreen was doing.

When we walked into the waiting room, I realized it was the same waiting room for the ICU that I had been in before. Then I saw that Ashley and Jason were already there waiting for us. Josh and Natalie got there a few minutes after that. I now had all my kids there with me waiting. Waiting to see what would happen with mom. I sat in a corner chair, and each one pulled their chair closer together. Each couple was sitting together, and I noticed that it had formed a circle.

The mood was tense and somber, but they were quietly having conversations with each other and doing what they could to help pass the time. I was very quiet and hardly spoke. Even though my mind was going a million miles an hour, it wouldn't slow down long enough for me to put a sentence together. The "would have", "should have", "could have", and the giant two letter word "if". "If only" and "what if" dominated every thought that flew through my head. On top of the emotional frenzy my mind was creating, the anxiety from each minute that passed added to the stress level that was already overloaded. Every minute felt like an hour.

After sitting there for a while and watching my kids interact together under these circumstances, I finally spoke. As I tried to compose my emotions, I said, "This is what life is all about." I held my arm out and made a circle while I was pointing my finger at each one of them. "This, right here," as I pointed around the circle again, "this is what it's all about. Family. It's not about the money. It's not about the size of a house or what kind of vehicle you drive, or even about the vacations you take. It's this." I pointed around one more time. "This right here, right now, this is what life is all about. Your family." Then I was quiet again. I wanted to share with them just how important a family bond can be, especially in tough times. That bond was the very thing that was keeping me together during this horrendous nightmare. I hoped they understood the importance of what I had just said.

As more time had passed, I glanced over at the clock for the 200th time, and I was getting very concerned. It was now two hours and fifteen minutes, and no one had come out to talk to us yet. Was there something wrong? Once again, my mind went into hyper-drive.

It wasn't very long after that when I saw Dr. Roswell walk through the door looking for us. I couldn't move. I couldn't tell by the expression on his face whether it was good or bad. He walked over to us and said, "I found the leak and I was able to repair it. She's still in very critical condition, but at least she's stable for now." He gave us some more details about how he checked every inch of her intestines for any tears, and that the leak came from where the PEG feeding tube had been inserted through her stomach lining. It hadn't closed properly, even though it had been sutured into place.

He also talked about how they divided her insides (literally) into four quadrants, taking each quadrant out separately to examine one by one to make sure there weren't any other tears or problems. He finished by telling us that someone else would come out to get us when she was ready to be moved to a room. When he left, I just sat there thinking about everything Doreen had just been through. I knew she wasn't even close to being out of the woods, but for right now, she at least made it through the surgery. Thank you God!

It was well over an hour later when a nurse came out to talk to us. She said Doreen was going to the ICU section, but not the one on the second floor that she had been in before. There were no beds available in that department. They were going to take her to the third floor Neuro Trauma ICU department which had only one bed available that day. She took us upstairs and showed us to the waiting room for that ICU. We again had to wait for a nurse to come get us once Doreen was situated in her room. Just like before, the minutes felt like hours, but at least this time I knew she was still with us.

Finally, a nurse came out to get me. As we walked into this ICU department, I immediately noticed it was much smaller than the ICU on the second floor. It was just one straight line of rooms on the left side, and a couple of nurses stations on the right with some other doors in between the stations. Doreen was in room four.

I took a deep breath in as I walked inside, and when I saw her, I exhaled in a sigh of relief. She looked pale, fragile and completely exhausted which was what I expected considering she just went through hell and back. Once again, my emotions took control, and the tears ran down my face. I had struggled immensely during the past fifteen excruciating hours where I didn't know if she was even going to make it, and a portion of those hours I didn't even know where she was.

Now, there she was, alive and breathing. She had fought hard to stay here with us, and now she would have to start her recovery process all over again. As selfish as it sounds, that didn't matter to me. She was still here. That was all that mattered. Besides, everything still looked the same as it had for the last three weeks since I first saw her in the hospital. She still had so many tubes and wires and at least eight to ten IV bags of various sizes, and of course, the ventilator. There was only one thing noticeably different now compared to before. She looked so weak and extremely frail, much more than before. I knew she needed as much rest and quiet time as possible, so I went back out to the waiting room to let each of the kids have their time with mom.

That ICU section had the same policy of only two people in the room at one time, so each couple took their turn being with her. They each took the time they needed with mom, and when they finished, they would say goodbye to me and head home to let the grand kids know how grandma was doing.

Since we had been there all day with four vehicles, it worked out that each couple could leave after they saw mom. Bryan and Ashley would meet me back at the house after they picked up their kids, while I stayed and went last to see her one more time that day. Heather stayed back and waited to take me home. It had been a long, long day and everyone was ready to get home and rest…and thank God.

Starting Over

The next day Bryan and I went up to see mom. She looked extremely frail and weak, just like she did the first time I saw her after her quarantine. The only difference now was the vent was hooked up to the trach in her neck instead of a tube down her throat. What seemed like progress over the last thirty days was just a mirage. The reality was, she was only at the beginning…again. But this time, she was even weaker. Here we were again in our dark version of *Groundhog Day*, starring at the machines for hours, and trying to quietly make conversation. The only bright spot in our "movie" was that our "star" was still with us, and for the most-part, she was stable.

They were still constantly adjusting her meds to find the right levels where her body would tolerate everything that was being thrown at it. There had been numerous times during the previous stay where the doctors had talked about the "*fine line*" they had to take with all her medications. It would be the difference between keeping her balanced and stable, or putting her into withdrawal which could be fatal in her condition.

So, like before, we would make notes about where the numbers were for some of her meds so we could share with the other kids when I got home. I had no idea what those numbers meant, but I knew if they went down, that was good. We had stayed for several hours before we left. Another day down, and so far, so good.

Now it was Thursday. Both Bryan and Ashley came up with me to see mom. That would be the last time they could visit because they would have to go home the next day. I knew leaving would be difficult for them under the circumstances, but there was no other choice. They would have to go home and live this from eight and a half hours away. I was just grateful the timing of their visit allowed us to be together at this critical moment in our family's existence.

Once again, we made our way back to her new ICU room on the third floor. We were only supposed to have two people in there, but all three of us went in and no one said anything to us. Again, we watched the machines and looked at the levels of meds she was on. The main drugs that we paid the closest attention to, were the Fentanyl and the Propafal. Those were the "heavy" sedation drugs as some of the nurses called them, so that's why we looked to see where they were at every time we walked in the room.

We were there for a little while when one of the nurses came in to check her incision and change the dressing. I'm not sure exactly what they called it, but it looked kind of like a girdle with Velcro. It was used to try and keep everything firmly in place to give the incision a chance to heal properly. The nurse had asked if we wanted to see it or stand back and don't look. Ashley and I stayed by the bed so we could see just how much of an incision there was.

When the nurse took the compression girdle off and removed the gauze, I was shocked to see so many staples holding her together. I don't know how many there were, but she was cut from just under her rib cage down past her navel at least three inches or so. I had never seen an incision that long before. I think even Ashley was surprised by the size of it. The nurse told us that everything looked pretty good with it so far, but it would probably take a while for it to heal under the circumstances.

Even though Bryan and Ashley understood exactly what mom's circumstances were, I think it helped them a lot to have spent some time being there with her, holding her hand, giving her a kiss and telling her how much they loved her. We stayed for a while longer, but it was time to go. At least now they would have an image in their minds and in their hearts of where mom was at.

Up until then, they could only envision what I would describe to them over the phone when we talked. It's one thing to have something described to you, but it's another thing to see it for yourself. What they had just witnessed over the last several days was horrendous, but I believe it was good for them to be here and go through it with all of us. We were all able to lean on each other and support each other *together*. That's what family is all about.

Friday morning would be a sad time. Tennessee was calling. It was time for them to go home. After they got ready and packed up, we went out for a good breakfast before they went on their way. I love breakfast, but that one was bitter-sweet. While we ate, I stalled as long as I could, but the time had come to release more tears and say goodbye. My heart ached knowing how much I would miss them, but at the same time, there was a small portion of my heart that was at peace because they got to spend a little time with mom.

Even though she wasn't conscious, I think she felt their presence and their love while they were there. I truly believe that.

We kissed and hugged and said our goodbyes, and we left in opposite directions. I don't know how many miles it was before I stopped crying, but I thanked God for letting them be here for the time they were and asked Him to send a guardian angel to help them get home safe. I was on my way to Rockford.

I had only driven by myself a couple of times at that point, but it was time I gave the kids a break from having to "baby-sit" dad. I have to say, it was a little strange driving by myself. The only company I had was my own thoughts. During this whole ordeal, my mind was on an unbalanced swivel. One moment it would be under control, and the next moment it wasn't. Frankly, my emotions were in the exact same state.

There had only been two other times in my life where my emotions had been so raw. That was when my dad passed, and then my mom a few years later. As emotionally difficult as that was back then, going through this extreme hellish emotional roller coaster now, coupled with uncontrolled and unanswerable thoughts, were at times, almost more than I could bear. The only thing that kept me together was the fact that I had to be there for her, no matter what. I promised. I went every day to be by her side, but now, I was going there on my own.

I finally got to her room and went in, like so many days before, but this time, a nurse came in and told me that I would have to put on a disposable gown and latex gloves to be in the room. I didn't understand. I didn't have to do that yesterday or any other day before that. She proceeded to tell me they tested Doreen for MRSA (sounds like "mersa") which is a bacterial staph infection that is contagious and can become very serious and even life-threatening. I stood there stunned. In her condition, what was that going to do to her? She just barely started the long journey of recovering from a major emergency surgery, and now that.

I had heard of MRSA before, it's a "super bug" that is resistant to antibiotics and it can be very dangerous. The nurse assured me though there were new types of antibiotics available now that work on fighting these bacteria, but to keep it from spreading to others, I needed to use the disposable garments every time I would enter her room. Now when I would hold her hand or touch her face, I would have to have a latex glove on. I understood the reason why, but it just wasn't the same touch that I was used to.

Up until her surgery, we were able to use her own favorite skin lotion on her hands and arms (carefully around everything that was attached to her), her feet and even on her face. Her skin was so dry and looked like it was getting thinner. Except for her face, it appeared as if she was rapidly aging, especially her hands. They were getting to be just skin and bones. There were times when I would rub her arm and thought I was going to tear her skin if I wasn't too careful.

Our daily routine now entailed having to wear gloves. I would have to be even more careful now because she just didn't need anything else to go wrong, or to go any farther backwards than she already had. It had been a horrendous battle for her so far, and it had also taken its toll on the rest of the family. After spending several hours there, it was time to go home and fill the kids in with the newest curve ball that had been thrown at mom. It would take several hours on the phone with a wide range of emotions, a routine that had become far too common for our family.

It was now Saturday, the fourth day after surgery, and I made my way back to Rockford on my own. It would be

DE-ja-vu from the previous day. The only exception was there were no new issues in the past twenty-four hours that would plague Doreen. Everything looked the same as the day before with all the tubes and wires, and she was still so weak, but at least she was stable. So, it was a good day. At least she didn't go backwards.

I then followed my standard routine: I went home, did chores, talked to my kids for a few hours and went to bed. Physically, not mentally. I still couldn't shut my mind off. It's amazing how loud your thoughts are when it is completely silent around you. We were still in a place of so much uncertainty, I couldn't help but try to find and question every possible outcome. If you're not careful, it will drive you crazy, Trust me, I know. Fortunately, "the law of exhaustion" would eventually take over, and I eventually would fall asleep.

Sunrise would always come quicker than I wanted, but that day would be a little better because I would have some company for the ride up and back, and for the hours in between. Heather came with to see mom. She had to gown up which is a little scary the first few times you do it. After we were there for a short time, the nurse came in and told us she wasn't doing well, and they had to stop the feeding tube because she had been vomiting earlier. Her stomach and intestines were not moving very well like they should be which was causing the oral meds not to be absorbed. So, they stopped the oral meds.

When they said orally, it meant the pills were crushed into a powder and mixed with water. Then they used a syringe to push it through her feeding tube. But everything now, including nutrition, would have to done through an IV tube. Once again, one step forward, two steps back.

The only bright spot that day was she had opened her eyes for a short time. I had witnessed that a few times, which makes you so excited to see her "awake". But then you realize that she had no idea what was happening because she was still so heavily sedated. It was a bitter-sweet moment just like the others. But it fueled the hope that one of these times she would be back to us and out of her prison. Even though Heather had gone with, and we were in there together, our visit remained very quiet and somber because of the events that had happened that day.

It was the same pattern of ups and downs. Good days and bad days. Moving forward and falling backwards. That had happened so many times since the beginning, you would think that we would be used to it by that time. But no matter how many times it happened, each time was as painful and heartbreaking as the time before.

We stayed for several hours, secretly hoping to see a sign of improvement, but nothing happened. The feeling of helplessness was exhausting, so it was time to go. We went home so I could complete my nightly routine and wait to go back the next day. Hopefully tomorrow would be a better day.

<u>Monday, October 11th</u>

It was the start of a new week. It was also a full week since Doreen's "free air" reared its ugly head and made her start the healing process all over again. Kirstyn didn't work on Mondays, so she went with me to see mom. Up until that point, she had been filling in and covering the office for Doreen just like she had before when we would go on vacation. It was only part-time, Tuesday through Friday, for the past several weeks. The idea was Kirstyn would keep mom's job in place with the hopes Doreen could return to work sooner than later.

We left a little before 10 a.m. and got there just before 11. When we went to the third floor and walked into the ICU rooms, I showed her where we could get the gowns and gloves on before we could see mom. After gowning up, I walked into the room and there was an elderly woman in the bed who was a complete stranger. A little confused and embarrassed, I walked out and over to the next room. The glass door was closed with the curtain pulled so you couldn't see in, so I stood there waiting for the door to open.

Kirstyn stood there looking at the puzzled look on my face, and then we heard a nurse ask if we were looking for Doreen. I told her we were, and I apparently forgot what room she was in.

She said, "She's not here. Didn't anybody call to tell you she was being moved?"

I immediately replied, "No, I didn't get a call and where did she get moved to?"

She apologized and explained they needed the room for another critical patient and had moved Doreen around 6:30 that morning. It was now 11:15 a.m. She then had us follow her to where they had moved her to.

When we got close to the new room, she pointed and said Doreen was in that room. We thanked her and walked a little further and entered the room. I was absolutely stunned and completely baffled when I saw Doreen in the bed with only the vent next to the bed. There was nothing else, absolutely nothing else. The day before in the other room, there were two IV poles that had at least eight to ten bags or more hanging from them. Now, everything was gone. Before Kirstyn and I could even come to grips with what we were looking at, the alarm on her vent went off. We both jumped and looked at each other hoping the other had figured out what the hell was happening.

Tragedy...or Blessing?

Within a couple of minutes, which felt like an eternity, the nurse who was taking care of that room walked in to check the alarm. I noticed right away that she was pregnant and could tell that she was very stressed and upset. She told us the vent alarm had been going off every few minutes ever since they moved her in that room, and she had three other patients to take care of as well. I heard what she said and how she said it, which didn't sit well with me.

I immediately responded with, "Where are all her meds and IV's that she was on? What the hell is going on? She's obviously struggling, so give her something!" By that time, I had regained my senses, but I was extremely upset. That didn't help the communication between the nurse and me, but it was very clear that Doreen was in trouble.

I knew exactly what the problem was. For the past four weeks, the doctors and nurses had talked about how they had to be so careful adjusting the sedation drugs and the other medications so it wouldn't put her into withdrawal. That was the "fine line" they talked about so many times. Well, guess what? Kirstyn and I were witnessing Doreen going through withdrawals with our own eyes, right there in front of us.

I will never forget what Kirstyn and I witnessed. It was the most gut-wrenching and completely helpless experience I had ever gone through. I had to watch the love of my life going through that kind of struggle trying to breathe, and to see the look of agony and pain on her face. Even though she basically was paralyzed, her body still physically twitched occasionally trying to cope with the shock of the missing medications.

It was only one week earlier that she had barely clung to life on the operating table, and now she was being tortured from the very medications that were supposed to heal her. How could this happen? When I looked back at Kirstyn, she had a horrified look on her face and was frozen in fear in the corner of the room. Every time that alarm would go off, our anxiety level would go through the roof. Doreen had been taken completely off all the drugs for almost six hours at that point, with only a couple of shots that the nurse had talked the doctor into.

During one of the many times the nurse flew in and out, I was finally able to get her to stop for a few minutes to help me understand what was happening. She explained this section of the hospital that they moved Doreen to didn't allow IV medication. She could only give her a shot of pain meds periodically because that was the only allowable option. She told us Doreen's chart still showed that she was on "oral" medications and hadn't been changed as of that moment. That "oral" order in the chart was the reason why she could only give her a shot which only lasted for short period of time.

She told us she had worked in the ICU department before, and patients like Doreen were moved *to* the ICU in her condition, not *out of* the ICU in her condition. There was nothing else she could do until the doctor changed the order. She said she had been trying desperately to get that order changed all morning so they could get Doreen under control and moved back where she needed to be. She asked if I wanted to talk to the doctor, which I think I answered "Yes" before she even finished asking. She left, and it was back to the nerve-racking wait, and to the horrendous warning sound of the vent alarm. You don't get used to that sound when it's happening to *your* family.

It took a while before the doctor finally walked into the room. I was standing on the far side of her bed. He stepped in closer to Doreen and looked to see with his own eyes what was happening. He introduced himself, which I don't even remember his name, but I immediately asked him as I started

Tragedy...or Blessing?

to walk towards him, "What happened to all her IV's? I don't understand what's going on here. Why is she like that?" as I pointed towards her. I think he was afraid that I was going to assault him, because he was back-pedaling towards the door. He was talking as he backed up, but I didn't understand a word he said before he was out the door. We had no answers.

Once again, the alarm went off and the nurse came back in. Even though I was extremely upset and angry by that time, I felt bad that I had miss-judged Doreen's nurse. I thought she was just cranky and had an attitude problem, but it turned out that she was under so much stress just trying to help Doreen. She had been doing everything in her power to fix the problem that Doreen had been subjected to.

She said she saw the doctor leave when she came back into the room and asked us what his response was. I told her I had no idea because he basically left us hanging with no answers. She told us she was going to go up the ladder of command to try and get the situation under control and resolved. She promised us that she would do whatever was necessary to get Doreen moved back into the ICU as quickly as possible. I thanked her multiple times for her efforts and determination to help Doreen and asked her to keep going until Doreen was safe. She promised she would.

We had been witnessing that catastrophe for over four and a half hours and it had taken its toll on Kirstyn and I, needless to say what it had done to Doreen. I was very concerned about Kirstyn because she still looked like she was in shock. Other than stay and continue to watch that nightmare unfold, I knew there was nothing else we could do to help, so I had to get us out of there and pray that God would take control. He did.

A few short hours later, Heather got a call from the hospital saying a bed had opened in the ICU on the second floor and they moved Doreen there. They said she was doing a little better and had her on a Fentanyl drip again. Her stats were better, and her respiratory rate had come back down into a tolerable range. With a sigh of relief, we could all breathe again. Another day from hell had finally passed.

The next morning still had some "carry-over" anxiety from the previous day's catastrophic event. The house was still quiet like it had been since Doreen left. I had tried watching TV a few weeks earlier to try and take my mind off everything, but that was when our troops were pulling out of Afghanistan which was being shown and talked about on so many channels. I thought I wanted to know what was happening outside of my little world at the time, but the visions of complete chaos and desperation were more than I could tolerate. My nerves were raw, and it felt like I was having a panic attack. No more television.

So, the many hours I spent at home by myself were in total silence, except for the kitchen clock: Tick-tock…Tick-tock…Tick-tock. The sound that once had tormented me had now become a pacifier that would give me a sense of calm peace. It seemed to be the only consistency I had. And then there were the two young pups and Tori. I would not have been able to handle living in that house by myself if it hadn't been for those three dogs. They truly brought me some comfort which I desperately needed.

The Voice of Jesus

I was getting ready to go see Doreen when I heard my phone. It was a text message from Jeff. He said he heard this song on his way to work that morning and thought of me and attached a link for the song. I played it and started to cry. It was one of the most beautiful songs I had ever heard.

From the very first verse, it felt like Jesus Himself was singing it directly *to* me. The song is called *"You Are Mine"* sung by David Haas, and it really needs to be heard for the full effect. (You need to look it up for yourself. It's worth the effort.) I sat there and replayed the song over and over again. It felt like His presence was in the room with me. Oddly, I felt relieved. God *did* hear my cries and my pleas. The words of that song contained His reply to me, precisely when I needed it.

A wise young man, whose faith is an inspiration to me, had told me one night during this agonizing journey that "God knows what we need *before* we know what we need". God certainly knew what I needed at that moment in time. Hope and Faith. It wasn't that I had lost all hope, or my faith, but they just needed a big boost right at that exact moment. I sat and listened one more time before I got ready to leave. I felt a little better, but I was still cautiously optimistic. I still had the visions in my mind of what Kirstyn and I encountered the day before.

This time when I arrived, I got off the elevator on the second floor and walked into the ICU that was very familiar, which immediately made me feel a little more at ease. Her new room was just three doors down from where she had been before, and as I walked past her old room, I couldn't help but look in. We had spent so many hours in there and it still looked the same, except someone else was in it.

When I got to her room, I gowned up and went inside. Relief! She was just lying there completely calm with no alarms going off. It looked like she was just sleeping. I whispered, "Thank you God!" and I leaned down and gave Doreen a kiss on her forehead.

When I stood back up, I heard a voice behind me say, "Hi Steve." I turned around and saw two familiar faces. It was Doreen's nurses from before, Molly and Hailey. I was so happy to see them because they were two of Doreen's special angels that had taken such good care of her the first time. Molly said, "It's so good to see you, but no offense, we were hoping we would never see you guys here again." I told them it was great to see them again as well, but unfortunately, it was under the same circumstances as the last time.

We talked for a few minutes, and I explained everything that had happened since Doreen left, including the previous day's episode from the third floor. They were completely shocked and dumbfounded on how that could have happened, and they even apologized for it. They obviously didn't have anything to do with it, but they felt so bad that Doreen had to even go through that awful experience. I knew they meant every word they said.

Now with Molly and Hailey as Doreen's nurses that day, I knew they would take great care of her, and I didn't have to worry about any missteps. They would be in and out throughout the day while I was there, and each time they would ask if I needed anything because they also cared about me.

During one of the many quiet moments I had with Doreen, I pulled my phone out to play the song that Jeff had sent me. I bent over by her side and whispered in her ear, "Jesus is singing this to *you*" and I hit play. I had the volume on low so I could hold it by her ear. I was holding the phone in my one hand and holding her hand with my other while we listened together. I was hoping and praying that she could hear it, that she could *hear the words* and *feel them in her heart*. God can do anything, so why not with this?

Over-all, it was a good day. There wasn't any noticeable progress, but at least there weren't any steps backwards either. Giving the kids the update that night was a lot easier than the last one.

Tragedy...or Blessing?

What a difference a day can make. That goes both ways, good or bad. I guess you could say that was the main theme for Doreen's whole journey so far, well, most of her journey anyway. We never knew what to expect when we walked into her room. Since it was Wednesday and Josh didn't work, he decided to go with me. That would be the best day we/I had visiting Doreen up to that point.

Everything pretty much appeared the same as it was the day before, but as Josh and I talked, I noticed Doreen had been making some faces. I wasn't sure if I was seeing things or not. I kept watching. Maybe it was just some type of subconscious reflex. I said to Josh, "Careful, I think mom's listening to us." As we looked down, she smiled and then quickly stopped. We looked at each other in disbelief. Did she just respond to us? How could that be? It was only two days ago where she was in a full throttle, uncontrolled withdrawal, and now she was messing with us? Yes, she was. She even had opened and closed her eyes a few times while we were talking to her. She was responding to us.

We were so excited. I still had a hard time trying to grasp the fact that it was even possible based on the previous forty-eight hours. But there I stood, watching another miracle happen before my very eyes. Once again, God knew what I needed, what our family needed at that precise moment.

We were only able to carry that on with Doreen for a short while before she drifted back into her dark isolation, but it was progress. Everyone all along said she would have to take baby steps, and that time, it felt like she did. When the nurse came back in, we told her what had transpired. She said it was great news and was happy for us, but we still needed to be aware there was a very long, long road ahead of Doreen. She told us not to get too far ahead of ourselves, and we should still only take it one day at a time. I understood exactly what she was saying. Our family had been living that for the past seven weeks.

Regardless, that was a great day! With my faith and hope restored, I leaned over and whispered in her ear, "I love you! I will see you tomorrow."

The next morning arrived, and I woke up refreshed. I slept a good portion of the night. Prior to that, I was lucky to get two or three hours of sleep at night, and not necessarily consecutive. I had some breakfast and went outside to do the normal morning chores with the animals, which took much longer now since I had been sick. It really was a chore because I would have to constantly stop to catch my breath before I could continue. I would say it took at least twice as long as it did before, both morning and night. After I got cleaned up and everything was in place, off to the hospital I went.

As I drove up, I was nervous again because I didn't know what I would find when I got there. Would it be like it was on Monday? Or would it be like it was yesterday? There was also the possibility it would be somewhere in between the two. I guess I was still feeling the aftershock from what we had encountered on Monday.

Fortunately, there had been enough quiet hours since that startling experience on Monday for me to reflect on what transpired that day. I came to realize that *everyone* had been pushed to the limit due to the pandemic, especially our health care professionals. The immense pressure and stress they were subjected to every day unfortunately lead to that clerical mistake about the "oral" medications. It obviously wasn't intentional, or even due to negligence. It was a simple mistake. We all make them. We're human.

Once I got there and did the gown routine, I went into her room. As soon as I saw her face, I forgot about all the questions that had gone through mind on the way up. I just wanted to kiss her and tell her that I loved her, and just *be* with her. I missed being with her at home so, so much.

But this is where we were at. It was going to take time, a lot of time before we could be together again at home. However long it would take us, it didn't matter. I had made a promise to her that I would be there every step of the way, and there was no way I would ever break that promise to her. As I talked to Doreen for a little while, she occasionally would open her eyes, look at me and smile. I think she actually recognized me.

The first time her nurse came in to check up on everything after I got there, she informed me that they had to stop the oral feeding tube because there was an issue with Doreen's stomach and intestines again. They had done an x-ray before I got there to see if they could figure out what the problem was. She said a special nurse practitioner (I think that was the title) would stop by to check on Doreen, and she could explain everything to me. I wasn't sure what to think, after all, Doreen had just been smiling at me. For some strange reason, time always takes longer when you are waiting for something that is important to you.

I was sitting by Doreen's bed doing my usual, watching the numbers on the ventilator and switching over to the blood pressure and heart rate monitor when the special nurse came in. I explained to her that I was Doreen's husband and asked her if she could explain to me, in layman's terms, what the problem was with Doreen's digestive system.

After she did her examination on Doreen and looked at her charts, she tried to tell me what was going on. She could tell I wasn't quite following her explanation, so she walked over to the wall where there was a dry erase board and picked up a maker. She drew a circle and said, "That's your stomach." Then she drew two lines that went back and forth down the board and said, "That's your intestines." She explained that the intestines basically move in a wave motion all the way through to the end. It's kind of like a snake that swallowed its prey, forcing it down with its muscles moving in a wave type motion. Since I've seen that before, I understood what she was saying.

In Doreen's case, her intestines were not moving in that wave type motion, so anything in her stomach stayed where it was because it wasn't being moved through the intestines. Even though it was all liquids, that motion was not strong enough to move anything, so her system backed up. That not only meant her nutrition, but also the medications they had ground up and put in water through the feeding tube were not going anywhere either, which meant her nourishment and meds weren't doing anything for her. That was the over simplified version of an illus (I think that's the correct word), but at least I understood what the issue was.

She also explained another important part of why her digestive system wasn't working. It was the fact that she hasn't moved a muscle on her own for the past six weeks. She continued explaining that to be healthy and have your body function properly, you must physically move your body. She couldn't stress enough how important it is for people to be physically active. She wasn't necessarily talking about working out in a gym, running or heavy activity, but just simply getting up and walking around for a while. That alone would make a big difference, which in this case, Doreen couldn't do.

I understood that as well because I had been watching Doreen get weaker by the day and wither away right before my eyes. She didn't have to convince me how important physical movement is for your body. I thanked her for helping me understand and she moved on to her next case.

Then, before I was ready to leave that day, I found out Doreen was approved again to be moved, and the Acute Rehab facility in Sycamore had a bed open for her. They were scheduling it for tomorrow and would be moving her in the afternoon. Finally, we were making progress on her journey home. I didn't even wait to tell the kids. I called them on the way home. Friday was going to be a great day!

I had a hard time sleeping that night because I was so excited. The next thing I knew, the sun was rising, and it was time to get everything done that needed to before I could go. I also had to make a pit stop before I could go to the hospital to see Doreen. I had to go to another hospital first, the local hospital in Dixon. A few weeks earlier, I had gone to my doctor for a chest X-ray because I had been coughing a lot back then. My kids wouldn't leave me alone about it, which is why I went.

Apparently, my doctor saw some kind of spot on one of my lungs and wanted me to get a CT scan just to make sure it wasn't something serious. I knew what the scan would be like, because I had the one done when I went to the emergency room back in August.

I wasn't comfortable going by myself, so I asked Kirstyn to go with me. I'm always afraid that I'm going to screw up the paperwork somehow, or not understand or remember what the doctor said. Just to make it clear, I rarely go to the doctor unless I absolutely have to. That was no exception, I didn't want to go, but I also didn't want to listen to the kids nag me about it either. So, I went and had it done.

When it was my turn, I went with the technician down a couple of hallways and into the room with the scanner. It didn't take very long before they were done. When she took me back to the area where Kirstyn was waiting, she made the comment to me that it was good I came in to have the scan done. I was a little curious why she said that which my first thought was that's how you get paid, so I asked her. She said she noticed I couldn't complete a sentence without pausing and taking another breath before I would finish what I was saying. I told her I never realized just how much air it takes to talk, and the other part of the problem was that I talked too much. She chuckled and told me the doctor would let me know the results as soon as they could get them over to him. I thanked her for being so nice and walked away, but I really was in a hurry to get going to Rockford to see Doreen before her ride took her back to Sycamore.

Kirstyn drove separately because she had to go back to work, but we stood by my car for a few minutes so I could call Heather and let her know that I was done, and it went smoothly. As we talked, she told me that the hospital in Rockford had called earlier, and everything was still on schedule for mom to go later that afternoon. I was so excited that I cut the conversation short and told the girls thank you, and how much I loved them. Off to Rockford I went.

It was a beautiful day, and the sun was shinning. Even as excited as I was to get there, I was smart enough to put the car on cruse control to keep me from flying a little too fast. I knew a speeding ticket would cost me time on the side of the road, and I wasn't willing to lose a single minute. She had only been back at the hospital in Rockford for ten days, but it felt like another month had passed. Once I got there and parked, it didn't take long for me to get up to the ICU second floor.

Forward, Backward, Forward

As I walked past the cluster of cubicles and desks, I saw our case worker, La'Nae, and said hello as I went by. She said hello and stopped me to ask if I knew that Doreen might not be leaving there that afternoon. Say what? I told her I had talked with my daughter only an hour ago and she was told that everything was on schedule for that afternoon. Well, sometime after they talked with Heather earlier that morning, Doreen had some sort of negative reaction and they had to bump up some of her sedations and meds, and her stats were all over the place. She didn't have any more details than that, so I went down to Doreen's room.

After I gowned up and went in, a couple of familiar voices came in behind me. It was Molly and Hailey again. If I remember right, they had asked to be Doreen's nurses that day because they knew she was supposed to leave, and they wanted to take care of her one more time. I was so glad they were there because I knew they would help me understand what the hell happened. They said Doreen seemed to be struggling a little when they started their shift but got progressively worse as time went on from the changes she went through over night. Changes, what changes? They couldn't give me the exact specifics, but the night doctor apparently ordered the reductions in the sedation meds and changed the settings on the vent.

I was frustrated and angry. It happened once again. They did too much too fast. Every time they lowered the meds too quickly, or they adjusted the vent too far at one time, Doreen would take three steps backwards. I didn't know if that was a standard practice which normally worked, but in Doreen's case, it backfired every time. But that time, it was going to cost Doreen a trip back to Sycamore. Not only that, but now she was back to being completely sedated and unconscious. It was just twenty-four hours earlier where she had recognized me and smiled, and now nothing.

As the time passed, Molly and Hailey continued to come in and out doing what they needed to do for Doreen. Finally, I heard another familiar voice behind me. It was Carrie from Sycamore. I looked at her and said, "Please help Doreen!" She told me she heard everything was on hold, which is why she came in to see what was going on. I explained how Doreen was the day before and how they had adjusted too many things at one time again. I pointed at Doreen and said, "And that's the result again".

She assured me they would hold the bed at their facility through the weekend to give Doreen a chance to get back to where she would be able to get released from this hospital. I then told her what Kirstyn and I had walked into on Monday when we saw Doreen going through withdrawals. She was shocked and very upset about what had happened, which she didn't know about, and with what was going on now. She clearly could see how frustrated and upset I was, so she told me she was going to make a few phone calls and would come back as soon as she had some answers.

It took about an hour or so, but she came back and told me she talked with the head doctor and the people in charge at their facility and explained the whole situation. They were contacting the people in charge at this hospital to clear the way to get Doreen released and moved as soon as possible that day.

When Molly and Hailey walked back in to change one of Doreen's IVs, Carrie asked them to stop and leave everything the way it was because her company was going to take over Doreen's care from that point forward. They understood and were happy that Doreen was going to be able to go, but they had to follow their protocol and check to make sure everything was cleared.

After a short period of time, they came back and said they were going to get everything prepped so when the transport got there, it would go as smooth as possible. They spent at least twenty minutes or more just following each of the IV leads to label them so the nurses at the new hospital didn't have to figure out that pile of tubes. I joked many times with the nurses that all those tubes looked like a big bowl of spaghetti. I finally could breathe again because it really was going to happen. Doreen was now ready to go, and all we needed was her ride.

Sitting there in anticipation was like watching a pot of water waiting to boil. It didn't really take that long for the crew of three guys to get there. I've never seen that much specialized equipment come from an ambulance before. They brought in their own special ventilator and a strange looking gurney made for transporting critical care patients. I was told that this transport was like a portable ICU department which was why there would be two of them in back with Doreen closely monitoring everything while they drove to Sycamore. I kissed Doreen on the forehead and went out into the hall to get out of their way.

I introduced myself to the one that was standing in the hall with the gurney, and he told me that he was the driver. I asked him if he could do me favor. I said, "Please take good care of her! Take it easy and make sure she has a smooth ride there…wait a second, I forgot these are Illinois roads; please avoid all the potholes."

He laughed, but knew I was very concerned about her travel, so he replied, "Don't worry. We're in no hurry to get there. We'll give her a nice easy ride."

I thanked him and asked again to make sure they take good care of her. I knew there was nothing else I could do there other than get in their way, so I turned around to walk away when I saw that Molly and Hailey were both by the nurses' station. I stopped to say goodbye and tell them how much I appreciated everything they had done for us. As I hugged each one, I could tell it was as emotional for them as it was for me. I said my final goodbye's and walked away with tears in my eyes. They really were a couple of Doreen's guardian angels there. I truly believe that.

Now I was on my way home, and Doreen was on her way to Sycamore. While I drove home, I called each of the kids to let them know about the craziness that had transpired, and how it had worked out. Mom was finally on her way to the next phase of her journey, hopefully for good.

We had already been down this road. It wasn't that long ago when Doreen had gone to Sycamore before, and this was exactly like it was the first time. Since she was transferred later in the day like before, they asked that we give Doreen a day to get settled in. It also would give them time to get her ventilator dialed in, as well as all the other apparatuses that she needed. She still had just as many wires and IV tubes as she did in Rockford, and still needed very close monitoring. She wasn't out of the woods by any stretch of the imagination, but at least she was one step closer (hopefully) to coming home.

At that point, we were still being told to take it one day at a time and don't get too far ahead of ourselves. When you hear those words as many times as we had, you kind of become numb to it and don't really focus on them anymore.

As long as I wasn't going to be able to visit that Saturday, I decided to get caught up at home with a few things that I had been pushing off and waiting for some time to work on them. One of those projects was closing the chicken coop and taking down the fencing around the side yard. Since we had got sick and Doreen wasn't home to help, the daily chores were getting to be too much for me to handle. Kirstyn was able to find a couple of people to buy our chickens which helped reduce the work load a little.

Letting the chickens out in the morning and locking them in at night, as well as feeding, watering and washing the eggs each night was only around a half an hour a day, which doesn't sound like much time. But with winter coming, it was going to be more of a chore in the cold weather, which I wasn't looking forward to. I was physically struggling every day trying to keep up with everything on my own, and I certainly wasn't going to ask for any more help from my kids. They had already gone so far above and beyond that I just couldn't ask. I still needed their help with so many other things that my daily chores didn't need to be a part of it as well.

Now that the chickens were gone, my calves and most of my cows were next on the list to go. We had found someone to buy some of the cows, and there was an auction coming up in a few weeks that would take the rest of what I needed to go. It would be another big sigh of relief once they were gone, but I would still have two cows and several of the kid's bulls at my house for the winter.

We have over-head water lines that go from one end of the barn to the other, so that was another big project which needed to be done before the weather changed. I needed to re-do the line because I had patched it so many times over the last ten years from every time it froze and broke. When Bryan was up last time, he helped me figure out a new way to run and drain the line and helped me get all the parts to replace the whole system. I had everything ready to go for that project, but that was too big to do by myself and I didn't have enough time that day. It would have to be done soon though, winter was coming, and the weather was already getting cooler.

During one of the many breaks I took because I physically didn't have the stamina to go too long, Heather had called to give me the update on mom. She talked with a nurse name Sherry who told her that Doreen had a "really rough entrance" and wasn't tolerating the new vent very well. Doreen's blood pressure had also plummeted, and it took them a while to get her stable.

They also had to bump up the Fentanyl and some of the other sedation and anxiety medications to help calm everything down and get her relaxed. That was not what I was expecting to hear. Honestly, I thought here we go again; we're back on that frickin' roller coaster. Even though I was physically tired, it would be another night of minimal sleep. Guess what I listened to? Yep: Tick-tock…Tick-tock…Tick-tock.

Sunday, October 17th

That was a start of a new week and a new phase in Doreen's journey. Technically, I guess it was a re-start of that phase. And it was a rough beginning, but I was hopeful the road ahead of us would start to get smoother and head in the right direction. The hospital's normal visiting hours were Monday through Friday, but since Heather had made the arrangements when she called the day before, just like the last time, we were able to go there on Sunday.

We knew we wouldn't stay very long that day because of how hard the transfer had been on Doreen. She needed as much rest as possible with the least amount of stimulus: me. I couldn't help myself whenever I was around her. I would hold her hand and talk to her and lean over every now and then to give her a kiss on her forehead. She didn't need that today though; she just needed more rest. I was okay with that, but I still needed to at least see her for a little while. After all, I didn't get to see her the day before. It was a short visit, but we left and went home so Heather could spend more time with her family. That was important too.

After I got home, I ended up calling the other kids to talk to them about mom's daily update, and then I called Aunt Sandy and talked with her for a while. Those calls with her always helped. That one was no exception. As I unloaded my burdens and concerns, and cried every now and then, she suggested I try something when I go to bed that night. She told me I should try kneeling by the side of my bed and then pray to God and give it all to Him. She said it has always been the most humbling experience for her whenever she did that. I've always thought that was something little kids do before they go to bed, but I never thought about doing it as an adult. Hmmm.

We talked for a while longer before we said our goodbyes and our "Love you", but I kept thinking about what she had said long after I hung up. I thought about all the hundreds of prayers I had said so far, and for all the prayers for Doreen that I had asked others to do. Surely God knew I meant them from the bottom of my heart, right?

The more I pondered about it, the more I realized that all my focus was just about me. Sure, I had prayed so hard for Doreen to get better...for me. For her to come home...to me. Not all, but many of my prayers were about what I wanted or needed even though I didn't realize it at the time. I was asking God to do *my will*, not His. I've been around for a long time, and I know how it's supposed to be: "...*Thy will* be done, on earth as it is in Heaven."

It suddenly dawned on me that I hadn't read my daily devotional book since I got sick. I still had plenty of time before bed, so I went in my bathroom and brought it out to the couch. It's a small pocketbook which has three months of stories in each quarterly release. Each page is one day, and it only takes a couple of minutes to read. I normally read it in the mornings while I'm getting ready, but I forgot all about it since we had gotten sick.

I was about two months behind at that point, so I sat on the couch with the pups by my side and started to read. I figured if I would read a couple of extra pages a day, I would get caught up in no time. It amazes me how some of the bible verses and the stories can relate perfectly to the circumstances you might find yourself in. Not every day or every story does, but I think God puts one there at the right time when you need it most, even if you don't realize you really need it.

It was now time for bed, and I decided to try Aunt Sandy's advice. It seemed a little awkward when I first knelt, but it didn't take long for me to understand what she meant. As I prayed, I asked for the same help and outcomes like I had said before, but this time, the tears started rolling down my checks as I spoke out loud to God. I have never felt so humble and vulnerable when I've prayed before. Even as bad as my heart ached for Doreen and my humble tears yearned for forgiveness, strangely enough, it felt good. It gave me a sense of calm, or peace, or connection, or all the above. It's hard for me to explain. I suggest everyone try it for themselves and allow it to happen. You must remember though, it will happen on God's time, not yours.

I still wasn't sleeping in my bed yet, so I got up and sat in the recliner in my room, expecting to listen to the clock all night. With the two pups in my lap and Tori lying on the floor, I closed my eyes wondering how much sleep I was going to get that night. To my surprise, I woke up only a

Tragedy...or Blessing?

couple of times, and when I looked, the clock had moved several hours each time. That felt pretty good.

It was Monday morning and time for everyone to go to work...except for me. Even though I still had a bad case of "dragon butt", I knew I was going to have to get back to work soon. Numerous times during our conversations, Jeff had told me he didn't want me back at work until I was feeling one hundred percent and back to normal. I had, of course, responded that I have never really been "normal". I appreciated his offer to stay home to build up my strength more, but I knew when the time came, I would need to take more time off to take care of Doreen when she got home. Honestly, I *finally* believed it was possible, and I hoped it would be sooner than later.

That workday started a new chapter in Kirstyn's routine. We had been keeping Doreen's boss, Richard, up to date with Doreen's progress as well as all the setbacks. Each time we would talk, he would ask if the doctors had some kind of prognosis on when they thought Doreen could come home. I unfortunately had to tell him the same answer every time: no two COVID cases were alike, and the only thing the doctors would say about it was to take it one day at a time. They wouldn't even hint at a time frame. I understood why he asked that question because in most cases, you normally get some kind of educated guess at least.

One other thing that wasn't normal in Doreen's case. Visitation was extremely limited, so I wanted just my immediate family, and it was only two at a time. Richard understood our situation, but he still had a business to run which I completely understood. He had been very kind to us by allowing Kirstyn to fill-in part-time so far, but now he needed Kirstyn to cover the office full-time until Doreen could come back to work. I think most employers would have hired someone else to take Doreen's position at that point because there was no end in sight of when she might be back. He said he wanted to hold it open for her because she was a very valuable employee. If Kirstyn agreed to go full-time, he was comfortable enough with her stepping in to help.

Richard had also been generous to us by paying Doreen for all her vacation time and for the balance of September. He then gave Doreen a "custom" maternity type leave to help us out financially. That was above and beyond anything we could have asked for and it was greatly appreciated. I would call him occasionally to give him updates, and to thank him again for his understanding, patience, and generosity. Hopefully it would only be a temporary arrangement, but so far it was working out okay for Richard, Kirstyn and for me. The office was in Dixon, so Kirstyn was also my grocery pick-up and drop-off which helped me out a lot. That was one less thing that I had to deal with or worry about.

A New Game Plan

The next day was a big deal. That would be the first of many at Doreen's "new" hospital in Sycamore. We would have a meeting every Tuesday at 1:30 p.m. with all the staff that would be involved in Doreen's care. Whoever would be available at that time, from the doctors and nurses to our case worker, from the pharmacy and the nutritionist to the respiratory and cardiology departments and everything in between. These were the team meetings where they would go over everything that happened the previous week as well as communicate what the goals were for the upcoming week. By doing that, everyone would be on the same page.

That was something new and very different from what we had experienced so far on this unwanted journey. I was rather nervous not knowing what to expect. Fortunately, Heather was also going to be there to help me keep everything straight and organized.

After we got there in Doreen's room, it didn't take long for everyone to come in to start the meeting. I was a little overwhelmed. I counted twelve people. Since that was the first one, they went around the room and introduced themselves and what department they were with. When it came to our case worker, she said her name was Angel. Before I could stop and think, I blurted out, "I see a lot of Angels here". I was a little stunned and embarrassed that I had just interrupted them. They all just smiled and told us that everyone will do whatever it takes to get Doreen back up on her feet and on her way home.

They also told us we should track her progress from week to week, not day to day. There will be days that might not go so well and look like she's going in the wrong direction, but if we looked at it from one week to the next, we would see progress. That was one of the purposes for those meetings. That sounded promising, but she was already starting out at the bottom so she could only go up, right?

They told us she had a one-hundred-degree fever overnight, and that the Fentanyl and other sedation meds had been increased. She tested positive for MRSA in her lungs and the infectious disease doctor didn't want to add any other drugs at that point other than what she already had to fight it. They also had the oxygen level up at fifty percent and had significant control of her breathing on the vent. Their primary goal for the next week was to slowly lower her sedation's and try to scale back the settings on the vent. They were going to start with baby steps in the beginning and see how she would respond.

That was the process I was hoping for. I gave them an insight of how Doreen had always struggled coming out of anesthesia after the procedures she's had in years passed, and how she had responded at the other hospital when they lowered everything too quickly. Everyone seemed to understand and now was on the same page as I was.

I felt the meeting went extremely well. Now let's see what happens. When we left that afternoon, Heather and I both were very comfortable with the direction of care they had talked about. We agreed that mom was in the right place with the right people, but we still needed to pray.

It had been a rough entrance for Doreen, and that first week wasn't much better. Every day seemed to have its own challenges from the previous one which was nothing new. We had grown accustomed to that pattern over the past two months. That repeated terrorizing roller coaster of ups and downs, twists and turns, and g-forces that made your stomach turn and your head want to explode. I was praying that ride would end once we got to this hospital. But it looked like the trial-and-error method would continue for a while longer until they could figure out how Doreen would respond to their system and protocols.

I knew that respiratory cases and ventilators were their specialty, and they would need a little time to dial in on Doreen's particular case. That didn't make the situation any easier for me, but it did offer some comfort knowing they were experts in that field, and it would be Doreen's best chance for coming home.

Since old habits are hard to die, I continued each day to write down the different stats and settings so I could let the kids know how she was doing each day. I'm not sure if it was from the move or something else, but her blood pressure was all over the place that week and they had her medications even higher than when she first got there.

There also had been issues with the feedings where they had to stop and start again a few times, and then there was the vent itself. It took some time to get that dialed in to where she was comfortably breathing and not anxious. Patience has never been my strong suit, but when you're placed in a situation like that, you have no choice. I don't know if I learned any patience here, but I did learn how to tolerate it. I also prayed a lot. I not only asked God to give Doreen the strength to fight this battle, but I also asked Him to give me the strength to keep up and do what needed to be done.

I knew it was time for me to go back to work, so on Friday that week, I decided to do a trail run. I drove to work and then to Sycamore to see how much time it would take. That would be my new routine starting on Monday the following week. I don't know why, but I was a very nervous about going back to work. I certainly was familiar with everything since I had worked there over twenty-nine years, but for some reason I felt very anxious and uncomfortable about it. I was off work for nine weeks and I certainly wasn't in the same state of mind, body, and soul as I was before.

Nobody knew I was coming, so it would be quite a surprise. I had lost almost forty pounds which certainly wasn't from Aunt Sandy's cooking, and my clothes were a little baggy. I felt like I had aged thirty years and lost just as many years of energy. But it was time.

When I opened the door and walked in, it was the reaction I was expecting. Everyone was so surprised to see me, and I think a little shocked at the way I looked. I made my way around to say hi to everyone, and I think they all noticed my emotional level had changed dramatically as well. I worked my way down to Jeff's office to visit with him for a little while, and he was completely surprised. I didn't even tell him I was stopping by.

My emotions got the best of me as I tried to express my gratitude for everything that he and his dad had done for us. From his genuine compassion and care to the financial bonus and his patience with my time away. But most of all, for all the prayers that he and his family had said on Doreen's behalf. He's a good man and comes from a great family! I don't know if he realized, just how much of the burden he lifted off my plate. The whole time I was off work, I didn't have to worry about my job or if I would even have one. That was a huge weight he had lifted off my shoulders.

I didn't want to be too big of an interruption that day, so I thanked Jeff again and told him I would start back on the following Monday. He once again was generous and allowed me to come in at 7 a.m. and leave at 1 p.m. so I could get up to the hospital in Sycamore to be with Doreen. I wouldn't take lunch, but I wanted to make sure the lunch period was covered. That was the least I could do to help since everyone had been covering for me the whole time. I said my goodbyes and told them I would see them on Monday, and off to see Doreen I went.

The weekend continued in the same pattern as the week had gone. Her blood pressure and stats would improve a little, and then go in the wrong direction. It was the same for the sedation meds and the vent settings. It was up…then down, better…then worse, day after day. That wasn't new, and of course, my emotions followed along in the same flow. Once again, I hoped and prayed that I would become numb to this seemingly endless whiplash, but that didn't happen. It just wasn't getting any easier. Poor me! Fortunately, clarity set in.

Poor me? With everything that had happened over the last couple of months, I only had to witness it. Doreen was experiencing and living it every single day. She had no choice and no say in the torture her body had to endure. I needed that reality check more often than I care to admit, but it did change the state I was in, and it brought me back into the right focus: Doreen, and what I needed to do for *her*. Her health and well-being were my number one priority, and I wasn't going to allow anything to get in the way of that. Even though my top priority was set in stone, there were countless other tasks that all jockeyed for position to get near the top of the list. I'm not sure if it's possible to multi-task multi-tasks, but that's what it felt like.

Back to Work

Monday morning was approaching, and I had to figure out exactly how much time I needed to get everything done so I could get to work by 7 a.m. It takes just under an hour to get to work, so I needed to leave no later than 6 a.m. to be there on time. I tried 5 a.m. and learned the first day that one hour wasn't enough time to get everything done, so 4:30 was the target time. I figured it would take several days or so to get a routine down.

There were a lot of mouths to tend to, and make sure they were all content because I didn't know exactly when I would be home at night. So, after everything was done outside, I would go back in and clean up, finish taking care of the dogs and head off to work. The hour drive to work would give me a chance to catch my breath and re-coop a little.

Work the first several days was very intimidating and uneasy. The work itself and the people there were still the same, but I wasn't. Obviously, my physical appearance had changed because of the weight loss, but mentally and emotionally I felt like a stranger and out of place. Having done this job for over twenty-nine years, I thought I would be able to just pick up where I had left off two months ago.

That wasn't the case. Everything felt awkward and unsure. The biggest fear I had was picking up the phone and having a customer realize I was back, and then ask a bunch of questions of what happened. I didn't want to have to explain everything repeatedly, not because it bothered me, but I didn't want everybody else at work to have to hear it either. The first few calls were the hardest, but as the day moved on, it got a little easier.

Even though I only worked for six straight hours that day (and for the next two months), by the time I left, I was physically and mentally exhausted. Throughout the day, and many days to come, I tried to keep my emotions in check, but I occasionally lost it in front of them and they saw a completely different side of me. That didn't bother me though, I was just grateful for everyone's effort picking up my slack while I was gone. I tried and did the best I could while I was there so when one o'clock rolled around, if all was good, I would head off to Sycamore.

It was about a fifty-minute drive, which gave me a little time to re-coop again before I would see Doreen. After my first day back to work, I was very excited to see how she was doing that day. My daily routine had changed so dramatically, and for some strange reason, I thought hers would be different too. But, when I walked in, it wasn't. Everything was the same at it was the day before. All the settings on the vent and the dosages on her meds were all the same, nothing changed. I was a little bummed, but then I thought, at least she didn't go backwards. I'd take that as a plus. After all, the goal was for more pluses than minuses.

Day two. Back to work was still rather cumbersome and awkward, but I was more excited and a little more anxious for my post-work hours. It was our second Tuesday meeting with Doreen's medical team. Heather met me there so she could take notes on what would hopefully be Doreen's progress. Now instead of writing down the daily stats, we took their suggestion to look at the weekly progression instead.

Once everyone was there, they went around the room like they did the first time. Each gave their report on how the previous week went, and what the game plan was for the upcoming week. The main highlight was that her lungs sounded much better than when she first came in. They had also taken out her staples (I didn't count how many, but there were a lot) that morning from the surgery. They had replaced them with sterile strips to help keep it together yet, and the incision looked like it was healing well.

They were still closely monitoring her blood pressure to try to get it under control and were also holding the vent settings where they were at because she was doing okay at those settings. There were too many other issues that needed to be addressed before they would start to wean her down on the machine. The infectious disease specialist said her white blood cells had been super high but were trending down, so they were hoping that the full broad spectrum of antibiotics, two IV and one oral, they had started her on would end soon.

Another big positive was that they had started to lower the fentanyl and other sedation meds. They explained how they needed Doreen to be more alert, not necessarily fully awake, to start the weaning process to get her off the ventilator. They were going to continue to lower the sedation each day if she would tolerate it. That was their primary goal, but it was also highly dependent on how all her other vital organs were functioning as well.

I had once again brought up how sensitive Doreen's system was to have too many things change at one time.

Everyone understood and agreed that in Doreen's case, everything would have to be closely orchestrated and in sync. After everyone left, I felt good about where everything stood, but I was still cautiously optimistic. I didn't want to get my hopes up too high like I had done so many times before, just to have them crushed when everything went backwards. But this time, it felt different.

The rest of the week continued with the new routine, and all went relatively smooth. The biggest draw-back was my energy level. All the new activity and extra travel was exhausting. The highlight of my day of course, was when I would walk in Doreen's room to visit. She has always been my security blanket, even before we were married. Even though I would visit every day, I still missed her so much. Not having her at home was absolute torture, so those few hours a day I got to spend with her were very precious to me.

It also helped that all the staff at this hospital, especially "my favorite" nurse Sara, were so friendly and kind and compassionate. Since I was there every day, they had gotten to know me and to see how dedicated I was to Doreen. They even were okay with me bringing a small portable CD player in for Doreen to listen to her favorite music, even in the ICU unit. I kept the volume down enough, so it didn't disturb any other patients, but I think the nurses really enjoyed the classic rock and even the custom CD I had made several years back for Doreen that I called "*Songs of my Heart*". My hope was that her favorite music would somehow help comfort and lead her out the darkness she was trapped in.

They also said we could bring in some pictures from home so when she would open her eyes, those images would help stimulate and motivate her to want to push forward. The nurses even told me there were several times where Doreen had opened her eyes and responded (smiled) as they talked to her. I hadn't seen any of that type of movement yet, but it certainly was the most promising development to that point. Every day I hoped I would catch a glimpse of that encouragement, but my timing only witnessed her resting. That was okay too.

Winter Preparation

Winter was coming quicker than what I wanted it to, and I was far behind in preparing for it. The one thing I had to get done in the barn for sure was replacing the water line. I wouldn't be able to handle another winter patching frozen water lines. Each splice only weakened the line, and there were a lot of splices from previous years. Since I had all the parts, I just need some extra hands to help get it done in one day.

I was able to recruit Josh and my grandson, Cayden, as well as my cousin Ken to be the laborers in the barn. I was also able to recruit Kirstyn and Natalie to go visit Doreen on that Saturday, so mom had company. Technically, this facility didn't have visitation hours on the weekends with only needed exceptions, but our family *needed* to be there every day, and they were so kind and graciously made the exception for us.

We started in the barn right away that morning and it was a little brisk outside. It didn't take us very long before we got into a rhythm. That wasn't anything new for Ken and me because we had worked together at the old lumberyard for several years and then again for a while at Lumberman's where I still work. We had always worked well together and made a great team. And to top it all off, we always had fun.

Ken and I always have been very close, and we always will be. He's like the little brother I never had, and I can always count on him to be there when I need his help. I couldn't ask for a better friend, one who just so happens to be a part of my family. That's awesome!

That day was awesome too. Everything had gone better than I expected with the tear down and replacement of the line. We put one hundred feet of pipe in with no splices, and even put all new heat tape on it to keep the line from freezing. Then the crew put all new pipe wrap and insulation to cover the pipe, and then put the plywood back up to finish. While they worked on the last ninety feet going to the tank, I worked on plumbing the first ten feet with all new shutoffs and draining. While we were busy having a good day in the barn, little did we know that Kirstyn and Natalie were having a great day with mom.

When they got back, they told us how much fun they had there because Doreen had been awake and had been responding to them. They even gave her a manicure and put a couple of pictures of the pups up on ceiling so she could look up and see her puppies. I was completely dumbfounded and blown away. That was absolutely the best day she had since before she got sick. My emotions took over again and I cried. That time though, they were tears of joy. No doubt it was another miracle, but that one was different from all the others I already witnessed. That gave my hope the biggest boost I had been longing for. And God was lucky too! He got to hear me pray a lot longer (a lot longer) that night. That was an unexpected great day.

I was so excited that I didn't sleep much that night. My mind was going a million miles an hour and I think I even made plans for our next vacation. Yep, you guessed it; I got way too far ahead of myself, as well as my expectations. But before I could go see her, I had to do the normal daily chores, and since I worked on the barn the day before, the house needed to be cleaned, and laundry needed to be done.

I usually had split it between the two days on the weekend, so now everything had to be done on Sunday. I had time because I couldn't go up until 2 p.m. anyway. I got up early and was able to get caught up with what I needed to. Why is it that when you are anxious to do something, time seems to drag on. That was how that morning went, but it finally came time to go and see that new development.

I had forgotten that it was Halloween until I made my way into Sycamore and saw a few kids that were dressed up in their costumes and already walking around. When I walked into the facility, even some of the staff had dressed up for Halloween. I was dressed up too as an over-excited husband who couldn't wait to see his wife. With high expectations of being able to interact with Doreen, I walked in only to see her eyes closed and no response to my arrival. I got the "trick" and not the "treat".

So, I followed my usual daily procedures and kissed her on the forehead, turned some music on the CD player, pulled up a chair and sat beside the bed and held her hand. Even with all that activity, there still was no response. As disappointing as it was, I was okay because I was there with her. That was all I really needed anyway.

I might have been on the third or fourth CD when I noticed she had opened her eyes. I stood up next to the bed and looked down at her. She looked directly into my eyes and smiled. My heart jumped for joy. I had seen her eyes open before, but that time it felt different.

Previously in the past when she had opened them, she would either stare off into space or most times, she just looked right at me but didn't connect. That time though, she looked directly into my eyes, recognized me and smiled. With tears in my eyes, I responded back, "I love you!" Then she smiled back at me again. Praise God! Looking in her eyes I knew my Doreen was still in there! She would close her eyes and fade back out, but every now and then, she would open them again and be aware.

During one of those moments, one of the nurses who was working that day had her granddaughter come in to trick-or-treat. She looked to be around two years old and was dressed up as a cute little chicken. I asked Doreen if she wanted to see the little girl's costume, and to my surprise, she moved her head from side to side to say no. I was stunned. She just answered my question coherently. That was an enormous boost in my confidence that we were on the right track. I couldn't wait to tell the kids what happened, which started when I pulled out of the parking lot that night. That month had started out in terrorizing fear, and now had ended in absolute hope.

> ¹⁰ So do not fear, for I am with you, do not be dismayed, for I am your God. I will strengthen you and help you, I will uphold you with my righteous right hand"
>
> Isaiah 41:10 (NIV)

[8] When Jesus spoke again to the people, he said, "I am the light of the world. Whoever follows me will never walk in darkness, but will have the light of life."

John 8:12 (NIV)

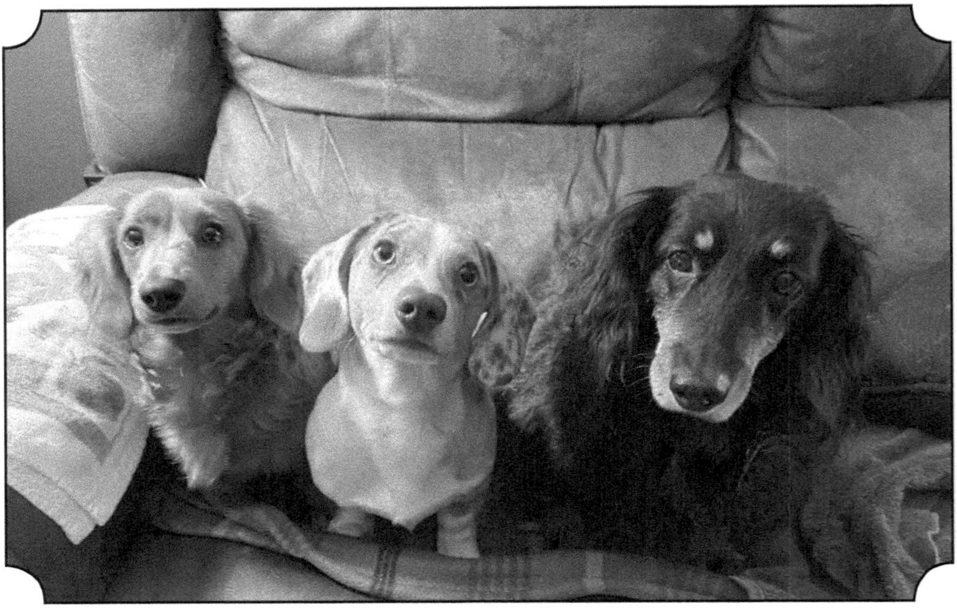

Chapter Four: November 2021

- Uphill, but Forward -

The day after Halloween always has a "left-over" sugar buzz. The energized buzz I had going was not from sugar though. I was still on a high from looking into Doreen's eyes the day before. I saw she was still with me and acknowledged it with a smile when I spoke. I think I still had a smile on my face when I woke up to go to work on Monday morning. I got up and went through my normal morning routine and headed off to work. Everything seemed to go extra smooth. I think it was because I was still flying high from the day before. It didn't matter what you called it, I had a spring in my step that day. After I breezed through work, it was off to see Doreen.

Unfortunately, my expectations were a little too inflated from my excitement, and I got a reality check as soon as I walked in her room. She didn't open her eyes, and she didn't respond to me when I told her that I loved her. The nurse came in and told me she didn't have a very good day so far, but maybe my visit might help. Dang it, once again I got a little too far ahead of myself. So instead of standing there looking at her smiling at me, which is what I expected to see, I went into autopilot and followed my usual routine. I turned on some nice music, grabbed the lotion and put it on her hands, arms and feet, pulled up a chair along side of her bed and held her hand. I had done that so many times by now that it felt like my comfortable security blanket.

I left deflated and there wasn't much to report to the kids, so the ride home and a couple of short phones calls at home took care of the updates. After I was done with the calls and did all the chores, I got everything ready for the next morning. I was positive the next day had to be better, at least when I got down on my knees and prayed that night, that's what I asked for.

The next morning followed the same pattern. Got up, did chores, went to work. That was only my second week back to work and I was still having a really hard time trying to get back into the real world outside of my COVID nightmare. No matter how hard I tried to focus on work, my mind would frequently wander back to Doreen and the hellhole we were still in. It would take several more weeks before I felt somewhat comfortable at work again, but even then, I continued to struggle being focused and present. Fortunately for me, everyone was understanding and patient which I was very grateful for, especially on Tuesdays. That was our meeting day with Doreen's caretakers and today was that day.

I was getting used to the drive from work to Sycamore and used that quiet time to pray some more. God had been hearing from me so often that I now would start by saying "Hi God, it's me again…" which I hope He chuckled instead of cringed. I had over two and a half hours a day of quiet driving time now, so if I wasn't talking with my kids, or Aunt Sandy, or anyone else, I was talking to God.

It used to really irritate me when I would see people talking on their cell phones while they drove, and now I turned into one of them. I rarely used my cell phone before, and now I couldn't be without it, just in case. I joked with my kids that once mom got home and things went back to "normal", my cell phone would live back on the counter in the kitchen. But until then, it was stuck to me like glue.

I had just finished my prayer as I pulled in the parking lot and saw that Heather was already there. She had been taking half-days at work on Tuesdays so she could meet me there for our meetings. I was really starting to feel bad that I had been dumping everything on her plate, and I was depending on her way too much. She had her own life and family to handle every day, and I had become another child she had to tend to. I knew we were getting close to the time where I needed to cut the cord and stand on my own.

Heather had been thrust into this situation without consent and had been doing a phenomenal job helping me navigate down this path of unknowns and sharp unexpected changes. The immense strain and additional stress from the last two plus months hadn't been good for her nerve disorder and her overall health. That additional stress took its toll on all my kids as well and my constant dependency on them didn't help the situation.

Before Heather and I went in, we talked about it being time where she shouldn't have to take off work anymore to be at those meetings. But being the kind of person Heather is, she said it was okay with taking the time off and it wasn't a problem with her boss, and she would continue if I needed her to. I just didn't want her to keep using her vacation time up in case she would need time off later. We decided to see how this meeting would go, and then decide.

We walked in just in time as the group was coming to her room. Once again, they went around the room, department by department and gave their report and their goal for the upcoming week. Most of them had made the comment that Doreen had finally settled in and was doing alright. She was starting to make small steps in the right direction. The scary drug Fentanyl was down to forty-five that day which was a big deal. She had been at the max dose of 300 not long after she got there.

They also reported that her incision had opened in a spot and a surgeon would come in to look at it tomorrow, and they would keep a close eye on it. Her respiratory had been doing a little better and was going in the right direction, but her blood sugar level was in the 190's and they had been giving her insulin shots. We talked about her being a diabetic, which I told them she wasn't prior to COVID. They thought she was based on her charts from the other hospital in Rockford. They said it was possible that her elevated sugar level might be from some of the medications combined with the liquid nutrition she was on, so the nutritionist said she would adjust her "food" to a lower carb formula.

One other positive highlight that day was from the pharmacy department. She said Doreen was not using the full allowance available of the anxiety and pain meds. That was very positive to me because during this entire journey, the doctors and nurses kept saying how Doreen was an anxious person which made it harder to keep everything stable. The continued primary goal for the following week would be lowering the sedation medications so they could start concentrating more on weaning her off the ventilator. They needed her more awake and alert for that process.

Over-all it was a very encouraging meeting, but they also made sure we understood that Doreen still had a long road ahead of her, but at least it appeared to be heading in the right direction. Since we were finally starting to see some progress forward, Heather said she would come to the next meeting but agreed it was time for her to stop using her vacation time. Besides, we had no idea of what lie ahead once mom would leave that place, and what amount of care and monitoring would be needed at that time. The unknown next "phase" was always scary to think about, but eventually it would be here, and we would have to deal with it.

The next few days were on repeat. It was the same routine with the same outcome. It felt like I was back in the movie *Groundhog Day* all over again. Speaking of movies, there was another movie plot I somehow managed to work into my routine during our Sycamore experience. It became a part of my daily routine for most of the time during that phase.

The movie had a unique character that had the ability to transfer an illness from an infected person into his own body by taking a deep breath in as the sick person exhaled. I had spent so many hours just sitting by the side of her bed, starring at her while she breathed. Countless times I prayed to God to let me switch places with her, so she didn't have to suffer. God was the only One who could hit the re-set button and put me there on that bed. I had even begged Him that if He wouldn't make the switch, at least let me take it from her…now. I would sit there for hours and time my breathing to hers, watching as she breathed out, I would take deep breaths in hoping to draw out the evil that had put her in that dark place.

Over and over, I would try to take it from her, the wholetime begging God to give it me. I know that's not how God works, but I had to at least try. I figured Jesus would understand why I wanted to do that since He had made the *ultimate* sacrifice for all of us. I was only asking to do that tiny sacrifice for her, and *love* was the same force behind it. Besides, God only has Himself to blame. He's the One who gave me the capability to love her the way I do. And I thank Him every day for that undeserved blessing.

Another Miracle

God not only has blessed my life in so many ways over the years, but during this journey, He also showed me the power of His love and miracles firsthand. He showed me another one on Friday that week. I had gone through my normal rituals like all the other days, but when I walked in to see Doreen that day, I couldn't believe my eyes. She was out of bed and sitting up in a chair. I was completely surprised and totally caught off guard as the nurses clapped and cheered while tears rolled down my face.

She had been slowly coming around and awake on and off (mostly off) when I had been there the last several days but seeing that was way beyond all my expectations. The nurses mentioned how she was doing better in the mornings, but by the time I usually arrived, she was always sleeping. That was okay too.

Right now, the only thing that mattered was what my eyes were seeing. I pulled out my phone and took a picture. She was even smiling on top of it. I couldn't wait to show the kids what I had just witnessed. It was nothing short of a miracle. There's no way that was even possible just a few days prior, and yet, here she was sitting in that special wheelchair.

The nurses told me they waited until early afternoon, knowing what time I would be there, to get her up and in the chair to surprise me. Surprise was an understatement. We sat there sitting together for a while enjoying the moment, and the whole time I was still in shock. It was hard to believe that she was sitting right next to me. But as we sat there, I could see she was struggling.

Imagine what it would feel like being strapped in a chair with no control over what was happening to you, and not being able to communicate on top of it. She was only able to stay sitting for an hour or so, and then they had to reverse the process to get her back in the bed. That was rather uncomfortable to watch, but worse, it was quite strenuous on her and her body.

They used a special hoist on wheels so they could maneuver it around and hook the four corners of the sling that she was sitting on. Since she literally couldn't lift a finger to move on her own, they hoisted her out of the chair and moved it over the bed and lowered her down. It took two of them to maneuver it because they also had to deal with all the IV tubes and wires that she was hooked up to, and with the all-important vent. I could see by the look on her face she was overwhelmed and fatigued. That was a major ordeal for her.

It makes you stop and think about the simple tasks we all take for granted. As difficult as it was for her, I couldn't help being so excited when I left that I didn't even get the car started before I started calling the kids to tell them the awesome news. It was a great ending to a long week.

I basically had two different routines going, one for the work week, and one for the weekend. The weekend routine had a much larger list of things that needed to get done at home, but it still included a trip to Sycamore. That went against their standard visitation rules (I think because of the pandemic), but by now they had gotten used to me being there and appreciated my devotion to Doreen. Whenever I was there, I always made sure I stayed out of the way and was quiet, even while playing the music.

I would even offer to help with tending to Doreen. I would assist them in moving her position, which had to be done every two to three hours to help prevent bedsores. They were certainly capable of moving her on their own because that's part of their daily routine with patients, but I always offered to help since I was just standing there doing nothing anyway. They were hesitant at first, but after a few times, I think I got pretty good at being an assistant. I wanted to do something to help them since they were taking such good care of the love of my life. That was the least I could do, and I would make them laugh when I could.

It is important to me to always be humble and kind as possible, and that wasn't hard to do because I was so grateful for all their efforts helping Doreen and our family. Kindness and humility really do go a long way in this life. I wish more people would try it. What a difference that would make in this world, but I realize that's a lot easier said than done. I know, because I got a big dose of "humble pie" that evening.

After I got back from visiting Doreen that Saturday, I called the kids to report in like usual. When I got to Bryan and Ashley, I filled them in on how the day had gone with mom. After chit-chatting awhile, Bryan had asked me if they could bounce something off me. They shared on how the siblings had been talking about the medical bills that were flowing in daily, and what some options might be that could possibly help.

I knew there was a small mountain of bills piling up because I was the one who got the mail every day. I would open them up and put them in a box on the counter, and then they would go to Heather's house. For the time being, problem solved. I told them I wasn't really concerned about the bills right now because there were a lot more important things to worry about other than those bills. I didn't care about the bills, I only cared about Doreen and getting her home.

The conversation continued around the issues of my heart, which obviously they understood. They wanted to make sure I was also looking at the realistic financial obligations that lie ahead and wanted me to consider the idea they had all talked about. For some dumb reason it never dawned on me that the kids had been talking among themselves during this journey. If they had mentioned it to me, I obviously didn't listen or didn't remember.

But now I knew, so of course I would listen to their proposal. In comes my huge dose of humility. They asked if it was okay to set up a Go-Fund-Me page to help us out financially. I was taken back at first, but then a wave of guilt and shame and even embarrassment began to overwhelm me. I got a lump in my throat and my emotions were raw as I proceeded to tell them that I didn't really want to do that. Mom and I had always worked our tails off and paid whatever was due. We never wanted anything we didn't earn, so I didn't want to ask for any charity. I also told them how I was brought up to take on my responsibilities and don't just look for the easy way out. I think it came across that my pigheaded pride wouldn't allow it.

After some more conversation about it, I finally had to explain it wasn't my stubborn pride that was holding me back. The truth was from all my previous life-long actions… or should I say lack of actions. From the moment they mentioned that fund, my mind had a wave of flashbacks to the many times I failed to help someone else in need when I could have. After my past neglect of others, how could I possibly ask someone else for money to help me out? I would be such a hypocrite. There was no possible way I would be able to live with myself by asking for that help. During that whole conversation, my tears of shame rolled down my face.

******

Do unto others what you want done unto you.

******

I had lived those words throughout my life when it was convenient or easy, but I had failed so many times when someone truly needed or could have used my help. God, please forgive me. At that point in our conversation, they understood my reluctance in asking for help, but the reality of our situation still needed attention. Their persistence was coming from a place of love and concern, which I was truly grateful for, and I knew deep down they were right. Regardless of the truth, I still couldn't help but feel like a failure.

I finally agreed and asked them to take care of whatever needed to be done. That was the biggest and toughest lesson in humility I had ever learned in my life. It was a long quiet night after we hung up. It was a short prayer that night, but God already knew.

One day left of the weekend, and I was up at sunrise like all the others. Both the weekend and weekday routines always started the same way with taking care of the animals first. The outside creatures got fed and watered first and then the inside ones, which were just the dogs.

There were a couple of times where our old dog Tori had stopped eating and drinking for two or three days, and I had to contemplate putting her down so she wouldn't suffer. That was a gut-wrenching thought process because Tori was Doreen's dog. If I had to do that, I would also have to tell Doreen about it once she was alert enough to understand. Doreen would have been so devastated and heartbroken, and I was concerned on what that would do to her physically since she was so weak. Thank God I didn't have to do that because Tori snapped out of it and had started eating and drinking again each time. It had been an emotional drain like so many other crises we encountered throughout this journey.

Well, speaking of the dogs and routines, there was a particular routine that developed rather quickly with the two young pups. Several weeks back, I had finally built up enough courage to move back into Doreen's room because it was just easier. I didn't sleep under the covers though. I would just lie on top of the bed and throw a blanket over the top of me and the pups would curl up next to me under the blanket. Ever since Aunt Sandy taught me how to humbly pray, I knelt by the side of the bed every night before bed, and the first thing in the morning when I woke up.

I noticed after the first few times of doing that, Smokey would go under the bed and turn around and lie down so his nose stuck out and would be right by my knees. Bandit would come along side of me and lie down by my leg making sure he was touching me. Both pups would just lie there with their heads down on the carpet and wouldn't move while I prayed out loud. Whether I prayed for a few minutes, or it turned into one of my marathons, the pups stayed quiet and still until I finished. It made me smile and gave me a sense of peace while I prayed. It was the darnedest thing. I called them "my prayer-pups." They always made me laugh though, because after I finished, they were full of piss and vinegar again until the lights went out. No question about it, they definitely were my comfort dogs.

They were also little terrors at times because they were bored during the day. There were many days when I had to do a quick vacuum after I got home at night because they brought pieces of corn stalks that blew into the yard or clumps of dirt into the house and had fun. Vacuuming and laundry and yard work were a part of the weekend routine, but those knuckleheads must have thought I needed more to do during the week. Even though I got irritated with them because of the extra work, it never lasted very long because they made me laugh, and because they were so darn cute. I guess they had their own routine for me just like I had for them.

Tragedy...or Blessing?

Sunday morning flew by, and after I finished with my cleaning and laundry, as well as getting my things ready for work the next day, I left and headed up to see Doreen. I was excited to get there that day because I wanted her to know that she would have a special visitor tomorrow. I was praying she would be awake and responsive so she would understand what I was telling her, and that she would be excited to hear the news.

Throughout the day, she would open her eyes and respond a little as I talked, but I don't think she really was aware or understood what I was saying. I would have to wait until the next day to find out if she comprehended or even remembered what I told her.

The next morning, I woke up before the sunrise and got moving. Today was going to be a special day. I breezed through the morning chores, and off to work I went. I don't know how it happened, but the clock at work moved extremely slow that day. I looked at the clock every two hours, and the hand only moved fifteen minutes. It was like watching paint dry.

It always has amazed me that when you want time to go quickly, it drags on, and when you want it to go slow, it flies by. I don't know how that's possible, but that's how it works. That day was no exception. So, after forty-seven hours of work that day, one o'clock finally arrived.

I booked out of work to go meet Aunt Sandy in Sycamore. I was careful not to let my excitement control the gas peddle, but I still made it there in record time. I sat there for a few minutes before she pulled into the parking lot. I got out of my car and walked over to hers to let her know I was there. I hadn't seen her for several weeks since the last time her and Uncle Chuck dropped off my menu request. She got out of her car and the first thing she said was, "Oh my goodness, you look like a little old man!" She never saw me in my baggy work clothes before. After we hugged, I told her I really felt like an old man as I chuckled.

I didn't know what Aunt Sandy was expecting to see, so I filled her in a little on what things looked like and how Doreen may or may not respond to us. I thought seeing Doreen in that condition might startle or even shock Aunt Sandy.

Once we got inside and down to Doreen's room in the ICU and stepped inside, Aunt Sandy walked right over to Doreen's bed and held her hand and told her how happy she was to see her and how much she loved her. Doreen had opened her eyes and smiled and I'm sure she recognized Aunt Sandy. But she had a hard time keeping her eyes open, and it didn't take long before she drifted back to sleep.

The whole time we were there, Doreen would only open her eyes briefly and then close them again. I think she knew Aunt Sandy was there and was fighting to stay present with us, but just couldn't because of the sedation meds. It didn't turn out to be the experience I was hoping for, but it was still a great visit. Now Aunt Sandy could better understand what I would talk about on the phone because she saw it for herself. Since the evening shadows were coming sooner in the day at that time of year, Aunt Sandy had to go so she could be home before it got too dark.

I always stayed as long as I possibly could before I would leave to head home. Visiting hours were only until 6 p.m., but they never kicked me out. Staying later always made me move as quickly as possible when I got home, so I could get the evening chores done as well as my "update" phone calls. That was one of the reasons I still looked skinny. I sometimes would forget to eat because I was so wrapped up with making sure everything else was taken care of and ready to go for the next day. It's amazing what a little adrenaline can do, even if you're totally exhausted.

Soon to be Solo

The next day would be Heather's last staff meeting in Sycamore. The morning rush went as planned, and my quiet drive time was spent with, "God, it's me again. Thank you!" until I would pull into the parking lot. It was hard to believe, but that was the fourth meeting already because Doreen had been there over a month.

Just like clockwork, everyone gathered, and the reports came from around the room. Her incision that had opened was finally closed and was looking good. They were still struggling with getting her blood pressure consistent but were keeping a close watch. The sedation meds were still being lowered which allowed her to respond and be more alert.

Since she had become a little more responsive, they were now starting to adjust the ventilator more frequently to see how she would respond. That would be a total trial and error approach because when she struggled with an adjustment, they would have to move it back to calm her breathing, so she didn't over-exert her lungs. When that would happen, she also became very anxious which messed with all her other vitals. Once again, they explained it was a marathon and not a sprint.

Over-all, they were happy with her progress over the past week. The plan would be to continue the same course for the next week. So far, so good. She was making some progress forward and only a few minor steps backwards. That was a far cry from the whip-lash events we had experienced previously. She was still very frail and weak, but we all could see her strong will was trying to fight to come back. Even though Doreen was still under some sedation, I think she was trying to stay awake and alert enough to hear what was being said during the meeting. She tried, but there was too much going on and she would fade in and out until it was done.

After everyone had left, Heather and I visited for a while before she had to get going. I stayed and went into my usual routine. After I put the music on, I got her hand lotion out and took care of her arms and hands before I moved the sheet to put lotion on her legs and feet. Her skin was so dry and thin, and she had very little muscle tone, like a very elderly person. I had been watching her slowly deteriorate right before my very eyes and there was nothing I could do about it.

I had a conversation a while back with Kayla, the special nurse from the hospital in Rockford, and she told me what happens to people when they can't move physically like in Doreen's case. It wasn't an exact science because everyone is different, but basically for every day that there was no movement (normal daily activity), there would be a week worth of muscle loss. That would explain why Doreen's muscles looked like they were disappearing. Even though she was getting the liquid nourishment needed to sustain her, the lack of movement using her muscles and ligaments made her extremely weak and frail.

One major issue which was becoming more and more pronounced was something they called "drop foot." That's where the tendons that control the movement of the foot contract and tighten and make it difficult for the foot to pivot to a ninety-degree angle which allows you to stand and walk. Since she was on her back in bed for so long, and not capable of moving, the tightening tendons made her foot almost straight with her leg. If she would be standing up, she would be like a ballerina balancing on the tip of her toes. The longer she would be in this "paralyzed" state, the higher the risk of it staying like that, or she would at least have some sort of permanent disability with walking.

Both hospitals understood the potential damage from that condition, and both places used a special "boot" to try and correct the ongoing battle with her feet. Her ability to stand or walk up until that point in time was not high on the long priority list the doctors were focused on. They had to concentrate on such a vast array of her other health issues before worrying about any mobility issues. Without addressing and "fixing" those things first, the ability to walk wouldn't have mattered anyway.

Her left foot wasn't near as bad as her right foot which had really dropped by that point. The thought of her having to live the rest of her life struggling to walk, or worse, having to be in a wheelchair was one of the million thoughts I would have during my solitude time at home. Many of those quiet times were agonizing moments, which some might rightly say self inflicted, but nevertheless, they were agonizing.

Stay focused and positive. Lean on your faith. Take control and move forward. Those things sound like something out of a self-help seminar, which I remembered some of the basics of. Back in 1989, I had used Anthony Robbins self-help program called *"Personal Power!"* ® to help me quit smoking. It worked and is still working well to this day.

My many issues now though were in a completely different realm and level than where I was back then. I know many of the principles still apply, but this time I needed more help than just Tony's. I had to go way over his head straight to God. I know He had a hand in helping me back in 1989 as well, but the journey this time needed His Divine intervention.

I believe He intervenes all the time, just sometimes it's more noticeable to us than others, or we may not even notice it at all. I was fortunate to see glimpses of His work as that week moved on. Doreen was finally becoming a little more alert each day. They had been trying to adjust the vent settings down, but she was struggling when they got to a certain point, and then they had to bump her back up to where she was before.

While I was there one day, one of the respiratory therapists, Lindsey, came in on her normal rounds. I should stop for a moment to explain why she was an exceptional therapist. She already worked full time at one of Rockford's major hospitals and took on a three month "second shift" at this facility.

I had asked her why she put herself through that kind of commitment. She told me she wanted to see what the next step in the recovery process looked like, and how well the patients moved through that next phase. She had only witnessed how the patients were doing when they left the ICU at her hospital, and she wanted to witness the success of how the patients recovered afterwards. I think she wanted to see that she was making a difference in people's lives. Her love for her job and her compassion for her patients were obvious, and I was glad God put her in our journey.

I had talked with her many times, but on that day, she told me how much Doreen was struggling with the adjustments. She explained if Doreen couldn't get past that one setting, she would more than likely have some sort of mechanical form of assistance to help her breath for the rest of her life. I told her I would have a talk with Doreen to see if I could help some how. But how?

Then it dawned on me, I needed her to change her focus. At that point of the weaning process, they were able to get her to that one setting and she wouldn't tolerate it for very long. It was understandable to me why she would become anxious and why her focus was on the struggle of that moment.

I can't begin to imagine what that must feel like, feeling like you're not able to catch a full breath of air, and not just for a moment, but constantly.

I knew I had to have a heart-to-heart conversation with her that would be difficult, and it would make me feel like I was being cruel. It wasn't that I was going to tell her to "suck it up and deal with it", but it would have to be tough love. One thing I had going for me though was Doreen's very strong will.

I started by telling her how well she had been doing and pointed out some of the major hurdles she had already conquered. Then I had to tell her about how I was told she would have to stay on the vent, or best case, stay on oxygen for the rest of her life if she couldn't get past that setting of the weaning process. I reinforced how she had taken control and conquered the vent up to that point in the weaning process, and she had the strength and the will to beat it the rest of the way.

You see, Doreen not only has a very strong will, but she can also be very determined. I knew if I could show her what her life would be like if she didn't get any further on the vent settings, her strong determination would kick in. It worked. The next time I talked with Lindsey, she said my talk with Doreen made a difference because they were able to lower the settings, and they didn't have to change it back. She was on her way to the final goal: getting off the ventilator. After thirty-nine years of marriage, I know my wife.

As the days passed by and the everyday routines continued, Doreen's progress continued moving forward. Her body was learning how to breathe on its own again. That sounded so bizarre to me in the beginning when we got to this acute rehab hospital. I was told Doreen would have to *learn* how to breathe on her own, how to talk again, how to eat and drink again (which they had just started by getting her to practice swallowing), how to sit up and walk again among so many other daily activities. What? How is that possible? Those weren't new activities she hadn't done a million times before. Why wouldn't she just be able to pick up right where she left off?

You can imagine the number of questions that spun off that information over time which occasionally whipped my mind into an endless frenzy. After months of waiting, at least she was on step one and moving in the right direction. When it was discussed, that progress would be baby steps, they weren't kidding. At least by this time, we weren't still on the vicious roller coaster. It was more like the "kiddy coaster" now. Fingers crossed and a million prayers later.

Now, the day finally arrived that I was on my maiden voyage. It was Tuesday again; time for the weekly meeting and Heather wouldn't be there. I was still a little nervous because I was afraid I wouldn't remember all the details so I could report them back to the kids. I was more than comfortable around all the staff because I had interacted with so many of them during all my daily visits over the course of the last four and a half weeks.

The meeting started like usual with everyone giving their input from their department as they went around the room. They had mentioned before, once she reaches a certain point in the process, which was different for every person, she would start to improve at a much quicker pace. From the reports that day, they were confident she was at that point or at least getting very close. They were very happy with her progress over the last week.

They saved the best news for last. Later that day she would be moving out of the ICU section and into a regular room. The news overwhelmed me, and my now common tears

Tragedy...or Blessing?

rolled down my face. After eleven extremely long weeks, she was finally moving out of an Intensive Care Unit. My heart was bursting with joy and gratitude, and as I looked around the room, everyone there was as happy and excited as I was. The genuine concern and compassion from Doreen's caretakers throughout this whole journey had deeply touched me, and they truly were "Super-heroes" to me and our family. I thanked them repeatedly and said, "When do we move?"

Within a short period of time, a small army of staff came in and moved everything, and I mean everything, out of the room. I offered to help, but the best thing for me was to stay out of the way. In literally a matter of minutes, Doreen was in a different section of the hospital and in her new room. Her new room was basically a semi-private room because it had a small nurse's station between the two beds with only sliding curtains to separate them, and it also had a shared bathroom in between. I taped up the various pictures we had brought up for her to see glimpses of home and set up the CD player so we could listen to some music.

That new room would be very different than the ICU room we had been accustomed to. There was only one bed in her previous room, and there was only a sliding curtain instead of a door so the nurses' station could always hear and see into each room. This room was also across from the nurses' station, but there was an actual door that could be shut.

However, there were only a couple of curtains separating Doreen from the other patient that was there in the other bed. I had put on some music, and we quickly found out her new "neighbor" was a man when he mentioned the music was okay but asked that we turn the volume down. It was a new experience having a neighbor basically in the same room, but you just couldn't see each other.

I obliged and turned it down and realized I would have to pay closer attention not only to how loud I talked, but also on what I would say. I wasn't too concerned though because I was just so happy that Doreen was really progressing down the right path. That's all I really cared about. It would take some adjustment with the new surroundings, but each day there was a noticeable improvement. What a difference a couple of days can make. My days were on repeat, but Doreen was conquering the machine and making great steps forward.

Friday, November 19th

I will never forget that Friday afternoon. It had only been a few days after she left the ICU, when I made my way to her new room. As I walked in and over to her bed, I noticed it was quiet and that the ventilator was unplugged and pushed over to the side of the room. I was stunned and unsure of what was happening. Doreen's nurse for the day, Josh, was in the room with a big grin on his face. He had been Doreen's nurse a couple of times since she moved, and he was a cool nurse. I was very confused as I stood on the opposite side of the bed from Josh.

Josh looked down at Doreen and said, "Are you ready?"

Doreen looked at him and nodded her head. He pulled the oxygen hose off that was attached to her trach and put a red plastic cap over the trach to close it off. Doreen turned her head towards me and said, "Hi, I love you!"

I immediately burst into tears as I leaned over and put my head on her chest, hugging her as best I could. I remember every muscle in my body shaking with emotion as I cried. I had been waiting for that moment for what seemed like an eternity, and it was finally here.

All those countless hours where I wondered whether she would even be able to speak again had just been answered. It took me several minutes to regain my composure before I stood back up again. Josh just stood there smiling at me. I was so caught up in the moment that I forgot I wasn't the only one there who heard those amazing words. I was so overjoyed and emotional that I couldn't even make a coherent sentence.

There were multiple major events that took place in literally less than twenty-four hours. The first one was the ventilator. It was shut off. Lindsey had told me that each time they adjusted the vent down, they would leave it there for a day or two until Doreen would adjust to that setting before they would attempt to lower it again. I apparently lost track of how long it had been, and how far they had got in the process. I thought she still had several more days before they would be able to switch her over to the trach collar that she obviously was now on.

The trach collar was the final phase in the weaning process because it didn't use the oxygen from the ventilator itself. It was designed to use the regular oxygen line coming out from the wall which blows the oxygen over the trach and not directly into it. That meant Doreen had to pull the oxygen into her lungs by herself. She was breathing on her own with no mechanical assistance! That was a miracle; one I had been praying so hard for.

Josh then explained that this special red cap (Doreen called it her "ruby" cap) was called a Passy-Muir Valve. It capped over the trach and allowed her to breathe in through it, and then would shut when she exhaled so the air went out through her nose and mouth which allowed her vocal cords to work.

All I could focus on was that she **told** me she loved me. I had just witnessed yet another miracle firsthand. By God's grace, and His alone, Doreen had just surpassed a major milestone on her excruciating journey. As you might imagine, my update calls that night were filled with tears of joy as I passed on what I encountered that day. Even the pups got to experience my joy by having to lie still on the floor that night for a long time while I prayed "God, thank you, thank you, thank you, thank you!"

I slept well that night. I finally felt, for the first time, that I could let my guard down a little. Even though some weight had been lifted off my shoulders the day before, there still was a lot of work to do coming up, so the weekend routine would not be normal like all the others. How appropriate that the following week was Thanksgiving.

I had so much to be thankful for, far more than usual. Doreen's progress the last few days was at the top of the list. Even though there was so much to be grateful for, that Thanksgiving would be a tough one for our family, especially for me. Doreen and I had never missed celebrating a holiday at home together for over forty years. That would be the first. From our very first date up until now, we were always together for those special occasions. Always.

Normally, each of the kids takes a turn hosting either Easter or Thanksgiving, and we would host Christmas at our house. It had worked out well over the years, but under the current circumstances, we decided to have Thanksgiving at our house for whoever could make it. I knew that Bryan, Ashley and the kids were coming up from Tennessee for sure and would arrive on Wednesday. Heather and her family would be able to come as well. Since it was such a last-minute decision, Josh and Natalie had already made plans to go to her brother's house, and Kirstyn's family was planning on

Tragedy...or Blessing?

going to Arkansas to see Jason's mom for the holiday. With the guest list completed and the menu planned, the low-keyed Thanksgiving get together had now been finalized.

I still had a few other phone calls to make to finalize the head count for the "barn-raising" event at Heather's father-in-law's farm the following weekend, because that's where they lived. Those calls would have to wait until I got back from visiting Doreen that afternoon. I was anxious to get there so I could hear her say "I love you" again. Those words had never sounded so comforting and uplifting, even though I heard her say them so many times before over the years. Obviously, I was a little excited to see her. Also, we would have extra company visiting as well. Kirstyn was coming up later after she went to the dentist.

I got there early afternoon on Saturday, and she smiled as soon as I walked in the room. It was amazing how such a simple gesture could make such a huge impact on me. That smile, now coupled with a voice, made all my fears and heartache completely melt away. We were able to talk to each other, which made it so much easier to communicate. From that point forward, it wouldn't just be my voice in the room during our conversations. So, I proceeded to tell her about all the plans for the upcoming week, and that she would have a few other visitors there to see her since I would be busy over at Heather's house.

We could only talk for a short while before it became difficult for her. The nurse would have to take the red cap back off and put the oxygen hose back on the trach collar. Even that part of the process would require baby steps. She would have to build up the strength and tolerance in her lungs which would take some time. But now she was moving forward and time wasn't an issue to me any longer.

Kirstyn got there later and brought me some dinner from Portillo's. That was one of Doreen's favorite places to eat, so I stood behind the curtain so she couldn't see me eat it. We laughed and joked and had a great visit that day. It was getting time for us to go, and Doreen said she was not comfortable being there with that guy in the other bed because he always seemed agitated. He even had been cursing and throwing things across the room at his company who was visiting him that day.

Doreen had told us she was afraid to be alone in the room because she was immobile and would not be able move or defend herself. I could see the fear in her eyes when she asked me to spend the night with her. Kirstyn stayed with her while I went to find the night supervisor to see if that would be possible.

A nurse told me to go down the hall to an office and ask for Dawn. She was in charge for the night. The door was open, but I knocked anyway and asked which person was Dawn. She introduced herself and asked what I needed. I told her I was Doreen's husband and then proceeded to explain the situation with the gentleman in the other bed. I explained how upset and scared Doreen was to be alone in the room, and that she asked if I could spend the night with her. I told Dawn I would need a few hours to go home, do chores, and get back again. If she would be kind enough to allow me to do that, I would be extremely grateful.

Dawn responded by telling me she had been watching over Doreen from the very first night she arrived. She had made sure that Doreen was always taken care of and was comfortable. She said Doreen was a very special patient and that everyone loved her because she always smiled at them when they would talk to her. She asked if I would give her a little time and she would see what she could do for us.

It was only about fifteen minutes or so before she came in a said they were going to move her to a private room. Just like a few days ago when she was moved out of the ICU, several people came in and away she went. So, within a few short minutes, Doreen was in her own room.

Dawn came in a few minutes later and asked if that new room would work and told Doreen she would personally keep checking in with her throughout the night to make sure she was alright. I was once again blown away by the true compassion and care that Dawn had just demonstrated. I was so thankful that God had placed this guardian angel in Doreen's life. She was amazing!

It was getting late, so Kirstyn left while I stayed for a little while longer to make sure Doreen was settled and comfortable. Dawn had stopped by the room again and told me that I needed to get some rest too, and everything would be okay because she would make sure of it. I had only met her two hours ago, and I knew I could completely trust her with taking care of Doreen. Knowing she was there watching over Doreen put my mind completely at ease. I left and went home and said an extra prayer of thanks to God for placing Dawn in our lives.

There wasn't enough time for any extra phone calls that night because I got home so late. Actually, I didn't even do any chores other than feed the dogs. I figured I would be doing chores all over again in just a few hours, so I decided to call it a night and take care of everything in the morning. I was completely exhausted and fell asleep before my head even hit the pillow. It felt like I just closed my eyes, and it was time to get up. How does that happen?

It was time for the morning weekend routine, but it would take a little longer than normal because I had to make up for what I didn't do the night before. I didn't mind it though because I knew Doreen was comfortable and felt safe after last night's efforts. That was more important than anything else. I hustled as fast as I could getting the laundry, dishes, and vacuuming done so I could get up to see how Doreen's night went. I figured if I got there a little earlier, I could get home a little earlier and make those couple of calls I needed to for the big project next weekend.

Once I got there and walked into her new room, I immediately could see that she really felt comfortable. I could also tell that she had a decent night sleep, as best you can in a hospital. I felt relieved that all of Dawn's efforts the night before had paid off. That was exactly what Doreen needed to focus on moving forward with the rehabilitation program.

At that point, I felt she was past the illness stage and now was working on the "re-learning" stage they had talked about several weeks earlier. All those baby steps didn't seem like she was going anywhere at the time, but when I looked back at where we were when she got there, she had made enormous progress. I was so proud of her for all her strenuous efforts, and I was extremely grateful for everything this hospital staff had done for her.

Like usual, the hours flew by while I was there, and I told Doreen I had to get going so I could do chores and make those calls I needed to. I always felt guilty leaving her, especially since she never wanted me to go. It usually took me an hour or so to leave, but that day, I really had to get going. I knew she understood, but I think she just wanted her best friend there.

By that time of year, it was getting dark early, so I had to do the evening chores in the dark. Once I finished and had everything ready for the next day, I made my first call to my brother Dave. I had already called a couple of weeks earlier to line up his help, so this was just to confirm he and his crew could be there next Saturday. He had lined up my nephew Davey and two of his employees to give us a hand. We also confirmed what tools he'd bring and the steel plates he had made for bolting the concrete blocks together. He came through yet again, and his "can-do" work ethics are contagious. Everything was good to go, and they would meet at my house early Saturday morning.

The other call I made was to my cousin Ken. I always knew I had to call Ken last after all the other calls because we usually were on the phone for two to three hours. If we had a one-hour conversation, the problem was he only talked for ten minutes and listened for fifty. Ken is one of those people you can always count on no matter what. I don't know what I've ever done for him to deserve that kind of commitment he's shown me over the years, but I am so grateful to God for allowing Ken to be a part of my life. Even though we don't see each other as often as we would like to, it doesn't matter, because when we do see each other, we pick up right where we left off like there was no time lapse at all. We have a unique and special relationship, one that doesn't come along very often in this life. What a blessing that is! Everything was now in place, so let the "barn-raising" proceed.

Somehow or another, those three workdays before Thanksgiving absolutely flew by. Each day was on repeat. Get up and get chores done, go to work until lunch was done, go see Doreen (time really flew then), go home and do chores and go to bed. I was fortunate Doreen was doing a little better each day, but I still had a hard time leaving each night. I missed her being at home so much.

But now with our upcoming schedule, I tried to get her excited about having some other visitors later that week, but I noticed she still was struggling a little. I'm sure a lot had to do with me going ninety miles an hour explaining all that was happening over the next several days. Since I had been waiting so long for her to come out of that dark fog, she was now awake and more alert, and I acted as if she was back to normal and would understand everything.

Obviously, there were some residual effects from the months of heavy sedation meds that she had been on, and she would need a lot more time for those things to work out of her system. I just needed to slow down and pay more attention to her pace of recovery and not try to speed up the process. She had only recently "learned" how to breathe on her own again and had just started "talking" again. Both of those giant steps were still very challenging and exhausting if she pushed too hard. I had learned a lot through this ordeal, but I still had a lot more to learn.

I don't know how many times I had heard the professionals say, "This is a marathon, not a sprint" and yet, I continued to lose track of that fact. During that Tuesday's meeting, everyone's report was very positive about her progress for the week, and before we finished, that quote was mentioned again. Sooner or later, it was bound to sink in; hopefully.

Either I'm a slow learner, or possibly because my mind over the last few months was always going in a hundred different directions at the same time, and I had a hard time keeping up with it. Maybe it was a little of both. Regardless, I had to really concentrate and focus on Doreen and all the upcoming tasks in front of me.

O Give Thanks…

Thanksgiving was only a couple of days away and there was plenty to do. Bryan, Ashley and the kids would be here sometime Wednesday evening, so the sleeping locations had to be ready for when they got there. Our Thanksgiving dinner

Tragedy...or Blessing?

would be here also, so there were things to get ready for that as well. Under the circumstances, this holiday had been put in place in short order, and it wouldn't be the same fuss and detailed dinner like those of the past. It already wasn't going to be a normal Thanksgiving because Doreen wouldn't be there, but we all made the best of a bad situation. But there was still plenty to be thankful for.

The sunrise Thursday morning came quickly, and the kitchen already started to smell like turkey. Once breakfast was done, we started prepping some more of the feast. Heather was at home making some dishes to bring, and we had decided to eat earlier than normal that day so I could go see Doreen. Bryan's family would go to Ashley's parents to spend the day with them when we were done, and Heather's family would go back to their house because they had to get ready for our crew coming over to work on the new building that weekend.

At the last minute, Kirstyn's family didn't go to see Jason's mom in Arkansas because our grandson Landon had been exposed to COVID in school, so their family had to stay home and quarantine for Thanksgiving. I would have asked them to come over, but I didn't because I was going to see Doreen later. I wouldn't let anyone come around even if they only had the sniffles. With everything we were going through, I just couldn't take the chance of possibly exposing Doreen to anything.

Dinner was finally ready, and there was plenty as usual. We gathered around the table like so many holidays before, but that one was different. That was the first time Doreen was not at the table. After we all said the common table prayer together, I continued with thanks to God for His healing grace for Doreen and for keeping our family together. Then our grandson, Emerson, read his prayer that he wrote. He thanked God for the food we had and for helping grandma get better. My emotions were especially raw that day but listening to his prayer opened the flow of tears again. The purity of a child's heart should be something every adult tries to strive for. What a blessing that is!

After we were done and everything was cleaned up, we all went our separate ways. I spent the rest of the day and part of the evening with Doreen and had a nice Thanksgiving with her. She had turkey for dinner also, but it wasn't the same as at home. She was eating "regular" food now, which I thought tasted pretty good. She still wasn't eating very much yet, partly because she's a pretty picky eater. I was happy just to see her have the capability to eat again. That was just one of the multitudes of things that I was thankful to God for on this Thanksgiving Day.

Doreen knew those next couple of days would be different because I would not be there to see her. I would be over at Heather's house working on their new building, but I made sure Doreen would still have company. I had asked Bryan and Ashley to spend Friday with her since they would have to leave the next day to go home. I thought it would also be nice for them to spend some alone time with mom, just the three of them. While Bryan and Ashley would be doing that, I went over to help make sure everything was in place and ready for Saturday when the full crew would be there to start putting the building jigsaw puzzle together.

That would be the first time any of us would be assembling a © Clear-Span hoop building, and that one was sixty-five feet wide by one hundred forty feet long by twenty-four feet high at the center. For the base of the structure, they used pre-formed concrete blocks that were two foot square and four foot long which weigh around 1,800 pounds a piece and were stacked two blocks high. If you do the math, there were a lot of them. Fortunately, most of them were already in place by that time, but we still had a few to set that day and make sure everything was square.

Once that was done, we went through all the parts and pieces we would need the next day to assemble the eight giant three-inch round tube steel trusses that were the main structure. In between the trusses was two-inch round steel tubes that were twenty feet long which would allow the enormous special tarp to stay formed and tight over the top of the structure. It took a little while, but we found all the parts we needed.

I figured with all the extra help coming the next day, we would be able to at least get the trusses assembled in the morning and have at least half of them up by the end of the day. It sounded simple to put together, but like all the projects I tackle, it wouldn't go as quickly as planned. I also had not calculated that the sun was going down much earlier than just a few weeks ago. After all these years of countless projects, you would think I would know better by now that nothing ever goes exactly as planned. Nope, and this was no exception.

It was late Friday afternoon, and we finished getting ready what we needed to start the next morning. I headed home because I wanted to spend some time with Bryan and Ashley and the kids that night. I would be leaving very early the next morning before they would be ready to go because Dave and his crew, and Ken, would be meeting at our house so they could follow me over to Heather's.

Once Bryan and Ashley got back with the kids, we had a couple of cocktails and talked until it got late. I always enjoy our visits, but somehow the time always seems to fly by. We said our goodbyes, which are always tough to do anyways, and everyone headed for their pillows. Tomorrow would be a long day, and since I wouldn't be able to go see Doreen, I had asked Josh and Natalie to go visit on Saturday so she would have some family there to visit with her and not have to be alone that day. Everything should be in place.

We planned to have everyone meet that morning between 7:30 and 8. Everyone was there by 7:30. There was my brother Dave and Wendy, my nephew Davey, two of Dave's employees, Mike and Nick, and Cousin Ken. After all the introductions, everyone jumped in their vehicles and followed me to Heather's. It was like a parade because just about everyone drove separately. After we got there, it would be the round of introductions again.

It was fairly cool outside, and everyone was ready to get started to just to stay warm. We went around back into the pasture where all the steel truss parts were unloaded and got the generators set up and all the tools out while a few of us looked over the blueprints. It seemed straight forward and detailed down to every nut, washer and bolt size. Since we found all the correct boxes with the right sized bolts and brackets we would need for assembling the trusses, we were able to get started quickly. Like any project that has a few people who never worked on something like that before, and who had never worked together, it took a little while for us to get a rhythm going.

On top of it, those pieces were large and heavy. Each truss had four large sections to make the main arch, and two smaller pieces, one for each side that came down to a point where they would bolt onto a large base plate which would be anchored to the cement blocks. Sounds easy, right? Not really, because once each one was assembled, they were sixty-five feet wide, and I have no idea how heavy they were. Once we finished one, we used the skid steer to pick it up the middle as high as it could go and had two people on each side to help pick up the ends so we could move it to the side and out of the way. We started with the last truss needed and worked our way to the first one needed so we would stack them on top of each other to make it convenient for when it came time to move them in place.

I think we were on the second or third one when we realized it was going to be a full day just getting them all put together and stacked up. Like any first-time job where there is a learning curve, we made a couple of mistakes and had to go back and fix them, but over-all, it went pretty well. We only stopped once for lunch and worked until the sun was starting to go down. I can't speak for the younger crew, but I was physically exhausted. After we finished with the last truss, we had time for a quick beer, and it was time to pick up the tools and sort who brought what and load up to go.

I was extremely impressed with how well everyone had worked together, as well as how hard everyone worked with no complaints. Even though we didn't come close to my over ambitious goals for the building, we did accomplish a major task. Those enormous trusses were completely assembled and ready to go. We had just celebrated Thanksgiving a couple of days before, and again I was thankful to God for everyone who came and helped just because I asked. I don't know what I've ever done to deserve so many good people in my life, but I am truly honored and grateful to every single one of them.

I spent the next few days recuperating. Even though we only managed to assemble the trusses and not the full fledged "barn-raising" event I thought it was going to be, it had taken a toll on me both physically and mentally. It wasn't necessarily because of one day's hard work, but more from the accumulation of the past few months along with a little hard labor that did it for me. I would have to say I was physically only at seventy percent of what I was pre-COVID. Couple that with my mind being on constant over- drive for so long and I was completely spent.

I did feel somewhat satisfied though that we were able to get a good jump-start on the building. We had been talking about getting it put up long before Doreen and I had got sick. But, under the circumstances, at least we accomplished something on it even if it wasn't what we had planned from the beginning.

Now that the building was started and we were past that project, I could now focus all my attention back on Doreen. I would get back in my daily routine and continue with the daily progress she was making. She still had a long, long way to go, but at least she was moving forward. November was ending, and it was hard to believe Doreen was finishing with her third month in the hospital.

> **[6] Do not be anxious about anything, but in everything, by prayer and petition, with thanksgiving, present your requests to God. [7] And the peace of God, which transcends all understanding, will guard your hearts and minds in Christ Jesus.**
>
> Philippians 4:6-7 (NIV)

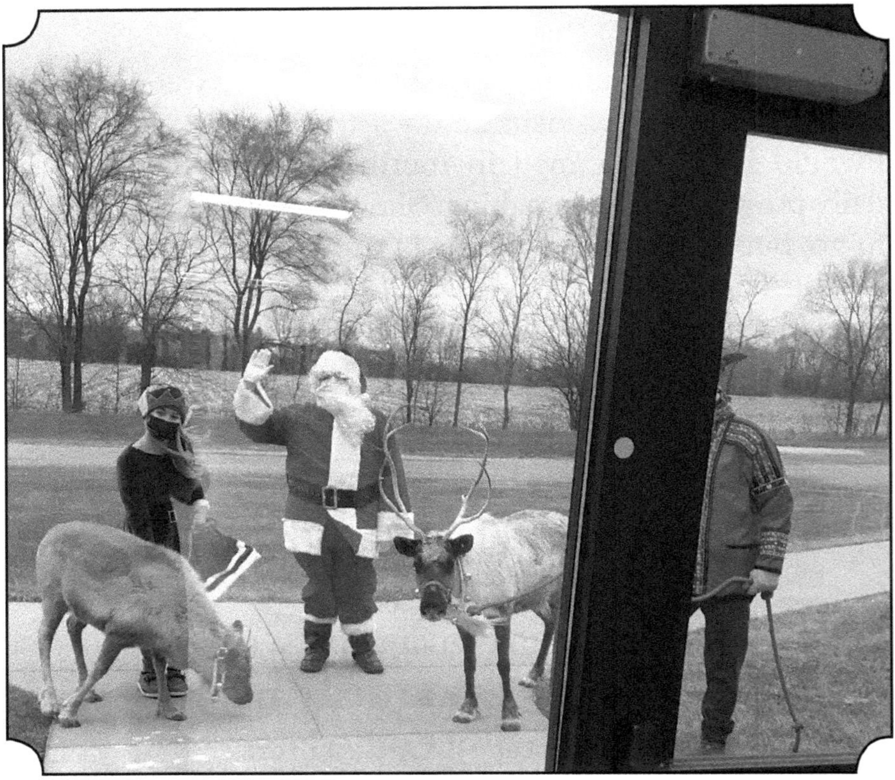

Chapter Five: December 2021

- Slow & Steady...Almost There -

Normally, that time of year always takes me a while to get used to because I only get to see my house in the daylight on weekends. During the week, I leave in the dark in the mornings to go to work and then I don't get home until it is dark again. I don't know if there's any actual proof behind it but doing chores outside in the dark always seems harder and more exhausting than when I do them in the daylight. I'm sure part of that is due to the temperature drop once the sun goes down, but it was already getting colder out during the day anyway. Now add the events from the last three months, and my physical energy level dropped to a low I wasn't used to. That didn't matter though because the daily chores had to get done no matter what because there were so many mouths that needed attention.

It basically went like this: I would let the dogs outside while I went out to do chores. I had to fill the water tank both morning and night for the cows, and feed small bales of hay to use up what I had before going back to the large round bales again. The weekend cow routine included spreading fresh cornstalk bedding which was a physical challenge all by itself. Over-all, it probably took the longest to feed the bees.

The bees were Doreen's passion, and I wanted to make sure I kept them alive for when she would get home. She had thirteen hives going. Since the food sources for bees were almost non-existent at this time of year, we fed them a special mixture of sugar water, vitamins and minerals. We use a special box which goes on top of the hive, so the jars are internal and only the bees in that hive have access to it. I would go to each hive and loosen the tie strap that held them down and move it out of the way. Then I would take the top cover off and put two one-pint jars of sugar water in upside down with the lids that had tiny pin holes in them. After that, I covered the jars with burlap and put the top cover back on and strapped it back down. It doesn't sound like much, but it took at lot of time.

I kept the hives strapped down because I didn't want to take a chance that a storm might come through while I wasn't there and possibly blow the hives over. The mornings consisted of putting the jars in the hive, and at night, I had to remove the jars to fill them back up and to keep them warm overnight. The sugar water gets too thick when it's cold and doesn't go through the tiny pin holes. It also made the jars hard to open to re-fill.

Also, since it was always dark out when I did chores during the week, I wore one of those head-band flashlights so I could see what I was doing. We had hives all around the yard and that was the only light I had. I'm sure the cars driving by were wondering what the crazy person was doing going into the hives in the dark. I just needed to keep them going for Doreen. I never really paid attention before to how much time it took to do everything. Now, I just did what needed to be done.

My daily routines for the past several weeks had become quite repetitive and mundane. Doreen's daily routines on the other hand, were progressing forward and becoming very exciting to watch. One of those daily activities we all take for granted was mealtime. Just a few short weeks ago, she had to learn how to swallow on her own all over again. As crazy as that sounds, the dietitian had to make sure Doreen would be able to handle drinking and eating with the trach in place.

She started by adding some blue food coloring in a cup of ice chips, and then gave a spoonful to Doreen. She then put her fingers on Doreen's throat to feel her swallow. After doing that a couple of times, she then had to use the suction tube that was hooked up to the vent tube through the trach. She had to push it down into Doreen's lungs to see if any of the blue dye went into her lungs. I had already watched that suctioning process so many times over the months, and that torture never got any easier to watch. After doing that for a couple of days, she was able to move on to water using the same technique. Once she passed that, on to pureed food. That was a thrilling day! She was able to have "real" food.

Well, sort of real food. I don't recommend the pureed cinnamon roll. Once she graduated the pureed process, she went on to regular food that needed to be chewed. During that process, Doreen told them they couldn't supplement with the liquid feed tube anymore. She was done with that type of nourishment. It doesn't sound like much, but those couple of weeks had been enormous progress!

Another area where she had made leaps and bounds moving forward was in her awareness and in her communication. Prior to Thanksgiving, there were times when she would be awake and responsive to what was going on around her, but I believe during those interactions, she was aware but wasn't totally present in that moment. I say that because the next time we had an interaction where I thought she was completely coherent, I could tell she couldn't recall the previous conversations, at least parts of them. Granted, it had only been the past few weeks we were even able to communicate to each other, but the past week or so since Thanksgiving, there definitely had been a noticeable improvement.

We were told by the team that once she was off all the sedation medications, it would take several weeks or more for the drugs to work out of her system. At that point, she would be able to cognitively function in a more "normal" fashion. They were spot on. That was a phenomenal step forward because we were now able to have conversations that actually progressed forward each day and not just for a particular moment. I could tell she still had a fair amount of "brain fog", but obviously that was to be expected. Heck, I was still a little foggy and I certainly didn't endure anything even remotely close to what she had to. I was thrilled with the progress she had made and with the momentum she now seemed to be accelerating at.

I wasn't the only one who had observed her noticeable changes. The rehab team had been monitoring her progress and was as pleased as I was. So much so they told me the time was quickly approaching for Doreen to move on to the next phase in her rehabilitation. The following Tuesday would be our last group meeting. It was a unanimous consensus from each department, the progress Doreen had been making recently was enough to move her to the final step to get her home.

The goal all along had been to get her home, but it always felt like it was so far away and out of reach. It had been talked about so much throughout this journey, but for the first time, it hit me that it was really going to happen. I had been afraid for so long to get my hopes up like I had so many times before, only to hit a wall and be crushed by some unexpected curveball. But this time, it really *was* going to happen. Her slow and steady progress forward was making it possible. Just a few more steps and we were almost there…home.

Time flies when you're having fun. At least that's what they say. I certainly wouldn't describe any part of this journey as fun by any stretch of the imagination. In fact, it would be the polar opposite of fun. But the next several days absolutely flew by. It had been the fastest days I think I ever had experienced. The daily routines and activities had all melted together from one day to the next.

Tuesday, December 7th

Before I knew it, Tuesday had arrived and that would be the last group meeting with this very special staff. The morning went as planned, and then I was off to Sycamore. Shortly after I arrived, everyone entered her room like so many times before. The meeting started and each one gave their assessment of Doreen's progress over the past week and added what they would like to see over the coming week. From the very start of the meeting, everyone knew the discharge date would be Tuesday December 14, 2021.

After they gave what their goal would be for Doreen for the following week, each one stated how happy they were with all the progress Doreen had made and encouraged her to keep pushing forward. Some of them had made a very special bond with Doreen, and I could tell how emotional it was for them because they cared so much for her. We were so fortunate to be in the care of so many good people during such a critical time in our lives. After the last one had finished and everyone was ready to leave, I asked them all to stay for a couple of minutes. I had something to say to all of them which I felt was very important, at least to me.

I began to speak, "I have to say, I have learned more about life in the last sixty days than I have over the last sixty years. I've learned what's most important in life, and what I've taken for granted. Over the last few months, Doreen and I have been on the same path, but my journey has been different than hers. There's been my physical journey, which obviously pales in comparison to the one she" I pointed to Doreen "has gone through. Mine wasn't even close to what she's had to endure."

"Then there was my emotional journey. It has been the most excruciating and horrendous emotional roller coaster I could have ever imagined. I cried a lot. I used to think that my tears were a sign of weakness. What I've learned over the last couple of months was that they're not a sign of weakness, but a true sign of honesty and humility."

"And then there's been my spiritual journey. Now, I know that God can do miracles. I've known that my whole life, ever since I was a little kid. But through this, I have seen so many of His miracles on this journey happen right before my very eyes. What I've learned though, is God doesn't always perform those miracles by Himself. He puts the right people, in the right place, at the right time to help in those miracles. So, I want to thank each and every one of you from the bottom of my heart. Thank you for being a part of Doreen's miracle. I am forever grateful! Thank you…thank you…thank you!"

As I finished speaking, I looked around the room and saw that a few tears had formed in some of their eyes. I could tell they felt the words of gratitude that had come straight from my heart. I just wanted them to know that the work they do, and the effort they put forth doesn't always go unnoticed. They really do make a difference in people's lives, and I wanted them to know they had made a difference in our family's lives. Through their combined efforts, Doreen would soon be on her way home to us. That was a miracle, and they *truly* were a part of that miracle.

That last meeting could not have gone any better. Everyone was pleased with Doreen's progress, and confident in her future outcome. Having worked with her as long as they had, they knew she would push herself to get back on her feet. They had met the real Doreen. I already knew what she was capable of doing, and I was so excited about having a real future with her again. There's a song that John Denver sings about a *"Rocky Mountain High."* My "high" was better. With the end date now in place, the only thing left to do was to get a physical rehab facility lined up.

There was less than a week to pull that off, but Angel was confident she would find a place for Doreen. It was a little nerve racking to wait and see where she would go because our family wanted to go some place as close as possible. Since I would be traveling from work, I didn't want to travel more than an hour or so from home. I already spent over two and a half hours of driving as it was, and I didn't want to add too much more on top of it. But if I had to, I had to.

When I got there on Wednesday, I checked in with Angel to see if she was able to come up with something. Not yet, but she was working on it. Even though the clock was ticking, I was doing okay with the waiting game. I knew God didn't bring us that far just to leave us hanging now. I stayed there while Doreen had her dinner, and then stayed past the visiting hours like I had done so many times before. She never wanted me to go, and I never really wanted to leave either, but she knew I had all the chores to do before I could go to bed.

Before I left though, we got a visit from our favorite nighttime supervisor, Dawn. She stopped by to see how Doreen was doing because she had heard about the good news; Doreen was ready to go on to the next step. I can't say enough good things about Dawn. I honestly believe she was Heaven sent.

During the course of our conversation, she asked what facility Doreen was headed to. We told her we wanted to go to a place in Rockford that we heard so many good things about, and because it would work out well logistically for us. She knew exactly which place we were talking about because she had a cousin that worked there.

Earlier in our conversation she had told us how her kids always asked if she had a favorite patient to which she would reply that she cared about all the patients. But she told them, occasionally there would be one who was her favorite. She looked and pointed at Doreen and said "*She's my favorite*" which brought a big smile to Doreen's face (and mine). We talked for a few more minutes before she said she had to keep making her rounds. Since Dawn had mentioned she knew someone at the facility we wanted to go to, I put my arm around her and said, "Since Doreen is your favorite, can you make a call to see if they could take her?"

Dawn smiled and answered, "Of course I will, just for her," as she pointed at Doreen again. "I'll see what I can do."

That's all we could ask for, and it was worth a try. We still had a little time yet, and everything was coming together nicely, or so I thought.

The next day when I got there, I was told Doreen had been accepted to the Physical Rehabilitation Center in Rockford. The Center would have a bed available, and the insurance company had approved it. Perfect, that's exactly where we wanted her to go. I don't know for a fact, but I think Dawn came through for us. The "high" kept getting higher. Doreen and I were having a wonderful visit that afternoon because of the good news. She was a little nervous and unsure, but she knew she would have to go that facility first before she could come home.

It had only been two or three hours after we found out the good news when I was called down to the administration office to talk with our case manager, Angel. When I walked in, I could tell by the expression on her face that there was an issue. She told me the insurance company was now refusing the transfer to the facility we wanted, and she would have to start the process all over again to see what other facilities might be available to accept Doreen. What the hell just happened? How could they say yes just a few hours ago, and then change their minds and say no? I was a little upset to say the least.

Angel told me she would try to get some other people in their company involved to make some calls and try to get this straightened out if possible. The high I was on just a few moments ago had suddenly made a crash landing. You would think I would be used to that roller coaster by now from the countless other times that s**t happened. I must admit though, that crash wasn't nearly as horrifying as the previous multitudes had been in the past.

It only took about an hour or so (a very long hour), before Angel came back to Doreen's room and said that she was good to go to the rehab center in Rockford again. She told us the people she contacted were able to advocate Doreen's case to the insurance company and why it was crucial for her to go to that facility to finish her recovery. I was dumbfounded. She did it. It was a job well done, literally by an "Angel". I gave her a big hug and thanked her for all her efforts. That was quite an exhausting day from the up, then down, then up again.

Big Surprise!

The next day was very, very emotional, far more than the day before. When I walked in her room like usual, she had a huge grin on her face. I noticed the grin immediately, but I didn't notice just a few inches lower. It took a few moments before I realized what the enormous grin was for. She no longer had the trach tube in! It was totally gone with just a small hole as a reminder. The tears of joy flowed like the Mississippi river. We had waited so, so long for her to reach that moment, and now she was there.

I couldn't wait to tell the kids when I left, and poor God, I think that was one of the longest marathon chats I had with Him. Hallelujah, it looked like all the final pieces of the vent-weaning puzzle were now in place and Doreen would be leaving in just a few short days.

There had been so many wonderful people at the Acute Rehab Hospital who had helped Doreen throughout that portion of her journey. I unfortunately did not write down all the names, nor did I personally thank each one of them at the time I could have. I sincerely apologize for my missed opportunities to those who deserved my gratitude. Though it may not have been expressed directly, know that my heart will always be grateful for the help and care Doreen had received while in their care.

We were able to share a small token of our appreciation after Doreen had the ability to communicate and make decisions on her own. It had only been within the last couple of weeks where she took control of her own personal "thank you" to the people she felt had done a lot for her. Keep in mind there were so many others who played key roles in her care prior to her getting to that point. I thought it would be fun (and therapeutic) for Doreen, so I brought in some one-pound jars of honey from her bees to give to those special individuals. That honey was her pride and joy from the hard work and love she put into those awesome tiny creatures.

It was so much fun to watch her motion to me to get a jar for her to pass out to that person. I could see the physical and emotional boost in her as she handed the jar to the individual as she told them thank you for what they had done for her. It was also a joy to watch as the people accepted it from her, and how appreciative and even emotional they were when she gave it to them. Witnessing that pure and genuine interaction of thanks is something I will never forget. I'm sure all those involved will remember Doreen for many years to come as well.

Now, I certainly couldn't end this phase of our journey without giving recognition to a very unique and special person who had been with Doreen every step of the way. He took such a personal interest in her and showed a level of dedication to Doreen like I had never seen before, ever. His compassion was honest and genuine, and the care he showed to his patients was extraordinary. I believe he truly loves his patients and gives them every ounce of energy he has to help them. His name is Dr. Dartazz. He was Doreen's primary care doctor while she was there. I will be eternally grateful to Dr. Dartazz for everything he did for Doreen (for both of us), and I thank God for placing him in our journey.

He played a key role in Doreen's miracle, as well as touched my heart and soul with his pure and humble service to others. I did not meet him the first time Doreen was there but had my first encounter with him a couple days after she was there the second time. He pulled me out of her room and found a quiet spot in the hallway to explain to me what he was going to do for her, for us. He promised he would do whatever he could to get her back on her feet so she could walk out of there. My first thought was he had too much caffeine and was a little over-confident. At that point, Doreen literally couldn't even lift a finger let alone be able to walk out of there in a few weeks.

From the moment she got there, the process was to find the next facility for her to go to because they had to re-apply every week to the insurance company to continue. That was nerve racking enough to hope she would be approved to stay for another week. Dr. Dartazz told me not to worry about that because he would make sure the focus was on helping Doreen get better. He told me numerous times during that first talk to trust the system, and to trust him. I had just met him, but for some odd reason, I felt I could trust him. I think it was the constant positive energy that poured out of him which gave me that comfort level.

For the ten weeks we were there, I had numerous encounters with Dr. Dartazz. Most of them were rather brief because he was always on the go (he was very high energy), but there were a couple of those moments with him that were very special to me, which I will never forget. He seemed to have taken a special interest in Doreen's case, and he even had called her his "sister" numerous times. I believe, in his culture, family is most important, so I was honored when he called her that. That meant a lot to me because my family is extremely important to me as well.

There was one particular day when I was sitting by Doreen's bed in the ICU, and I was holding her hand like I always did. I was rather surprised when I saw Dr. Dartazz out of the corner of my eye lean over and kiss my shoulder. I was a little startled and immediately stood up and turned around to face him. I think my reaction startled him, and he promptly apologized multiple times for doing that. I told him I wasn't upset, but it had just caught me off guard.

He proceeded to tell me that it is a custom in his culture to kiss another as a greeting and a sign of respect. I was honored by that, so I returned the gesture back to him. I stepped forward and gave him a big hug and told him "This is how my family does it!" The table had turned. It was kind of funny to see the shocked look on his face by my "custom".

After that, there were a handful of times when I was there, and he came in to check on Doreen. I would walk over to him and put my arm around him, give him a little squeeze, and told him "Thank you" for everything he was doing for her.

There was one other time where I saw him walking by and called him into the room. When he came in, he saw Lindsey, Doreen's special respiratory therapist, and said hello to her and asked how everything was going. As I started walking over to him, he said "Oh, another hug" which made me chuckle. I had something else in mind. As I stepped close to him, I took my hands on each side of his head and leaned over and kissed him on the cheek and immediately followed that with a hug. He was totally surprised and dumbfounded by my actions. I took a step back and said, "Dr. Dartazz, you said in your culture it was a custom to kiss someone. In my family, we hug. I think this world right now could use a lot more kisses and hugs in it! What a difference that would make!"

As I took another step back, I looked over at Lindsey and saw that she had a big smile on her face, and I think I saw a tear in her eyes. When I looked back at Dr. Dartazz, I could see that he had a tear in his eye and was a little emotional. I think it was because I had just honored his culture and customs, and I showed him respect. Even though we come from completely different cultures from opposite sides of the world, kindness and love are universal and can be shared.

The tiny gesture I gave that day pales by comparison to the love and respect that I have for Dr. Dartazz. He really is one of the good people on this earth, and truly is an amazing humble servant to his fellow human beings. I pray that God continues to bless Dr. Dartazz as much as He has blessed Doreen and I.

Our time at this amazing facility was ending, and it was time for me to share the good news with the rest of our family and friends. I had been writing updates periodically and had Kirstyn send them to the group on Facebook Messenger. As you might guess, the updates started in darkness and desperation, looking for light and hope in the first stretch of our marathon. Then as time passed, the message would occasionally ride the emotional roller coaster I was on, and slowly worked up to glimpses of progress and improvement, and now this. With the season of Good News coming upon us, I wrote this update on December 11, 2021, and sent it out to the group:

> *"Hi everyone – This is the season of God's greatest gift to us all…Jesus! I wasn't really sure how I would be able to handle Christmas this year, whether my heart would be filled with joy or be burdened with sadness. I know that my heart should be filled with happiness and excitement because of Jesus' birthday that will be here very soon.*
>
> *However…my heart is bursting at the seams because my Christmas Blessing from God has come early! Doreen no longer has the trach in, and she is completely tolerating breathing on her own! I have once again witnessed God's Amazing Grace before my very eyes! God has not only heard all of the prayers for her, but He has answered and continues to answer them.*

Doreen has also been accepted to the Physical Rehabilitation Center in Rockford. They specialize on her physical needs, and their goal is to have her home in a few weeks, not a few months. I can't help but cry as I write this to you all. God has blessed me so far beyond my comprehension that I can't understand it and ask Him, "Why me God? I don't deserve this much of Your love." But here's the answer and the best part. I don't have to understand, I just have to trust Him and accept it! And that's all because of Jesus!

So this year, maybe we should say "Happy Birthday" to Jesus and "Thank You" to God for sending His greatest gift of all. I know that's what I'll be doing. Thank you to all of you again for all the prayers, love and support you have given to Doreen & I! May God Love and Bless all of you as much as He has Blessed Doreen…and especially me! I love you all! Steve"

That, of course, was by far the easiest and best update I wrote the entire time.

From the very beginning, time almost felt like it had been standing still. And now, it was hard to believe that Christmas was just around the corner. The kitchen clock: Tick-tock… Tick-tock…Tick-tock was always consistent and never varied in speed, but somehow, the days were passing by quicker and quicker now. Maybe it was the anticipation and excitement of the next short phase which would lead to Doreen's final destination…home. Throughout this entire journey, that was what we all had been praying for. In just a few weeks, all those prayers that went to straight to heaven would soon be answered.

Tuesday December 14th

The day finally arrived to move on to the next phase. Hopefully, that would be the last move for Doreen before she would come home. I always tried to remain positive throughout this ordeal but based on the past three and a half months of experience, I had become guarded, and sometimes even skeptical, whenever things appeared to look like they were progressing forward. There had been too many times where my hopes and anticipation were hit hard by reality which was traveling one-hundred miles an hour in the opposite direction. Let's just say that I was cautiously optimistic…again.

The day had come for us to say goodbye to all the wonderful people who had helped Doreen get to this point. I thought it would be such a joyous occasion, but it turned out to be bitter-sweet and a little frightening, especially for Doreen. The obvious sweet side of that day was she had "graduated" the vent-weaning program at that facility and was moving on to restore her physical mobility. That by itself was a miracle. But at the same time, the routines and the atmosphere that both of us had become so accustomed to was about to change dramatically.

Doreen was extremely nervous and scared because it would be at a new facility with all new people, and on top of all of that, there were all the questions of her unknown physical capabilities and how would she be able to handle those. It was over-whelming for her. You must put yourself in her shoes. She had been unconscious and was immobile for almost three months. It only had been since Thanksgiving where she was fully awake and coherent, which by that point had only been a few short weeks.

During that short time though, she had become comfortable with her surroundings and with the all the people who took care of her. My comfort level at that facility was even higher. I had only missed four or five days the entire time she was there, so I felt very comfortable in that environment. But now, in just a short time, everything would change.

While we were waiting for the ambulance to arrive that would be transferring her, a steady stream of staff would stop by her room to say goodbye (including a few tears) and wished her well. They even had a small group come in to take a picture with her so they could post in on their Facebook page and write a brief story of her successful journey there.

I noticed as they said their last words to Doreen, each one told her in their own way they absolutely knew she would get better and back on her feet because of the focus and determination she had shown over the past few weeks. They knew whatever she would put her mind to would be possible. They had watched her do just that once she became fully alert and in control of her mind. They were all as proud of her as I was.

There was only one person who didn't stop in to say goodbye that we had been hoping to thank one more time. That was Dr. Dartazz. We asked if he was there, but a few people had said he does not handle saying goodbye very well. Doreen was very comfortable with Dr. Dartazz and completely trusted him, and I had become pretty attached to him. We both knew how much he wore his heart and his emotions on his sleeve, and it would have been a heart wrenching encounter for all of us. I just wanted to give him one last big hug and tell him I was so thankful I trusted him, and to also say, "God bless you and your family!"

Time was up. The transfer paramedics pulled their gurney into her room and got everything ready to go. The last step was moving her onto the gurney and out the door they went.

I had already taken most of her things home the night before, but there where a few small things along with some paperwork that I had to take. I walked down those halls for the last time and said a few more goodbyes as I walk out the door to my car. I had told the paramedics I would be following them to Rockford, so I would be behind them. I barely had my car started and they were already driving past. I had to try and keep up even though there were no sirens. Let's just say that they didn't let any grass grow under their feet.

We made it there quickly, but I had a brief flashback of the night Doreen went back to the previous hospital in Rockford for her emergency operation. As quick as we had just made it there, what took so long on that horrific night? That hospital was only a couple of miles farther than the new physical rehab center. But I didn't have time to ponder about that anymore because I had to park and learn a whole new routine on where to go and who to speak with.

As you can imagine, there was a whole new list of questions and uncertainties in my mind that I would have to navigate, as well as all the new surroundings and people. For my entire adult life (yes, I said adult), Doreen had always been the one to take charge and control of whatever we were doing. I have never had a problem with that because I will be the first to admit, she's by far the smarter of the two. She does the thinking, and I do the lifting. Up until this point, that had always worked for us.

So now, without my security blanket, I had to be the front person and carry that unfamiliar load. I masked up and walked through the front door of the new physical rehab facility for the first time. There was a small, but very nice sitting area just inside the doors. Just a few steps farther in and there was a counter area with a person sitting where I needed to check in. It was the start of my new routine. I had to sign in along with the time, in and out, and the room number. Since we just got there, I obviously didn't know which room Doreen would be in. It only took a moment for the nice lady to look it up, and she instructed me on were to go. She had also mentioned that our case manager, Alissa, would stop in to go over everything after Doreen was settled in. She then chuckled as she told me to go down the hall to the North Pole and turn left.

I was a little puzzled, but I headed off in the direction she said to go until I saw exactly where she had mentioned. The "North Pole" was the circular nurse's station that was decorated for Christmas. I sort of forgot about the upcoming holidays because I was too busy trying to keep up with all my daily activities around the house and with work, just so I could spend as much time with Doreen as possible. Plus, Doreen had always been the one who took care of decorating our house for Christmas. She wasn't there to bring the Christmas spirit in the house. It was just me and the dogs, and the possibility for Doreen to be home by Christmas had already come and gone.

I made a left at the festive station and walked down to the second room from the end on the right. I noticed as I walked down the hall and then into Doreen's new room that this section of the facility had just been newly remodeled and updated and was beautifully done. Plus, Doreen's room was as big as a nice hotel room. They certainly didn't mess around. They were already in her room getting her situated as I walked in. I could easily see that it had been a very big day for her, and she looked exhausted.

After the nurse left, as I was sitting there looking around, it hit me that *this* was the final stop for Doreen before she would be able come home. In case you couldn't tell, my emotions throughout this journey had been a little on edge, and that moment was no different. I had tears in my eyes when I leaned over and kissed Doreen's hand and told her that she's almost there. Just one more step and she'll be home.

It wasn't very long after that when Alissa walked in and introduced herself. She was a very nice young lady, and I could tell she loved her job and was probably pretty good at it. She gave us a binder that was called "My Health Journal" which basically described everything we would need to know about the facility, as well as a journal to make notes and keep track of the progress made. She explained that Dr. Hunee would be her physician while she was there, and who Doreen's therapists would be as well as the first day's schedule starting the next day.

There was so much more she went over during that initial introduction that it felt a bit over-whelming to me. I occasionally glanced at Doreen and could see that she was as well but was also scared. Before we finished with Alissa, I asked if I could bring in some pictures from home as well as the CD player so she could listen to her music. She said it wasn't a problem and they even had a bulletin board next to the bed just for that.

After Alissa left, the nurse came in with the dinner menu to get Doreen's request for the night. After he left, I went back out to the car to bring in the pictures, the CD's and a suitcase with some of her clothes. I was told ahead of time to bring in her daily clothes because she would be getting dressed everyday in her own outfits and pajamas. No more hospital gowns for her. I wasn't sure how that was going to work, but that's why she was there.

After she ate a little dinner, I stayed for a while to try and help ease her uncertainties. I told her how proud I was of her that she conquered breathing on her own again just a few short weeks ago, and then conquered talking again, and then eating and drinking again, all when she put her mind to it. Now, it was time for her to conquer the physical challenges just like she did with all the other challenges. I believed in her and I knew she would be able to do it. I totally understand that over-coming extreme challenges are a lot easier said than done, especially when you're not the one who must conquer them.

I used the word extreme intentionally because Doreen's "drop-foot" would be a major hurdle, and the fact she could barely sit up on her own without someone there to help steady her because she just didn't have the core strength to do that simple task on her own. I knew exactly how big and steep of a climb it would be to conquer her physical mobility mountain. I promised her many times that I would be there every step of the way.

I'm sure my words helped comfort her some, but still, the fear of the unknown continued to haunt her. I could see it in her eyes, which by that time were getting very heavy. I put on some soothing music to help her relax a little and kissed her on the forehead and told her again how proud I was of her, and that I loved her more than anything. I said goodbye and I would see her after I got off work the next day. What a busy day it was.

The next morning started with the usual regiment of duties and then off to work for me. Doreen on the other hand, started her day in a completely new atmosphere and with completely new activities. She would be introduced to a wide variety of caretakers and specialists that would be starting her in a whole different direction than what she had become accustomed to. As strong of a person as she had been before on the inside (and still was), her physical body had been so devastated that it would put her very will to the ultimate test.

She knew I was at work, and I would be there if I could, so she understood she had to dig deep because she had no choice but to start the last phase on her own. Having felt her agony the night before, I had a hard time concentrating at work on the tasks in front of me. I couldn't help but wonder how she was doing with her new surroundings and how well she was handling the different tasks in front of her. Jeff had allowed me to continue with my shortened hours at work, so once they were done with lunch, off to Rockford I went. It was about an hour and a half ride, so God got a little extra time with me. I did all the talking.

After I got there and signed in, I went down to Doreen's room to see how she handled her first day so far. I was both excited and nervous at the same time because I had no idea on how it went for her. When I walked in, she smiled as soon as she saw me. Well, I thought, that's a good start. I thought she would tell me how well all her activities had gone, and it wasn't as scary as she thought. That's not exactly how it happened.

Her day started with breakfast and then morning hygiene: brushing teeth, washing up, brushing her hair, etc. After that was done, her primary physician, Dr. Hunee, had stopped in to go over what they would be doing and to answer any questions she had. He was very familiar with everything she had gone through and with all the medications she had been on and was still on.

His goal was to over-see her progress and to make any adjustments needed to keep her rehab moving in a positive direction. He encouraged her to take control of her situation, and not be afraid to speak up about anything. She told me her first encounter with Dr. Hunee went well, but it would take some time to get used to this new world she was now in.

The morning had been busy for her because she also had the respiratory therapist stop in to check on her oxygen levels, and to do a couple of breathing tests. On top of all that interaction, her nurse for the day had been in and out numerous times throughout the morning with grooming, eating, medications, the notorious bed pan, insulin pokes and taking her regular stats. And there were also times when the nurse stopped in just to see if she needed anything.

She also had met one of the therapists named Kristina. She was a speech-language pathologist who specialized in helping people relearn how to talk again, along with thinking and even swallowing skills. Those were things I never even thought about through this ordeal, but when someone goes through as much trauma as Doreen had, those things we take for granted don't just automatically come back. Doreen said she was very nice and explained each step of the process and why it was important to the end goal. Doreen liked her and seemed very comfortable with that portion of her rehab, plus that session would be in her own room. She certainly wasn't bored so far that day.

Not long after I got there, the physical therapist named Steve (I liked him already) walked in. After the introductions, he went through the program he thought would be the most beneficial for Doreen. From what I understood, everyone who would be involved on Doreen's team had already read about her case before she even got there and had been involved in a group discussion on whether or not their program could even help.

Steve already had a good idea of the challenges she faced. But on this first encounter, he still needed to hear what she wanted out of the time with him, and he also wanted to let her get comfortable with him. He was very clear that he would never force her to do anything she didn't want to, but he would highly encourage and push her to go beyond her comfort zone because that would only speed up her over-all recovery.

He had her do a couple of small tasks in bed just so he could see what range of motion she had, and a few tests to see her level of strength. Now, after seeing what she could do and where he thought she was at physically, he said he would go back and fine-tune the program he had already laid out.

He also explained how the rehab programs there really encourage the patient's family members, especially the ones who would be caring for the patients when they got home, to be "trained" as well and to be there as much as possible for support. An important part of the process was to show me how to continue Doreen's rehab at home, and how to do it properly and safely.

When Steve made that comment, it suddenly hit me on what it would be like once Doreen got home. Many times, I had thought about the numerous possibilities of what it might be like when she came home, based on what her capabilities would be at that time. But those were just thoughts and "what ifs?" It seemed so far off back then and there was plenty of time to figure it all out. I had been praying for so long for her to come home, and now suddenly, we were actually getting close.

As our conversation progressed, I could tell that certainly wasn't the first time he guided people down the path to recovery. He was good, and I felt comfortable with him, but more importantly, Doreen felt comfortable. He finished up by letting us know there would be two sessions a day, one for physical therapy and one for occupational therapy. Each one was an hour and a half, either in the morning or in the afternoon, Monday through Friday and no sessions on the weekends. He told her he would see her in the morning, and the sessions would be in her room for a while until she was comfortable.

After he left, Doreen and I agreed it went well with him and this was the right place for her to be in. Before the afternoon was over, Doreen's occupational therapist, Cortney, stopped in to go over her portion of the program. Since we had never been involved with a facility like this or any programs like this before, I asked what the difference was between the physical and occupational therapies. To me, occupational therapy seemed like it would have something to do with her work, and the physical therapy would obviously work on all her muscles. I also told her I thought the speech therapy was odd also since she was already talking and was easy to understand.

Cortney just smiled and said many of the people who come there have the same idea about what the different therapies do. She then gave us a brief general description between the three therapies. Speech therapy would deal not only with her vocal communication, but also with her cognitive state. Since Doreen had been down for so long, they would work on her mental concentration and retention as well as focus on her throat region because she was on the vent and trach for that length of time. Next was what the physical therapy focuses on. Basically, it works from the waste down. It concentrates on your core strength (stomach muscles) and works everything down to your toes to build up to walking again.

Cortney's area would basically be from the waist up. She explained that there was some over-lap between the physical and occupational therapies, but the upper body function was where her area of concentration would be. That portion focuses on the fine motor skills that revolve around the use of the arms and hands. I understood what she was saying because up until that point, Doreen could hardly even hold and control her cell phone. Now it made sense to me how the three different therapies all worked in conjunction with each other, and why each one was so important to Doreen's recovery.

She finished up by telling us how Doreen would also stay in her room for that portion of her therapy until she progressed enough to go down to the gym for more advanced sessions. She described a little of how those sessions would be and finished by asking us if we had any questions. My mind was rather numb by that time from all the info we received that afternoon, and Doreen appeared to be a little over-whelmed as well. I thanked her for helping me understand and grasp what was in front of us.

Doreen's first day of therapy was complete, and it was comforting to know she had three therapists who obviously were very compassionate and who genuinely cared about their patient's well-being. Again, I knew Doreen was in the right place. In the back of my mind though, I wasn't quite sure how Doreen would be ready to go home after only the two-to-three-week time period everyone talked about. Given Doreen's physical condition, how would that even be possible?

I guess I was afraid of what the answer might be, so I didn't ask that question. Since we had never been anywhere close to a situation like that before, I figured we would have to just wait and see. Considering where we came from up until now, a few more weeks were a drop in the bucket.

The new revised routine was up and running. My mornings and early afternoon had stayed the same, with only the second half of the day slightly modified. Doreen's entire routine had changed dramatically from what she had been used to in Sycamore. Obviously, there were all the new sites and sounds, and all the new faces, but she now had to start the process of taking care of herself, with some help of course.

She had lost a lot of weight and muscle tone over the past three months, so everything was a daunting task that would drain her energy quickly. Couple that with the all the different therapies each day, and she would end up completely exhausted. I could sense some frustration on her part, mainly because her mind was willing, but her body wasn't able. I tried to keep reminding her it would take time, and unfortunately, there weren't any shortcuts or quick fixes. If there were, I would do everything in my power to make that happen.

During one of my many conversations with the special nurses at the large hospital, they had told me about what the lack of movement does to the condition of one's body when it's not used. Here's my over-simplified version of those conversations: For every one day of no active movement, the loss of muscle tone would be equal to seven days of normal physical activity. So, if that were true, then Doreen would have lost around 110 days worth of muscle through this ordeal.

That certainly would explain why she looked so fragile, and why she was so weak physically. It made my heart ache to see her struggle physically during her rehab, especially since her mind and her will to get better were so strong. Time. She just needed some more time.

During the first few days there, time had given her another birthday. Everyone there had wished her a happy birthday and gave her words of encouragement for her present. My primary boss of twenty-nine years, Ron, remembered how much Doreen loved a special Italian pizza called Focaccia. Ron also remembered it was her birthday. He drove all the way to Cicero to his cousin's unbelievable deli (Freddy's Pizza) just to pick up a couple of focaccias, and then dropped them off at work so I could take them to Doreen for her birthday. I was so touched by his thoughtfulness, and his genuine sincerity and concern for Doreen. I am so grateful to work for a company that cares so much about their people, including their families. I thanked Ron for the great surprise and told him how thrilled Doreen would be to get his gift.

I was right. Doreen was very excited when I opened the box and showed her what was on the inside. She wanted me to take a picture of her taking a bite and send it to Ron, and to tell him thank you for the great birthday dinner. She had only been eating "regular" food for about a month, so this was a big deal to eat one of her favorites. I took the rest of the focaccia home and put it in the freezer so I could use it as a pick-me-up when Doreen would need a little boost in spirits at some point down the road.

Since her birthday had passed and it was now the weekend, she could relax for a couple of days from her therapies. After watching a few therapy sessions, I think most people don't understand how much we take such simple tasks for granted. I certainly acquired a new-found appreciation for all the "little things" we usually don't even notice.

Simple things like sitting up in bed and putting your legs over the side and not falling over. Or putting your arms through the sleeves of your shirt and pulling it down. Or the simple task of picking up your phone when it rings. There are hundreds of daily activities we do all the time without a single thought because those tasks don't require much concentration or effort on our part. Doreen, like most of the patients in that facility, would have to learn how to do those basic tasks all over again, and with an immense amount of effort.

Christmas 2021

Once the weekend was over and another week of routines started, I found myself getting somewhat anxious about the upcoming week. It was Monday, and Christmas was on

Saturday. Normally I would be so excited to cruise through that week of shorter workdays and holiday treats, but for obvious reasons, that time period was rather stressful. It certainly wasn't because of Christmas. That special day had seemed so far away for so long that I hadn't really thought about it. I had been so caught up in Doreen's breath by breath, minute by minute, hour by hour, day by day, and month by month recovery process that I almost missed the most important blessing of all…Jesus' birthday.

Well, obviously I wouldn't have missed it. I think the real reason I didn't focus on it was because Christmas is Doreen's most favorite day and time of the year. I knew the annual "glow" on her face that I had witnessed for literally decades would not be there this year.

She normally would spend countless hours of her time in thought and preparation for Christmas, not to mention all the shopping that needed to be done, and she loved every minute of it. But this year, that routine was missing, and all of her joy had been denied. There would be no Christmas celebration at Grandma's house this year. It broke my heart every time I thought about it.

Besides, at the moment, we needed to stay focused on the tasks at hand: Getting her ready to come home. That was all I really wanted for Christmas anyway. Even though Christmas was just around the corner, our family was in unfamiliar territory of not having a firm itinerary in place of exactly where everyone was going to be and at what time. Basically, it was every family for themselves while I spent that special day with my very special partner. So that was the plan that year.

Having spent the past several days at the new facility getting familiar with Doreen's new rehab team, one of the things they talked about regularly was the possibility of me spending as much time there as possible. Since the average length of stay there was only two to three weeks, they stressed the fact that I needed as much therapy training as Doreen required.

I needed to learn some basic rehab therapies so I could work with Doreen daily at home, but more importantly, I needed to learn the proper ways on how to move her around so neither of us would get injured. They were just as concerned about my safety as they were about Doreen's safety. I would be no good to her if I injured myself by not using the correct techniques. Or worse yet, I could possibly hurt her.

That weighed heavy on my mind. The million "what-if" thoughts now plagued my mind once again. Those thoughts fueled my fear and anxiety which resulted in an all-to-familiar stress level. But, on the other side of the spectrum was the elation of Doreen's long awaited return home. It felt like I was facing an impossible and cruel double-edged sword. If I made the slightest mistake, it could be very costly.

I knew I needed to talk with Jeff to see if it might be possible for me to take another leave of absence a couple of weeks sooner than I had planned. I already had talked with him about time off when Doreen got home, but I didn't realize how much I would need to know, and how much physical training I would need to learn before we could even bring her home.

I also told Jeff I had been informed by our case manager that there would be a visit by a trained staff member to check out our house to make sure it would be ADA compliant and safe for Doreen once she was home. I thought coming down to the "home stretch" would finally allow me to coast a little, but I quickly learned my nursing duties were only beginning to ramp up.

Jeff understood the situation I was in, but he asked if I could work the next few days because he had an announcement to make to the whole company. He hadn't asked anything of me the entire time, so I certainly wasn't going to question his reason. His compassion and generosity for us had been beyond measure during our unwanted journey.

And true to form, he surprised me and the entire company a few days later by giving everybody the entire next week between Christmas and New Years off with pay. He felt the craziness and stress over the past two years had taken its toll on everyone, so he wanted everybody to unwind and spend some uninterrupted quality time with their families. Everyone was excited and grateful, but no one more than I. Jeff once again had come through in my time of need.

By Tuesday, December 21st, Doreen had already been there a full week. She was slowly improving with each day, but I could see she was somewhat frustrated because her body couldn't keep pace with her mind. During each task, she knew what she wanted to do and how to do it. On the physical side of the equation though, her strength did not equal the effort she put forth. All I could do was keep encouraging and supporting her, but most importantly, I would constantly tell her how much I loved her and how proud I was of the effort she was putting in.

As a matter of fact, Kristina, the speech pathologist, had already released Doreen from her care. She said Doreen's speech, throat and mental awareness and capacity were exactly where it needed to be and there wasn't much else she could do for her. That was yet another miracle. Just a few short months ago, there was serious concern about brain damage, and now she already over-came that hurdle.

Another area Doreen was showing steady improvement on was her fine motor skills with her arms and hands. She was working on that with Cortney during the occupational sessions since she had got there. Since she was able to do more with her phone, Doreen decided she wanted to send out the update to everyone that day. We had been talking about how the girls posted my different messages all along, and now Doreen wanted to read them.

As she did, I could see how strange it was for her to read about what she had gone through, especially since she had no idea of what actually happened. After she finished reading the updates, here's what she decided to write (I'm typing it exactly the way she wrote it):

"Hi everybody- it's Doreen. I'm not really sure how to start. It feels at times that I am watching a dream, sometimes scary and sometimes good, but there are lots of holes in it. Everyone around me has been telling me some of what I've been through but it still doesn't feel real to me yet or at least parts of it. They say it will take more time to understand but I don't think honestly that. I thought I should say thank you and let you know how I am doing myself. After reading it from the beginning, it is so obvious to me that Steve & I have been blessed with such a great family and wonderful friends who care so much about us. We thank God for this very special Blessing! I want to say thank you to each of you for all the prayers that you prayed & for the love you have expressed to me and to my family. I can't tell you how much it means to me. Thank you from the bottom of my heart. I lao saw that there was a GoFund me to help with my medical bills. I want to say an extra thank you to those who helped with" She accidentally hit send and then continued with another text.

"With that as well. Steve says I shouldn't worry about that part but he isn't the one who pays the bills. So thank you again for your love & support. As far as my rehab I am getting a little stronger and better each say. It is hard and even strange to have to learn how to do literally all over again. I know I have to push myself because that's the only way I can get home. It's very exhausting but I'm looking forward to going home. I miss my puppies and stave. Hopefully the next time I talk to you will be I'm my way home. Thank you you for all the love and prayers that have helped me get through this! All my love, Doreen"

How amazing was that? Less than six weeks ago, I literally had to pick her hand up and place it in mine just to hold her hand. Now there she was, holding her phone and typing that long message to our family and friends, completely on her own. On top of that, she composed it all by herself without any help from me.

I was so excited and happy and proud of her that she was able to perform what normally would be considered a minor task by most people's standards. For her though, it was a monumental accomplishment that came with an equally sized amount of exhaustion. I could see both the satisfaction on her face and the drain it had taken on her physically. She needed to rest a while, so she closed her eyes and listened to the music. I had my chair pulled close to her bed with my back to the window as I followed suit.

The music was playing softly, and it was quiet and peaceful until there was a loud knock at the window which made us both jump. I could see she was as startled as I was. I jumped up out of my chair and turned around to see what that noise was. I started to laugh when I saw what I saw.

I stepped to the side so Doreen could see for herself. It was Santa Claus, two of his elves and two of his reindeer standing outside of her window waving and smiling and wishing us a Merry Christmas! We laughed and smiled and waved back at them. What a pleasant surprise it was, and much unexpected to say the least.

We found out later from the nurse that Santa pays a special visit there every year, but because of the COVID protocols, he could only stand outside of the patient's window to wish everyone a Merry Christmas and not in person face to face. No one on earth was immune to that microscopic demon that had mysteriously appeared, not even Santa.

Once she finished her dinner that night, we talked a little more about what my schedule would be for the rest of her time there and beyond. I told her earlier about Jeff's announcement to everyone which would allow me to be there all the time. I only had one more day of work on Wednesday, and then a half day on Thursday. Then I would be off for Christmas Eve and the whole following week.

At that point, we didn't know for sure what her release date would be. Everyone involved had talked about Doreen finishing up by the end of the year, but there was the possibility of her having to stay another week, maybe two, after that if necessary. If it were up to me, it would have been sooner not later.

But first things first. She needed rest from her very busy day of therapy and from that extraordinary accomplishment she did. I told her how much I loved her, kissed her and said goodnight. I left to go home and fulfilled my busy evening duties before I would go to bed. When I got on my knees to pray that night, I thanked God more than normal for letting me witness yet another miracle, and for His amazing grace and love that had made it possible.

The clock was ticking, and the time for her to come home was getting closer. It finally felt like a reality. Up until that point, there had only been hope, until now. She really was coming home soon, and there wasn't much time left (all of a sudden) to prepare for her homecoming. Over the next couple of days, the therapists talked with Doreen and I about the routines we would need do daily, as well as what modifications would be needed at home to make it safe for her to function. My lists were getting longer, and the time was getting shorter.

I must admit I was feeling a bit overwhelmed, but I never lost focus, not even for a minute, that it was all about Doreen. I had prayed a thousand times and then some for God to heal Doreen and let her come home. We were on the home (literally home) stretch, and all my prayers would finally be fulfilled.

During those days before Christmas, Doreen's drive and effort were very apparent, but I felt her heart was sad because she was "chained" to that bed which felt a million miles away from her most favorite place and time. She would miss her fifty-ninth anniversary of being at home with her family at Christmas.

I tried to make the best of it by bringing up some Christmas cards for all the kids and grand kids so she could sign them and put some money in the card, but that was only a quick temporary fix. She understood due to the circumstances we were in, but she still felt like she didn't do enough to make Christmas "Grandma special". I don't think she realized it at the time, but what made Christmas extra special was that Grandma was *still here* with us. I'm pretty sure that was what everybody in our family had been asking for all along.

So being the Blessed family that we are, everyone got their Christmas wish that year, especially me. Our family traditions would have to be put on hold until next year, but the Joy of Christmas was shinning as bright as ever because of Doreen.

One special tradition that Doreen and I have done for decades was going to church on Christmas Eve. It always served as a reminder of what the true meaning of Christmas is all about: Jesus' birthday. All the excitement of getting together and giving presents to each other is a lot of fun and brings much happiness, but going to church on that special night had always kept us anchored in the *real* Christmas spirit.

I don't know, I guess I've always felt we were honoring Jesus *first* before we celebrated the modern commercial day of giving and receiving. I think both are great celebrations, when done in the proper order. Now don't get me wrong, there were a few times over the years where we didn't make it to church on that night for one reason or another, but I can tell you, it was on those occasions when Christmas had felt a little off. Christmas Eve, December 24th, 2021, would be another one of those occasions, but with a slight difference because of the circumstances.

Christmas Day

That special morning had arrived. Normally in years past, I would be up extra early getting the turkey going and then go back to bed even though I wouldn't go back to sleep. I would eventually get up when it was light outside and go out to give all the animals a special Christmas breakfast. By the time I was done and came back inside, Doreen would be up and start getting the rest of the dishes she was making prepped while I finished any last-minute cleaning and setting the table for dinner. We always tried to eat around one o'clock, which rarely actually happened. The kids would start showing up around noon or shortly after, so it was always amazing how quick the mornings flew by.

We would then eat and visit for awhile before it was time to open presents. There were nineteen of us, so when you open presents one by one, it takes a little while to go through the process. That was okay though, for the amount of time and effort that everyone had put into the gifts, it was nice to take the time to enjoy the love and thought that was behind them.

After we would finish presents, it usually was time for dessert, which always was more plentiful than my waistline required. But I always enjoyed every one of them. After a few more festivities and some more time visiting, eventually everyone would make their way home. That was a very brief version of what our traditional Christmas celebration was like at our house. It was always very hectic and exhausting, but in a very satisfying way.

None of that would be the case this year. The only exception was I gave all the animals a little extra special feed for Christmas, and then off to Rockford I went. I wanted to be there as early as possible so I could spend as much time with Doreen on that special day, hopefully to comfort her and pick up her spirits. Christmas meant so much to her.

I knew our wonderful family traditions had been broken, but the absolute most important part was that she was still here with us. There will be more family traditions in the future to enjoy, but at that moment, we needed to be focused on where we were and enjoy the time we were in.

Throughout the day, each of the kids and their families had called to wish us a Merry Christmas and excitedly tell us all about some of the gifts they got. Doreen's face lit up with each call and throughout the conversations, but when it was time to hang up, I could tell her heart ached because we weren't there in person. That happened over and over, and each time with the same result.

That even happened when her folks had called to wish her Merry Christmas. They had been getting updates from Josh on a regular basis, but they were now calling Doreen directly since she was able to use the phone on her own. They also had not been able to visit Doreen in any of the facilities since they couldn't drive anymore, and didn't have a way to get there. I could tell Doreen even had a difficult time talking with them because she felt like everyone was so far away, and there were still a lot of foggy areas she was coping with.

Like she had explained in her update, there were a lot of holes in her journey that made it difficult for her to connect all the dots. I knew at some point, when she would be ready, I would do my best to fill in those blanks for her to hopefully help her complete that painful experience she had to endure, and hopefully find closure to help her move forward. But that moment wasn't here yet. I just had to help her get through that Christmas Day.

Before the day was over, I told her she would have Kirstyn there the next day to visit her without me because I needed to get the materials to build a ramp so she could get into the house. I also had to get some grab bars and a new shower head so she would be able to get in and out of the shower safely. I had already taken the shower doors off and put up a shower curtain in its place. The special shower bench she would use was designed to go on the inside and on the outside of the shower at the same time so she could transfer in and out, hopefully by herself. I still thought someone would be inspecting our house before she would be released, so I needed to get those things done as soon as possible. She was okay with that because she knew it had to get done, and I think she needed a new visitor anyway.

- Slow & Steady...Almost There -

I got going early Sunday morning so I could get to Heather's to borrow her pickup truck to haul the materials, drop them off at home, take her truck back, then go back home and start building. It was a little cool in the garage that day, even with a heater going, so I worked on the ramp for awhile until I got chilled. Then I went inside to work on putting the new shower head with a handheld wand up as well as mounting the ADA grab bars on the shower walls. Later, I went back out in the garage to work on the ramp some more.

While I was busy that day with my construction projects, Kirstyn went and spent the day with Doreen. She was able to see how nice the facility was, including the physical therapy gyms and all the equipment they had available. She was really impressed how nice Doreen's room was and how big it was. I don't know what the other rooms looked like in the other wings of the building, but Doreen was fortunate enough to end up in a newly remodeled room. They were still working on a few rooms in that wing of the facility, so I think Doreen was the first one in that room.

Kirstyn and Doreen had a great visit that day, and I was able to get most of the checklist done that was needed for her to come home. I took pictures of what I had done so far, but I needed to finish the ramp the next night. Doreen always makes fun of me when I build something because she says I always build it strong enough to drive a tank on it. I think I do that because I only want to have to build it once, so it lasts.

The next day I got going after my normal morning chores, and I was the second person to sign in that day. I got there very early, even before she got her breakfast. It had become my new routine now that I was off work. It worked out great because I was able to be there the whole time for each of her different therapies throughout the entire day.

It was quite the learning experience, and it was as intense for me as it was for Doreen. The big difference was she would be completely drained physically as well as mentally from her major efforts, while I was only mentally drained from my minor participation.

There was so much to take in. Each time we went through a task, I thought I understood how it needed to be done, only to fumble my way through the steps and would have to try again. It always looked and sounded so easy when the therapists showed us, but then trying the same task using my new skills always ended up with a completely different result from theirs. I felt so bad for Doreen because she was the one who had to suffer through my learning curve.

Many of the activities I was learning mostly revolved around coaching or guiding Doreen through some different exercises, but the one that challenged me the most (and terrified Doreen) was when I had to pick her up to move her from the bed to the wheelchair. She was only able to sit up on the edge of the bed by herself, which was a chore for her, but she couldn't stand or anything even close to that. She was only just starting to be able to use her arms to help her "scoot" a little down the bed. That doesn't sound like much, but that was huge progress.

Steve, her physical therapist, told us that over the next couple of days, we would be learning how to transfer in and out of the car. I could see the panicked look on Doreen's face with that news. Fortunately, she was done for the day. I told her not to stress out about that anymore for rest of the night. I tried to reassure her we would be okay, and she had to trust me that I would be able to handle it. I would never let her fall no matter what.

She needed to get a good night sleep because we had a big day ahead of us. I needed to get going so I could finish the ramp, and hopefully it would be sufficient to bypass a home inspection. I would still call the kids each night, but the updates were getting shorter. I think they were getting a little burnt out from my constant jabber anyway. I did most of the talking, most of the time.

I came the next day armed with my pictures of the ramp to show them how we would easily be able to get Doreen in and out of the house when necessary. They were impressed enough that the home inspection wouldn't be needed anymore, or it might have been that we lived almost an hour away. It didn't matter to me; I was just glad that one more box had been checked so Doreen could come home.

We got started right away after breakfast with one of her daily occupational therapies which was a group session down in one of the rehab gyms. There were several people that sat around the table as Cortney gave them different activities to try. Each person had their own story and unique challenges they faced, but all of them had to try and conquer those seemingly simple tasks. She had them try and shuffle playing cards, stack dice on top of each other until there were five high, roll a ball across the table to each other, and even pick up pennies, nickels, dimes and quarters and put them in a coin bank to mention a few. She also timed them during some of those activities to really push them to concentrate on what was in front of them.

As I looked around, simple tasks they were not. My ignorance around those who have physical control issues, or potential permanent disabilities if you will, was an eye opening and humbling experience that I witnessed first-hand. It was heart wrenching on one hand to watch as each one struggled with their own physical challenge, but on the other hand, it was also heart lifting to see some of them tackle the task with an "I'm not giving up until I conquer it" attitude.

Tragedy...or Blessing?

Doreen was in that category. Even though the clock had stopped, Doreen and a few others kept going until the task was finished. Unfortunately, some of them did give up trying.

After watching that happen a few times while we were there, I can only imagine how hard it must be for Cortney to deal with that every day. It was obvious to me how compassionate she was about her work and how much she genuinely cared for her patients. I watched and worked with her as she helped Doreen steadily progress. We were fortunate enough to have her as Doreen's occupational therapist. By that point, there would only be a few more days with her because the discharge date was finally set: Friday, December 31st, 2021. It was crunch time.

Not long after Cortney finished on that Tuesday, Steve came in for her physical therapy session. We were going down to the gym with the "mock car" setup to practice getting in and out of the car that day. By that time, Steve was letting me get my practice in with helping Doreen get out of bed and in the wheelchair. I can't stress enough that it was a hundred times harder than it sounds.

Since Doreen only had a minimal amount of strength in her legs, the only thing she could to do was to lean forward and put her head on my shoulder and try to wrap her arms around me to hold on while I grabbed the gait belt that was tight around her waist. I would have her lean towards me while I used the leverage of my own weight to pull back and pivot her towards the wheelchair while the whole time making sure her feet didn't slide out from under her. That doesn't sound that complicated, but trust me, it was a Herculean task that scared the s**t out of both of us every time.

Now on that day, we were going to practice that motion in a much more restrained area, a car. It was a rather unique simulated car setup which was able to raise or lower the height, depending on your own vehicle's height. It had a normal looking car door and a bucket seat as well as a dashboard. I was anxious to practice those movements numerous times because I knew once we left the facility, we would be on our own and wouldn't have Steve to help bail us out if we ran into any difficulties. Hell, I had plenty of those difficulties while we were there.

The entire time we were going over the proper steps I needed to focus on, I totally overlooked the most important part of the whole process, Doreen. She had to be relaxed and comfortable enough with everything, probably even more so than me. I was so caught up with my role that I didn't even think about how much we both had to work together so neither of us would get hurt.

We practiced the transfer a couple of times before I told Steve that I had an issue with that set-up. My car door didn't open to the full degree that the simulated one did. He tried holding the door closed more like mine would be, but that didn't work too well. Steve and I both could see this practice run was taking its toll on Doreen, and it was wearing her out. So, Steve suggested I bring the car I would be using back the next day, and we would practice getting her in the car outside in the real elements, which meant she would have to have a winter coat on also. Doreen was very hesitant, but knew that's what we needed to do since the real ride home was only a few days away. That was an exhausting day for her, for both of us.

The next day was even more intense with activities than the previous ones. We started in the morning right after breakfast with Cortney's routines in one of the rehab rooms, followed by Steve's planned outside auto transfer. Just getting Doreen ready to go out in the elements was a more detailed process than I thought it would be. Prior to getting sick, it would only take us about two minutes to get ready to go out

Tragedy...or Blessing?

the door, but our new way of life would drastically change our "old normal" routines.

Once we had her bundled up and ready to go, we had to move quickly so she wouldn't get too warm and sweaty. I was afraid she would get a chill from that because I didn't know how long it would take to actually get her in the car. I just didn't want to take any chances of her getting sick again.

When we got outside, Steve did the first pass in and out of the car, which obviously went perfectly. Then it was my turn. Well, let's just say my practice run outside sucked. I felt so bad because I was not giving Doreen the confidence she needed to ease her fears and anxieties for her journey home, and beyond. I knew the steps I needed to do in my head, but the actual physical motions just didn't happen the way they were supposed to.

Steve was very patient and encouraging as we did it over several more times, with Doreen grimacing each time I tried. I was supposed to be her knight in shining armor, but I looked and felt more like the court jester. As flustered as I was, I knew I had to keep trying and keep my emotions and body language in check because Doreen already had enough on her plate to deal with. I didn't want to add any more stress in an already stressful situation.

Steve continued to do a phenomenal job in coaching and reassuring both of us that we were going to be alright, and it would get a little easier as we repeated those movements over, and over again. I trusted Steve and believed he was telling us the truth. It would take time and practice, and as Doreen improved, it would get even easier. Once again, I felt blessed that God had put the right person in the right place at the right time.

But the day wasn't over. I had been advocating for several days to get Doreen's feed tube removed before we left there.

It was still attached through her stomach because of the "just in case" scenario of something going wrong, and it would have to be used again.

We were told the doctor who put it in should be the one to remove it, so I wanted to have Dr. Roswell from the large Rockford hospital remove it before we went home since we were only two miles away. I did not want to take her home only to have to turn around and bring her back to Rockford to get it taken out. We were right there. Besides, my skills so far of getting her in and out of the car where horrendous at best. One less transfer was a high priority for me, for us.

I'm not sure who the hero was at the rehab facility, but they were able to get it scheduled on short notice, which included Doreen's final ambulance ride (thank God!). Since it was set up last minute, we had the choice of getting the feed tube removed or stay at the facility for a scheduled meeting with a company that would measure and fit Doreen for leg braces and special boots due to her drop foot.

We decided the tube removal was most important at the moment, and we would be able to go to that other company down the road if she still needed that type of help. It was literally a minute-by-minute decision because in less than an hour, she was on her way to the outpatient offices where the surgeon would get her final "COVID leash" detached. Well, I guess I wasn't counting her oxygen hose, but at least that one wasn't actually attached.

I was able to be in the room when Dr. Roswell removed it, and they didn't even take her off the gurney she was on from the ambulance ride. We had no idea of what to expect since we didn't know how it was even attached. He apologized to her first as he put one hand on her stomach with his fingers around the hose and grabbed the hose with his other hand and wrapped the hose around his fingers. He said he was sorry once more, and then pulled up hard with his hand holding the tube and it literally popped out in one motion as Doreen's eyes nearly popped out of her head. It was like ripping a Band-Aid off except at a much higher pain level.

Dr. Roswell apologized again and checked out the hole that had caused so much agony a few months ago. I don't know if he remembered what transpired back then with the "free air" that entered her system because of that tube, but at that moment, he was only concerned with the wound it left behind and what our instructions were to keep it from getting infected once we got home. I guess you could say that she went full circle with Dr. Roswell.

It didn't take long for the paperwork to get done and back to the physical rehab center we went. The round-trip procedure only took a little over an hour. It would have taken us that long to just drive up there if it hadn't been done at that time. One more major box had been checked off the list.

But, with everything that had transpired that day, it had completely wiped her out and she was done for the day. It was only a couple of hours until dinner anyway, so no more therapies or other activities were needed. It was a big day for her. I couldn't wait to call everyone and give them the great news for the day. In just two days, Doreen would be home.

The Final Countdown

I didn't sleep much that night. A million thoughts went through my mind: Good ones and terrifying ones. I think I set a record for the "what-if" scenarios. I flew through the morning routine and was on the road before light. I was the first visitor to sign in that day. That would be her last full day there and I hoped we could get the most out of it since it would all be up to me starting tomorrow. I don't think she had been awake too long before I got there, and I was greeted with her big, beautiful smile when I walked in the door. I almost felt giddy, but at the same time, I was completely terrified. How is that even possible?

It wasn't long after when Doreen's breakfast showed up. I hope they weren't checking the volume of food consumed on her plate because I helped her clean her plate, or at least a part of it each meal I was there. I think some of the nurses there even liked me, because occasionally they had an "extra" tray and asked if I would like to have it. Of course, I said yes, because I can't let good food go to waste. I have to say, the staff was so wonderful, extremely helpful and accommodating at every level.

That was by far the shortest leg of her journey, but an enormous factor in the healing process for her ticket home. Because it was her last day for therapies, the first session of the day would be down in the rehab rooms, followed by lunch and a little rest, and then her final afternoon session in her room.

The morning session went okay, but I could see she didn't have her normal push that she's had the entire time there. I figured she was getting scared of all the unknowns that lie just around the corner; basically, the next day. She barely picked at her lunch, and I knew something was obviously wrong. When I asked, she said everything was okay, but she just "felt a little off."

It wasn't too long after that when Cortney came in to complete her last session with Doreen. She was going to help Doreen transfer to the toilet and then practice taking a shower. I could see in Doreen's eyes that something was really getting to her, and once we got into the bathroom, Doreen broke down and started to cry. She couldn't hold it back any longer and she sobbed so hard that her body shook. Both

Cortney and I were stunned by what just happened. Doreen said she was done and didn't want to continue with any more therapies. She just wanted to go home. Cortney was amazing and her compassion for Doreen was on full display.

We got Doreen back to her bed and helped her back in. Cortney was able to help calm her back down and told her no one would make her do any more if she didn't want to. She also told Doreen it was normal for people to get overwhelmed at the thought of going home and having to be on their own without the hands-on help she's been used to at the facility. After she finished talking with Doreen, she said she would talk to Steve and explain the situation.

A little while later, Steve came in to check on Doreen to see if she was okay and to double check on whether she wanted to do one more session. Doreen told him the same thing, she was done. He respected her decision as well and talked through a few more suggestions to help her with the transition home. They were both absolutely wonderful therapists who truly cared about the well-being of their patients. I owe them a debt of gratitude for all their efforts and care they showed Doreen and I during our short stay there.

The day wasn't over yet though, Doreen got a visit from the psychologist, Dr. Ross, who heard what happened earlier in the day. She was able to help put things in perspective from where Doreen had started her traumatic journey to the place where she was now, and how much progress she had made to that point. It was okay to have a wide range of emotions because of what she had been through, but just don't get stalled on any of the negative ones. She said she knew everything would be okay for Doreen because she heard about the support and love that was waiting at home for her, and those were the things she should look forward to. We thanked her for her kind input and said our goodbyes.

We still weren't done that day because the next visitor was Alissa, our case manger. She came in to give us a list of the things she was working on that would be essential for Doreen's discharge tomorrow. She was in the process of setting up a company called Homecare to deliver a hospital bed which we would rent, and a commode and shower chair which we would buy. She had them set up to be delivered to our house the next morning so it would be ready by the time we got there. She also arranged with that company to deliver the oxygen tanks and an oxygen concentrator machine to the house as well.

Another area of the discharge process she was working on was with a company for Doreen's home rehab care. That would include a RN nurse, an occupational therapist and a physical therapist that would come to our house for a six-week period to start. She was still working on finding a company who covered our area. On top of all of that, she was working with our insurance company to get approval for all the equipment and the home care team. Apparently, that portion of the discharge process was always on short notice, but very crucial for patients in Doreen's condition.

Honestly, I was very nervous that everything wouldn't be able to come together quick enough. It was only a few hours away. I wasn't sure what I would do if we got home and I didn't have a proper bed for her to be in. Obviously, our regular bed wouldn't cut it. Alissa told us not to worry about it because that's what she does all the time. She was very confident about everything working out as planned, so we trusted her with the details…but I still prayed that night for God to help clear the way.

It was now New Years Eve morning. This was it! Doreen's final destination from a long, long agonizing and heart wrenching journey…HOME! There had been countless times throughout this hellish nightmare where I didn't know if that day would even be possible. Yet here we were.

There were a lot of moving parts that day, and fortunately, the cavalry had arrived a couple of days earlier. Bryan and Ashley and the kids had come up for a few days for the holidays but would be leaving the next day to go back home. It worked out well because they would be able to stay at the house to let the people in from the home health rental company to get the equipment set up, including all the instructions on how everything worked. We have never been involved in a situation like that before, so I was thrilled for them to be here to help, although we didn't plan that ahead of time. It just so happened to work out that way. I left early to get to Rockford to make sure we had all the info and instructions from them on what to do after we left there.

After she had breakfast, one of the nurses came in to instruct me on how to check Doreen's blood sugar, as well as how to give her a shot of insulin. Say what? I didn't know that would be a part of my nursing duties, or at least I didn't recall it being discussed before that moment. I was nervous as hell because I never used a needle before, let alone using one on someone else. The nurse was very patient and understanding and walked me through step by step.

She then handed me a nine-page print-out of all the medications Doreen was currently on. There was the name and dosage of each pill, the times of day she needed to take them, as well as the primary purpose and possible side-effects of each drug. I was freaking out from the pages and pages of instructions just for her meds. As overwhelmed as I was, I did my best to keep my composure so I wouldn't put any more stress on Doreen that she didn't already have. On the outside, I stayed calm and cool, but on the inside, I was a complete nervous wreck. Doreen's very life would literally now be in my hands. No pressure...not.

There was one tiny relief, right after I gave Doreen her insulin shot in her stomach. One of her doctors came in and said she wouldn't need to have the insulin shot anymore because he had put her on a drug called MetFORMIN which helped control blood sugars. He had started her on that pill on Sunday, and her levels had come to the point where the pill could replace the shot. I welcomed that news because it was one less thing I had to stress about.

Shortly after that, Alissa stopped by to give us an update as well as find out where we wanted to pick up her medications. She had almost everything lined up, except for the home health care people and which drug store we wanted to use. One of the few setbacks of living out in the country was not having a lot of options readily available, especially when it came to specialized health care. She was able to find only one company, Home Health Care, which would be able to come to our house for weekly check-ups and therapies, but she was still working out the final details. She was confident it would be done before we would leave there.

As far as the medications, fortunately Kirstyn was still filling in for Doreen at the insurance company up in Dixon. She was only going to be there for a few hours, so we used the drug store chain which wasn't far from there. Kirstyn would stop by there to pick up Doreen's medications and bring them to our house, hopefully by the time we got there.

I felt like we were in a three-ring circus, well, more like a ten-ring circus. There was a steady stream of people coming in and out of her room. There were the nurses and the respiratory therapist who finished up taking her stats and finalizing paperwork, and then Doreen's primary doctor, Dr. Hunee who came in to finish his portion.

Even though we were only there for a total of eighteen days, including that day, some of the staff stopped by just to say goodbye and wish us well. We even got a special goodbye from Cortney and Steve. They stopped by to give Doreen one last round of encouragement and to share their gratitude with Doreen for the persistent efforts she gave every time, and for her great attitude. They really enjoyed working with her and expressed how confident they were that she would continue to improve and conquer this set-back that had changed our lives.

It was time to go. All the paperwork was complete, and the car was loaded. It was the last ride in the wheelchair there, but we had one more stop before we went out the door. I wheeled her in one of the rehab gyms over to a wall that had a bell mounted on it. It was a very special bell which would only be rung by a person who finished their program and was going home. Doreen reached up, grabbed the string and rang that bell. All the people in the room clapped and cheered as we waved and said goodbye.

Just a few more steps down the hall and Doreen was finally free…she would be on her way home! I had tears rolling down my face as I signed out for the last time. As I went out to bring the car up to the doors, I wondered if this was really happening or if it was only a dream. I had prayed for that exact moment for so long that it almost didn't feel real. But it was.

The nurse stayed by her side and then wheeled her out as I pulled up. I gave her my phone so she could take a picture of Doreen getting in the car to go home. I was confident I would be able to get Doreen in the car without any issues because we practiced it several times. I got her close to the car and locked the brakes on the wheelchair, got her to lean into me while I got a good grasp on the belt, leaned back and pulled her forward while she had her arms around me, and I pivoted to turn her back towards the seat so I could set her in the car. That sounded perfect, right? Except when I went to pivot, my feet slid on the salt that was spread on the driveway which also caused Doreen's feet to slide as well. It happened so fast, and it felt like my feet were on marbles while I was trying to not to fall.

The nurse was still taking pictures because she didn't realize what was happening. I yelled for her to go on the driver's side of the car so she could help pull Doreen into the car before I would lose control and go down. She heard the panic in my voice and ran around the car and reached in to help. We barely avoided a complete catastrophe. The last picture the nurse took before she jumped in to help shows the look of complete panic and fear as Doreen held on for dear life. That was a very shaky start to our maiden voyage home.

Homecoming!

It took several miles of silence before our nerves had calmed down enough before we were able to speak again. It was an emotional ride home, and at times felt very strange because of everything that had transpired over the last several months. Plus, I could see she was scared and over-whelmed. She kept saying how weird it felt being in the car driving down the expressway. I understood exactly the feeling she was talking about based on my own experience when I started driving after being sick. She obviously wasn't driving, but the motion of everything moving quickly around her was an odd sensation.

It was probably the quickest ride home I had the entire time, and we were pulling in the driveway before I knew it. Finally, she was **home** at last!

Tragedy...or Blessing?

Ashley had parked her car to the side so I could just pull straight in the garage and park. I closed the garage door and sat there for a moment because four months of emotional tension funneled down to that very moment. Tears rolled down my face as I opened the door to get out of the car. But, as soon as the car door latched closed, my new caregiver instincts kicked in and I immediately forgot about my own emotional state and focused on getting Doreen out of the car and into the house. I went in and got the wheelchair and asked Bryan to come help me. After my solo transfer getting her in the car, I knew I should have some help standing by just in case. And I needed it.

Doreen was already drained from all the commotion and stress of the journey home, and now she had to tolerate another rookie transfer just to get her in the house. Since Bryan had zero training in this area, he relied on my directions which were as jumbled as my brain. My fears had overcome my confidence which caused my instructions to sound like a foreign language, one I didn't even understand. Poor Doreen, she had no choice but to close her eyes and pray she wouldn't be dropped. It took way longer than it should have, but we finally managed to get her in the chair and up into the house. She could breathe again. She made it in the house.

Our living room would now be Doreen's new living quarters until she would be able move under her own power. Imagine what it would be like to be a completely strong and independent person who now had to rely on someone else to literally do everything for you. That level of frustration would now be Doreen's closest companion for an unknown length of time. But for now, that was Doreen's new reality.

After all the hugs and kisses and tears, I attempted my first at-home transfer from the wheelchair to her new bed that was set up in the living room. We had moved the couches out of the way the night before so the kids could have the rental company set up the hospital bed and the oxygen equipment in that room so she could watch TV and be able to look out the front window as well as out the back patio door to see the familiar scenery.

Once we settled in, Bryan, Ashley and the kids went over to her folks to spend part of New Years Eve with them and give Doreen a chance to settle in, relax and rest. It wasn't long after when Kirstyn stopped by herself to see mom finally home and to bring her medications. She only stayed for a little while because she knew mom needed time to rest from her exhausting homecoming. The day was not only physically challenging for her (and myself), but probably more taxing on us emotionally. After a few more hugs and kisses, Kirstyn left to go home.

I thought it would be nice and quiet so Doreen could rest, but I didn't realize how much noise the oxygen concentrator would make. We had it set over by the little entryway by the front door thinking it would be out of the way and around the corner to keep the sound down, but that wasn't the case. On top of it, I couldn't seem to get the oxygen level set properly and consistent which caused Doreen's stats to drop a little. Nothing dangerous, but certainly not at the optimum level she needed. I was a nervous wreck because I couldn't get it to work right, and because I was so afraid that I was going to screw something up.

The nurses had always made everything look so effortless, so how tough could it be? Well, within a few short hours, I quickly realized how strenuous and challenging that job really is. It is a monumental responsibility that requires a mental focus, coupled with a large dose of compassion and energy to get that job done.

Tragedy...or Blessing?

My new role had started whether I was ready or not, and I knew I would need a little help comforting Doreen to make her feel more at home. Fortunately, I had three little helpers that had missed her as much as I did. Her puppies. Now that it was just the two of us, I picked up the two pups and put them on her bed. She lit up like a Christmas tree and the smile on her face made my heart melt. I had prayed for so long to see that moment of pure joy and happiness. Then I picked up Tori so Doreen could kiss and hug her as well, and I had a sigh of relief that I made the right decision by keeping Tori around even when I thought it was her time to go.

Even though there were a few hiccups, Doreen's homecoming was yet another miracle I just experienced. It was a little after 10 o'clock when Bryan, Ashley, Emerson and Adalyn got back to the house. They wanted to spend a little time with grandma before bed because they were leaving in the morning to go back home. We had visited for a while when grandma decided to hand out the Christmas cards she wrote at the physical rehab center.

That would have to be the Christmas Doreen had missed. It wasn't the one she wanted or dreamed about, but at least there was one. We were going to have to get used to making the best of what was in front of us, and that was a start. The clock was getting closer to a new year and a new chapter in our life together. Thank you God for letting her come *home*... Happy New Year!

> **¹⁰ And the God of all grace, who called you to his eternal glory in Christ, after you have suffered a little while, will himself restore you and make you strong, firm and steadfast.**
>
> 1 Peter 5:10 (NIV)

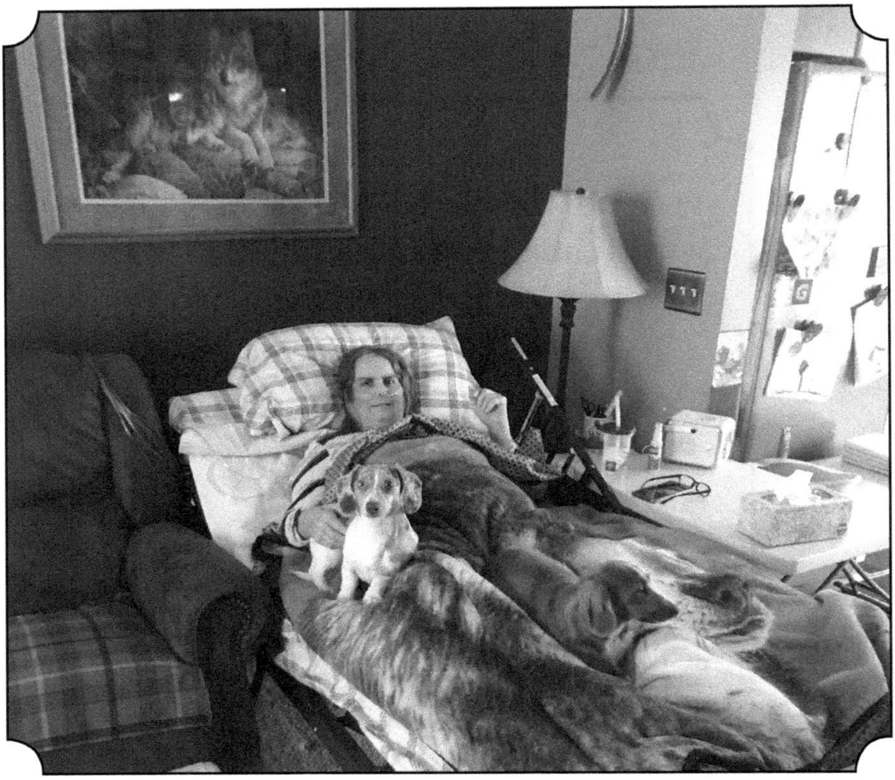

Chapter Six: Welcome Home to Our New Path

- Ready or not...Life changes -

Midnight came and went without a countdown, or the crazy party hats and confetti as in years past, but rather with a quiet "Happy New Year" in a dim lit newly renovated home hospital room. Doreen's new, and last, "hospital" room. Everyone had gone to bed before the calendar change because we were all exhausted from the excitement of Doreen's monumental accomplishment and long-awaited homecoming. Plus, the kids wanted to get going early in the morning so they could try to get back home to Tennessee before dark.

I'm not sure exactly how much sleep Doreen got that night, but I know I didn't sleep very much. It was a totally different atmosphere with completely different new sounds. The dogs were also a little confused with those strange new surroundings and activities because it was supposed to be bedtime.

On top of the changed environment, I couldn't calm my nerves. I kept picking my head up off my pillow on the couch to look over at the bed to make sure she was doing okay, and that nothing was wrong. There were a couple of times during the night when she called out because she needed to use the bathroom. We certainly were not capable of getting her to

Tragedy…or Blessing?

that room just yet, so the uncomfortable bedpan would have to be used for an unknown length of time. I didn't have any real experience with that, even though I saw the nurses help her with that numerous times. I learned quickly over time the proper way to position and maneuver everything, but it still was an uncomfortable experience for her each time.

We made it through the first night and before we knew it, the sun was starting to rise and shine through the back patio door. It didn't take too long before everyone was up and getting ready for the needed departure which no one wanted to take that day. It was bitter-sweet. There was the joyous tear-filled homecoming of Mom/Grandma which everyone wanted to continue, and then the sad tear-filled goodbye's that were just moments away.

Even though there were only a few shortened moments together with them, after the most excruciating longest four plus months in our family history, those brief moments spent together were a priceless treasure. I think Bryan especially needed to see mom home to give his mind, heart and soul some well deserved peace.

So, life moves on. It was time to go and to say goodbye. After the final hugs and kisses and many tears goodbye, they walked out the door. Normally, Doreen and I would stand in the garage and wave as they pulled out of the driveway, but not that time. That ritual would have to be put on hold for now, but hopefully not indefinitely.

January 1st, 2022 had already started out with emotional tears, and the day had only just begun. Later in the day would be subject to more tears from joyful reunions from the special people who experienced the same hardened journey as I did, one we all had to endure. We also all prayed the same prayers and asked God for the same result the entire time. Our prayers had been heard and answered! By God's Grace and His Grace alone, Doreen was now back at home with her family. How amazing was that!

I had talked with our kids about spacing out the visits because I didn't want to push Doreen too much because she obviously needed to rest and relax for a few days. We decided that Heather would go first with the kids, Jarrett, Owen and Ali. They would stop by for a couple of hours after lunch so mom could recoup a little after an emotional morning. Then, after Heather's family would leave and we had dinner, Kirstyn, Jason, Landon and Liam would come to visit for a while. Then Joshua, Natalie, Cayden and Ava would come by Sunday afternoon for their visit after the RN, Ulysses, from Home Health Care came to do his first at home check up.

That would be the schedule because everyone, especially the grand kids, needed to spend some quality time with mom/grandma because they all missed her so much. With everything that had transpired throughout this family nightmare, it felt like a lifetime since the grand kids had been with her. Even for our kids, there had only been a limited amount of time they got to visit her at the various facilities during the past four months.

So as each family got there, I could see the uncertainty of what to expect on their faces, even through the held-back tears. They all knew that grandma had an extremely bad case of COVID, which they had all talked about as a family, but to actually see the difference from before until now was a shocking reality. You could tell by their interaction with Doreen that they were struggling emotionally, some openly and some tightly holding back, and some in-between the two. I experienced all of the above. My emotions had been on hyper-drive for the past four months, so it didn't take much for me to get choked up at the sight of these extremely grateful families' reunions with mom/grandma.

Tragedy...or Blessing?

Another major tug at my heartstrings was Doreen's reaction to each one as well. She was so, so happy and excited to see each one, and to let each one know just how much she loved them and how much she missed them. Doreen is an amazing grandma and mom! Obviously by now, I think you should know how much she means to me!

Even though we didn't spend too much time with each family, we were able to get our postponed mini-Christmas in with each one. Each one only took a few short minutes to complete, unlike the decades of years passed, but I'm sure those brief moments will be well remembered by each one of them because we were still together as a *whole* family. That gift will not be soon forgotten.

With Christmas now "officially" over and all the first homecoming visits were done with each family, so far, so good...or so I thought. Once our seclusion set in on that Sunday night, I could tell something was a little off with Doreen. At first, I thought it was from the wind-down of the anticipation, you know, the same kind of feeling you get when the reality of your vacation is over.

But then it got worse, much worse. She said she was feeling nauseous and didn't even want to take a drink of water. My first thought was I had mixed up some of her medications and she was having a bad reaction to it. And then out of nowhere, she began to throw up, not a little, but violently. I freaked out. I didn't know what I could do to help make it go away.

For the next twenty-four hours, she continued to vomit, at times almost uncontrollably. We already had her first doctor's visit scheduled with Dr. Crawford on Wednesday morning, which was the earliest we could get. We called Kirstyn and Heather and explained what was happening to see if they could help figure out what was going on with mom. We tried to pinpoint what the difference was from the hospitals and rehab facility compared to home. Anything we came up with would quickly be dismissed, except for one. The only change we could come up with was the water. We have well water at our house which I'm sure those other places did not, so that had to be the culprit.

It was miserable to watch, and even more traumatizing on Doreen's system. I felt like a complete failure when Doreen looked at me and said, "If I get sick one more time, take me back to the hospital." She had only been home for a little over forty-eight hours and now she was already willing to go back, even after all those times when she desperately wanted to leave and just come home. There had to be something that was causing this issue. But what?

I started by counting the pills in each bottle to see if the numbers were correct, and then I looked over the pages of her medications that the Physical Rehab Center had sent home with us to see if we could figure something out. The last three pages were the possible side effects from each drug she was on, and as I read them to her, we came across one that pretty much described her symptoms to the letter. It was the one she had just started on a week earlier called MetFORMIN which was to control her blood sugar levels. The side effects listed were Nausea, Vomiting, Diarrhea, and Physical weakness. Out of everything else we tried to account for, that drug addressed every symptom she had.

After hearing the effects I had just read, Doreen immediately said she would not take that drug anymore. I saw her take charge like that once before in Sycamore. They wanted to give her the liquid nourishment again through her feed tube after they stopped for a few days once she started to eat "real food". They felt she wasn't eating enough on her own, but she refused to let them because she felt it wasn't helping her, especially with her blood sugar.

Doreen strongly advocated for her own health back then and I knew better than to push the issue since she was the one who had been dealing with those horrible side effects. I thought she should wait for the doctor to make the call, but it was only another day and a half before her appointment, so hopefully it wouldn't be critical for her to miss that medication for such a short period.

She made the correct call. In less than twenty-four hours, she was feeling better and wasn't vomiting any more. Talk about what a difference a day makes, that was a perfect example. Other than the visits with all the kids, those first three days home were extremely challenging for me and were absolutely miserable for Doreen. She had come home to start feeling better, not worse.

We were fortunate enough to have cleared the first hurdle, but that was just the first of many to come. So how many more hurdles would we have to clear? In track, you can count them up until the finish line. In life, you just take them one at a time as they come, and then move on.

It was early January in the Midwest. Winter was on full display. Up until then, the weather had been fairly mild through December. I had joked with people saying they should thank me for the descent winter weather so far because I had asked God if He wouldn't mind keeping the roads clear and dry while I traveled so many miles each day to be with Doreen. But I forgot to ask Him about continuing that trend once we got home.

When we got up on Wednesday morning and looked outside, the nasty winter weather had hit all at once. It looked like someone had shaken a snow-globe and then added thirty to forty mile an hour winds, along with plummeting

- Ready or not...Life changes -

temperatures. Damn, we had to get Doreen to her first visit at Dr. Crawford's office. I knew I wouldn't be able to do it by myself, so we called Heather to see if she could send some help over.

It didn't take too long before they got here, which I think it took us longer to get Doreen bundled up and in the car. That was an entirely new experience dealing with a wheelchair and an oxygen tank, as well as a nervous patient, a nurse in training and two rookie helpers. Now throw in a small blizzard and what could possibly go wrong? All things considered; we fumbled through it unscathed.

When we got to the doctor's office, we had to pull the car on the sidewalk as close to the doors as possible because the wind was blowing the snow so hard it hurt as it hit your face. We angled the car the best we could to block the wind, and we got Doreen out of the car as quickly as possible and in the chair. It only took a minute or two, but under those conditions, it felt much, much longer. I felt so bad for Doreen because there was absolutely nothing she could do for herself but sit there and wait for us to move her from place to place.

I can't begin to imagine what that must have felt like for her, previously having complete independence to now total dependency. Life had thrown her a hard, hard curve, and now she had no choice but to deal with what was in front of her. I had made a promise to her the first time I saw her when she got out of isolation that I would always be by her side, helping every step of the way. I guess I didn't realize it at the time just how big some of those steps were going to be, but with God's help, our focus would stay on looking forward.

Even though there were a few challenges during that first doctors' visit, the checkup itself went well. Dr. Crawford was up to speed with Doreen's case, and we had a game-plan for her future follow-ups. Now we just had to get her home through the same weather we started with. What a huge sigh of relief once the garage door closed at home and we were able to maneuver in much easier conditions. That two-and-a-half-hour ordeal used a full day's worth of energy for her, so once we got her settled back in the bed, it didn't take long for her to close her eyes and doze off. Finally, some much needed rest for her after her wild and nerve-racking adventure.

With our first outing now out of the way, we would not have to venture out for the next few weeks unless some unforeseen situation would arise. Winter was now on full display, including the temperature. I kept the thermostat in the house turned much higher than normal because I didn't want to take a chance on Doreen catching a cold, the flu or anything else.

I even took a big heavy quilt and nailed it across the large front window because it leaked the cold air so bad. On windy days, it could blow a candle out at twelve inches away. All our windows in the front of the house (which faces west) used to be insulated glass, up until our close encounter with a tornado back in June 2016. We were fortunate that it only clipped our house, but it popped all the seals on the glass which we didn't notice for a year or two later. Anyway, that's why I was over cautious with trying to keep the house warmer for Doreen. The constant temperature watch and control would now be a part of my new routine as Doreen's nurse and caregiver.

There were so many things for me to keep track of, like: all the medications, taking her blood pressure, and checking her glucose levels multiple times a day. There were also all the daily necessities which most of us take for granted because we can do it ourselves. She needed help with just about everything, like eating, getting dressed, brushing her teeth and hair along with other personal hygiene, restroom calls, and I even had to help her get to a sitting position on the edge of her

- Ready or not…Life changes -

bed because she had very limited physical movement on her own in the beginning. At least the hospital bed was electric so she could raise and lower her head and feet, but to raise and lower the bed up and down, I had to crank that by hand.

There was a huge learning curve along with lots of trials and errors. And it wouldn't be just my actions I had to be aware of. I fortunately caught a pharmacy error on two separate occasions. On Saturday nights I would take her pill organizer and fill it for the following week. It had seven separate days with multiple compartment times for each day. I would take one bottle at a time and put each pill in the proper slot. On those two occasions, I saw a different looking pill from all the rest which obviously didn't belong in that bottle. It clearly wasn't right. After that scare, I was over-cautious with everything. That could have been a disaster.

That was all new to us and it took a bit of time, but we were able to get the new routines working fairly well and semi-comfortable for both of us. We even had a bell she could ring in case she needed something, and I wasn't in the room. It also worked especially well at night when she had to go to the bathroom.

Now that she was home and we were together for twenty-four/seven, I was most impressed with Doreen's attitude and determination to get better. It was inspirational. However, based on the previous four plus months, I couldn't help but be the over-protective partner who didn't stop worrying about everything, and who didn't stop asking if she was okay or if she needed anything. I wasn't going to take any chances on her progress going backwards. No more roller coasters from now on…God please!

Pushing Forward

Another new routine that had started was the trio of professionals from Home Health Care who would pick up on Doreen's therapies where the physical rehab facility had left off. It was supposed to start immediately once we got home, but only the RN, Ulysses, had come by in the first ten days.

On his second visit, he didn't realize the rehab sessions hadn't started yet, so he made a few calls and was able to get the physical therapist, Art, and the occupational therapist, Josh, to come out within a few days. My guess was, there was a shortage of therapists, just like the shortage everything else. They were stretched too thin and over-worked from the pandemic just like all the other health care workers I encountered throughout our journey. The insurance company had approved ten hours for each of them per episode (ten – one-hour sessions) and would have to be re-evaluated and approved if more sessions would be needed. That was the starting point.

As each one arrived on their scheduled day, my job would be to lock the pups in the bedroom because they didn't like strangers in the house. Then I stayed out of the way for the time being so they could do their job. After a couple of sessions, Art and Josh gave me instructions and showed me how to work with Doreen on various exercises in between their visits to keep her progress moving forward. When each session was over, they would look at their schedules to figure out logistically what would work out best for the next session.

The territory they each had to cover was a lot of miles, in winter on top of it. There were a couple of times the weather didn't co-operate, but it didn't matter because we were very pleased with each one of them and with the progress Doreen was making. They knew what they were doing and were completely focused on helping Doreen get on her feet again. It would be a slow and tedious process, but with Doreen's and their commitment, I knew it would only be a matter of time.

It was also a huge help to have an RN come out once a week to check up on Doreen's condition, and the bonus was Ulysses compassion and genuine care about our situation. On each visit, after he took all her stats, we would sit and talk about how the week went and how each therapy was going. He would listen and take notes and then make suggestions on what might help make things more comfortable or even things we needed to be cautious about. He was very thorough, professional and trustworthy. We were able to have his help for a total of seventeen sessions which took us through the end of April. Ulysses was the easiest of the three for Doreen to deal with. He didn't make her do anything physical.

The shortest interaction we had was with the occupational therapist, Josh. There were some scheduling issues off the bat, and he only came three times in January, but then he ramped up the frequency of visits in February. He originally started working with Doreen on her fine motor skills until his fifth or sixth visit. Doreen had progressed rapidly in that area, which she had been working on constantly. He was very pleased with her progress.

She decided to show him how she "exercised" in between the sessions. She loves working on these pictures called Diamond Dotz ®. They are very tiny colored plastic dots which get placed one by one on a sticky picture that has specific numbers to match specific colors. She showed how the tool picked up and held each piece, and then she placed it on the appropriate spot on the picture and pushed down a little to make it stick and stay in place. He laughed and said his job was done and asked what else Doreen wanted to work on since he still had a few more sessions to reach the ten that was already approved.

Our biggest goal was to have her be able to stand up on her own (safely) and eventually walk again. So, for the rest of his time with us he focused on exercises for her legs, and with helping her get on her feet for short periods of time. I believe his added assistance with her physical therapy had helped Doreen tremendously with her mobility. He finished his ten sessions by the end of February.

The last and most challenging area for Doreen was the physical therapy, especially in the beginning. Ulysses and Josh were fairly easy on Doreen in their areas of expertise. Art, on the other hand, pushed Doreen on the physical side because he knew he had to once he saw what he was dealing with. Doreen's drop-foot was going to be a real challenge for both of them and he knew it.

Her left foot still was not nearly as bad as her right foot. She could not put her foot at a ninety degree to her leg like the normal position it would be in if you were standing. The tendon, or tendons, that control the mobility of the foot had been "frozen" in place for months from the lack of movement and would require some major work to stretch them out and make them functional again. On top of that, the muscle loss in her legs would also complicate the matter. She had lost over eighty pounds through this nightmare, which a lot of that was muscle.

If Art wouldn't be able to get it functioning properly, there was the distinct possibility Doreen would have to have a custom brace made for her leg(s) to help her get around. I think that possibility was one of the strongest motivations for Doreen to push herself the way she did, and to tolerate the intense pain from those rehab sessions.

The first several weeks were spent on stretching the tendons and muscles and to work on building up her core strength. It was hard to sit back and watch the grimacing expressions on her face as Art worked on her feet, especially the right one. I could see tears in her eyes, and Art would ask if he should ease up some or move on and come back to work on it again later. Each time she told him to keep going because she knew she had to. It was the only way she would be able walk again, sooner than later. After everything she and her body had been through, everybody, including me, would understand if she wanted to take it easy and not stress too hard.

But watching her now push through the frustrations and the pain to reach her goal of being able to walk again was truly amazing and inspiring to witness. The letter I wrote to her in the very beginning was spot on. Her drive and determination was second to none. I think Art appreciated working with someone who was as determined as he was to getting them back on their feet again.

It took a lot of trials and tears, but Doreen eventually was able to stand up for short periods (a few seconds to a minute, then two, etc.) which worked its way up to a few steps with a walker. It was a major milestone when that happened, and I cried with joy that day! There had been many times where I questioned whether it would even be possible. I thanked God for another miracle and asked for the momentum to keep going, and I also asked for forgiveness for my lack of faith. Art had done his job well and got Doreen up and moving, very shaky at first, but moving. She still had a long recovery ahead of her which still required her to work on her strength and stability, but at least she clearly was on the right path.

Art had a total of fifteen sessions with her and he made each one count. Doreen and I will be forever grateful to

Ulysses, Josh and Art for all their efforts and care they gave to Doreen. I was convinced once again that God put the right people in the right place at the right time. Doreen's journey was living proof of that.

Speaking of the right people, Doreen and I are so blessed to have such a great family and friends. The time had come to ask for some help because I would no longer be her full-time caretaker. We were in the first week of February when I got a call from Jeff at work. He was checking in like usual to see how Doreen's progress was going and to make sure we were doing okay. He filled me in on what was happening at work and then asked me if I had a date in mind on when I thought I would be back to work. I hadn't given much thought about it prior to that moment. My total focus had been on taking care of Doreen every minute of every day for the past five weeks since she came home.

I knew I would have to face that moment at some point, but the time had flown by so fast and now it was time to make that decision. Since I hadn't spent any time figuring out how to make sure Doreen would be taken care of while I was gone at work, I asked Jeff if I could have a couple of days to give him an answer.

After I hung up, panic set in. How the hell am I going to do that? At that point in time, Doreen still couldn't get out of bed by herself, or stand, or walk, or make her way to the bathroom, or anything else for that matter. She was totally dependent on someone helping her for literally everything. She had made phenomenal progress already, but she still had a long road in front of her. One that would require outside muscle so to speak. She needed assistance.

Doreen called Kirstyn and Heather to see if they knew anybody that might be willing to work as an in-house caregiver during the day while I was gone, and on such short notice. God answered yet another prayer and Heather had a lady named Rosalie who would be able to work for a few weeks or so. We asked her to stop by to talk and to make sure it would work for all of us.

When she came to see us, I was a little hesitant at first. She was a very nice lady, but she was a few years older than us and was smaller in size than Doreen. I was concerned how she would be able to help Doreen get out of bed and in the wheelchair among all the other physical activities that were required every day. It was true Doreen was getting a little stronger and better each day and was improving with being able to help with the processes, but I was so afraid of Doreen being dropped or falling. I was nervous about that happening when I moved her, and now I had to trust someone else who clearly wouldn't have the same strength as I did.

On short notice, we decided to hire her and try for a couple of weeks to see how it would go and see how much Doreen would improve over that time. If anything would happen, Kirstyn and Heather were only a phone call away and could be there a lot faster than I could. I also had a little comfort in knowing that Ulysses, Josh and Art would be there throughout the week to give any extra assistance if needed. I'm not sure if we really had our ducks lined up in a row, but we did have a game plan even though it might only be temporary.

I made my call back to Jeff to tell him we had help lined up and I would be back on Monday, February 14th, Valentines Day. After I hung up the phone, my nerves kicked in again just like they did the first time I went back to work. It was a strange feeling, like I was a kid on his first day of school and didn't know where to go or what to do. It didn't matter. It was time.

It was very hard to give my full attention at work when my mind was constantly thinking about what was happening at home. I couldn't help it. Our world had been turned upside down for the past six months and we weren't anywhere close to having any sense of control of it yet, or even what direction our new path was headed.

My mind and emotions once again would not rest. All the "W" questions (who, what, where, when, & why) now consumed much of my focus because I needed to have all the answers. My focus *should* have been on trusting God. After all, He was the One who brought Doreen out of the depths of that awful darkness up to that point. How could I forget that? Especially when He continued to provide us with everything we needed at the precise time we needed it.

For those first two weeks I went back to work, Doreen was fine. In fact, Doreen and her therapy team had pushed hard and made huge progress with her physical capabilities.

Friday, February 25th

That was a phenomenal Friday because I once again witnessed another miracle! Heather and Ali stopped by to visit for a while to see how grandma was doing. Heather used my phone and recorded Doreen standing up by the couch and walking on her own using a walker, with me three inches behind her being a nervous wreck. She went about twenty feet to the kitchen and turned around and sat down in a chair. When she finished, she said, "Ta-da". She was totally exhausted from that short venture, but the emotional joy overrode the physical deficit. That forty-five second maiden voyage was the farthest she had walked in over six months. That night, I know the tears flowed down quite a few cheeks after they saw that video.

Since Doreen had progressed as well as she did in such a short time, we decided to call in the cavalry. We made some calls and lined up a few people who would come out to be with Doreen and help her throughout the day. I was beyond grateful that we had the next two weeks covered so quickly, especially since it was on such short notice.

Doreen's new caretakers for the next couple of weeks would be Aunt Sandy, Pam and Debbie (our good friends from St. Charles), Janie (a friend of Heather's and an RN), Kirstyn and Heather. There was absolutely no hesitation when we asked for help, only "What do we need to bring?" Once again, my heart was humbled. God has blessed us with so many special people in our life who really care about us. They truly were a part of God's "Amazing Grace".

So, with our new plan in place, wait, let me re-phrase that; With God's plan now in place for Doreen's daily care, I would go back to work feeling a little more at ease because Doreen was in really good hands.

From the first day Doreen was home, I had been very paranoid about "outside" people coming around since COVID was still very active. That wasn't the only bug that scared the heck out me coming in contact with Doreen. Anyone who might have a cold or the flu or even the sniffles made me nervous. I only had her home for six weeks and I was afraid the slightest little illness would put her back in the hospital again.

I wasn't alone in those concerns, everyone who would be helping us, as well as many others, also understood Doreen's predicament. She was at such a high risk because her system had been so compromised and over-whelmed, so everyone took the necessary precautions to keep her safe. Aunt Sandy already had a little practice with that because she and Uncle Chuck had been our first visitors back in January, other than my kids and Doreen's therapists of course.

Even with the substantial improvements Doreen was making each day, I still only wanted a very limited amount of select people coming around. I also knew we had to be extremely careful around other people and places and understood that would be our "new norm". We were coming up on the end of February and winter still would stick around for a while. The weather cooperated enough though, so no one had any issues of not being able to get to our house for their shift. Was that a part of God's plan as well? You decide.

That was it. The cavalry had arrived and completed their gracious duty, and the time had come for Doreen to be on her own and take care of herself during the day. She was both excited and a little nervous at the same time about gaining some of her independence back. I, on the other hand, was only nervous. My brief comfort level from the past two weeks had disappeared. My focus during the workweek would now once again be divided between home and work. The truth be told, it wasn't fifty-fifty either.

Doreen on the other hand, had more than enough to keep her busy during the day. She had a lot of catching up to do with some of her previous duties she normally took care of. Heather brought back all the paperwork I had dumped on her while Doreen was in the hospital. Everything had been handled that needed to, but it now needed to be sorted and organized to go in its proper place at our house. It just lived in file folders and boxes at Heather's house.

I don't need to describe what the pile of hospital and doctor bills as well as the small mountain of insurance paperwork looked like. That would keep her busy for weeks, especially because there was an issue with one of the doctors being in-network, but the billing company was out of network. That was a nightmare, and a battle Doreen wasn't about to let slide. So, to battle she went and spent countless hours on the phone getting the paperwork straighten out. I, like most people, would have just waved the white flag and gave up. She didn't let it go like I knew she wouldn't because I had been witnessing her determination for months now. Having a background in insurance, she knew things weren't billed out correctly and she wasn't going to have us pay for something that we shouldn't.

During that process, she had to request a ton of detailed bills of what services were rendered to show exactly what the insurance company should have paid based on what the in-network pricing was. We obviously had met all our deductibles and then some.

One day while she was going through some of the bills, she came across one and set it aside to question me on. When I got home, she asked me about the bill from K-W Hospital in Sycamore. It was only two miles away from the Acute Rehab Hospital. She said I never told her about that hospital stay. I was confused because she never had been there. There had to be some mistake.

She handed me the bill and I looked at it to try and figure out what it was for. It had the emergency room and doctors as well as a CT scan and other X-rays. None of that made any sense until I saw the date of services rendered. It was October 4th & 5th, 2021. That was when Doreen had her emergency from the "free-air" they found in her system at the rehab hospital. I just found the missing six hours when Doreen left that night until she arrived at the hospital in Rockford.

Apparently, Doreen's stats had "crashed" within minutes of leaving the rehab hospital that night and the K-W Hospital emergency room was right there. We never got a phone call to tell us what happened that night. She was completely off our radar for over six hours, and we had no clue. Coincidentally, that was the same time frame where I completely broke down

Tragedy...or Blessing?

and told God: "I…got…nothing…left." And His answer that night was: "Trust God." I'm so glad I did!

So, the mystery of where Doreen was for those six hours had been revealed. That was both terrifying at the thought of what had happened to her, but also comforting to know that she received life-saving care. It's so much easier now because I know what the result was. Thank you God!

While Doreen continued to pursue answers and patiently wait for results, she had another large task which I gladly passed on to her. That task stemmed from September 7th, 2021, and was another constant reminder from that heart wrenching day when Doreen was put on the ventilator. That day was the once in a lifetime (hopefully) hailstorm that damaged our house and totaled my car. I had asked her to redesign the front of our house.

I had already made some decisions because of all the shortages going on in the building industry. I started by hiring a contractor back in October because he was totally booked and wouldn't be able to start until the following May or possibly June. He was the only one who responded out of the four I called for an estimate. Not only was labor hard to find, but some of the materials we needed would also be on a three-to-six-month lead-time.

While Doreen was still in the hospital in December, I got a variety of samples of steel roofing colors, shutter and siding samples, decking and column samples as well as new window info to show her. I think she was most excited about the windows; I know I was. The windows we had were absolutely awful, especially in winter.

Because of the abnormal circumstances with material, I went ahead and ordered some of the different items needed based on the potential extended lead-times. But I wanted her to draw it out somewhat to scale along with the color combinations to make sure we liked what was ordered. Once the material would arrive, we would be stuck with it.

I also wanted her to design a new landscape layout since I was adding a small deck on the front next to the small, covered porch so we would be able to sit out there and enjoy God's awesome sunsets. So, with her markers and ruler in hand, she drew out what the front of the house would look like. She even made cut-outs of various parts and changed the color so we could overlay it on the picture to see if we wanted to go with a different color combo.

I was impressed. It didn't take us too long to both agree on which one we wanted. The final design fortunately had the same colors I had ordered with the larger items like the roofing and siding. No changes needed there.

With any type of construction or remodeling, money always plays a major factor in the design and decisions. Lucky for us we knew exactly what our budget was because the insurance company had already paid out the hail claim back in October and the money was in the bank. It didn't take her long to create a cost spreadsheet of the materials needed as well as the labor costs which were already quoted. We had a pretty good handle on where every penny would be going, and I thought the budget was spot on.

The other enjoyable task I asked her to do was to figure out the different flowers and plants we wanted to have in her new design. We sort of had a flower garden in the front before, but it always got lost in the weeds and the over-grown shrubs. We knew we wanted to pull out all the ornamental and evergreen bushes because they had become out of control. She was going to be able to start with a clean slate. We measured the overall outline of the existing area and of where the new front deck would go.

With all the dimensions in hand, she drew it to scale including where she wanted a path to go through the garden. She spent many hours over many days watching the various garden shows on T.V. that had their spring sales. She would record the parts of the show which had the flowers she really liked, and by the time I got home, she had done her research on how big the plants got as well as the time periods they bloomed. She then would plot them out on her drawing. She was so excited and was enjoying it so much that it made my heart melt. After all those months of me watching her endure that horrendous torture, I was finally seeing her joy and passion for life again. That was priceless.

Then one day, I came home to see her a little on the deflated side and asked if she was okay. She said she was, but she used up our small budget we had set aside for the flowers and landscaping. When we originally came up with a number, I really had no idea how much to put towards it so we just picked a number. But now, I wasn't ready to let her revived joy and excitement go just yet. She just found that again. So, I suggested she keep going until the front was exactly the way she wanted it.

I then suggested she find something for the area in front of the evergreen trees as you pull into our driveway, and for the area between the bee hives and the backside of those evergreens alongside of the driveway going back to the barn. She immediately perked up again, but then paused and asked, "How are we going to be able to afford that?"

I had no idea how we would make that happen at that moment, but I did know I wanted to see her continue to have fun with it. She hadn't had any fun for a long, long time. I told her not to worry about it because we would figure it out somehow. She just needed to finish with her design.

You would think after sixty years I would know better than to believe everything will go as planned when working on a project. Just like the planned budget for the landscaping, the schedule for working on the rest of the hail repairs didn't go as planned either. I did get all the materials gathered up by the first week of May like I told our contractor I would, but now his schedule was running behind. We were going to be his first roof of the season, but now that was delayed.

At that point, Doreen was the one in contact with him and he thought he would be able to start by mid June. When that rolled around, he had come down with some sort of health issue and wouldn't be able to start for several more weeks. Getting the roof on first was now holding everything up, including all the money we invested in landscaping that was just sitting there. Doreen was spending countless hours watering everything just to keep it alive. All those plants needed to get in the ground. She couldn't get a firm date for starting from him and we decided that we couldn't stay in this holding pattern any longer.

The clock was ticking, so Doreen made a call to a roofing contractor she used to sell insurance to. He was so surprised and happy to hear from her, and once he heard our predicament, he said he would have a crew over to start within two days. Doreen called our original contractor to let him know, and to see if he would be able to give her a definite time frame. He was still swamped and still running behind schedule, so we all agreed to just cancel and move on.

Based on Doreen's conversation with the new roofing crew, I brought all the roofing material out of the barn and placed it in our "front garden in waiting" so they didn't have far to go with the material. Then two days later, the roofers showed up and started on the roof. Our long-awaited project had finally begun. As much as they got done on the first day,

I thought it would only take a couple of days to complete. That's what I planned on, but that wasn't the case. It ended up taking over a week before it was complete. Now, I could finally move forward.

New Plans

Sometimes when things don't go as planned, it can work out for the better. The over-run on our landscape budget was now completely paid for. The plan had changed from having a carpenter install the windows and siding to now doing it myself. We saved over six thousand dollars in labor. Great for our pocketbook, but boo for my soon to be aching muscles.

The added savings not only paid for the extra landscaping, but now it allowed us to extend the stone panels across the entire front of the house under the new windows. We were also able to upgrade to a self-adhesive house wrap that self sealed around any fasteners from the siding. No more winter winds blowing through the house!

First things first though, I needed help putting the three large front windows in. There was no way of doing that by myself. So, who would I call to help? The same person I always can count on in a pinch…Cousin Ken. He came through every time I needed his help over the last year, even if I just needed to talk.

So, without hesitation, he packed his tools up again and came out to help. I already had all the siding off, so we just had to work on taking out the old units and put the new ones in. It should have been an easy in and out project giving us plenty of time to have a beer or two afterwards. But that didn't happen.

When Ken and I got the first large unit up on the sawhorses, and we got on the ladders to put it in, it wouldn't go.

- Ready or not...Life changes -

We had to set it back down. What the...? It took a moment, but then I realized that back in October when I talked with our original carpenter, he had helped me measure the windows and I didn't double check the measurements before I ordered them. I'm not exactly sure what happened, but the new windows were one inch wider and one inch taller than the old ones.

Now we had to change the opening size in both directions. That just added a whole lot of time to what should have been easy replacement. All three units in the front of the house were the same size, which meant the other openings would have the same problem. They did.

Fortunately for Ken and me, Kirstyn and Jason showed up right before we had to put the third unit in. It was very hot out and the sun was baking us because we had been working in the full sun all afternoon. The extra set of hands helped us get done that much faster so we could get out of the sun.

We went inside to cool down, and what a difference those new windows made. Since the windows faced west, I ordered them with an upgraded glass that had an extra coating on it to help reflect even more UV rays than the standard low-e units have. As we were standing there admiring our handy work, I realized that finishing the inside would now cost more because the old jambs and casing were now an inch short in both directions. It's true; an inch can make a huge difference.

Poor Ken. He thought he was done with my projects. I needed some more of his help a couple of weeks later. The other area I needed the extra help with was the north side of the garage. It's only around sixteen feet to the peak, but I don't do very well with heights. But that wasn't the only reason for asking for help. If the truth be told, I wasn't anywhere close to the physical level I had been prior to getting

Tragedy...or Blessing?

sick. My energy, strength and especially my stamina were at levels I had never experienced before.

I knew Ken and I would need a little assistance on that side, so I had recruited some extra help from one of our good friends from St. Charles. Bob and Debbie were from our old neighborhood. Debbie had already come out in February to help Doreen when I went back to work. Bob was a real carpenter, unlike me, who was about to retire and not have to do that kind of work again. He graciously agreed to help us, and they came out early in the morning on a Saturday so we could make sure that part was finished. I was thrilled because I really needed someone who knew all the tricks of the trade.

The three of us made a pretty good team once we got started. Bob did all the measuring and cutting, and Ken and I did all the fastening and ladder work. We got done with that side a little faster than I thought we would, so we worked around the corner and knocked out around the garage door and up the side of the house that tied into the garage roof.

By that time, Ken had to get going home for another obligation. I will never be able to repay Ken for all the love and support he has given to me over the years and especially during Doreen's and mine darkest moments of this journey. I will never stop thanking God for allowing Ken to be a part of my life.

Within minutes of Ken pulling out of the driveway, Josh pulled in and parked. We weren't expecting him to stop by, but as he walked up, he asked "Where's Ken?" He came by after he got done with work so he could visit with Ken and Bob and Debbie. Well, I couldn't let a good opportunity go to waste, so I had Josh go up on the garage roof with Bob to help finish that small section.

Bob had found out quickly, as I stood and watched, the new steel roof was very slick and hard to stand on. Then I

- Ready or not…Life changes -

got the skid steer out and hoisted Josh and an extension ladder up to lay down on the roof so Bob had something to brace himself with, so he wouldn't slide down the roof. After watching that performance, I knew there was no way in hell I would have been able to do that on my own. So, we ended the day in exhaustion, with a cold beer, and I in complete gratitude.

With all the difficult areas out of the way, I could now concentrate on the front of the house, and we could finally get all the plants and flowers in the ground. Well, the landscaping schedule suddenly got an unexpected boost. I woke up on a Sunday morning and felt a little off. Ever since Doreen came home, any time I thought I might be catching something, I took a COVID test just to be on the safe side. That time, I tested positive. I came down with COVID again which scared the hell out of me. I was petrified I would get Doreen sick again. I would not be able to live with myself if something happened to her.

I called Jeff to let him know what happened, and he told me to stay home for five days which now was the new CDC protocol. He was very concerned about Doreen and how we would be able to handle that again. I told him I would keep him posted. Then first thing Monday morning, we called Dr. Crawford's office and told him what happened. Under the circumstances we were in with Doreen's case, he called a prescription in for Paxlovid which was a five-day pill regiment which helped reduce the effects and transmission of COVID in many cases…hopefully.

I started taking it right away and I made sure to stay on the opposite side of the room and wore a facemask any time I was in the house. It started out like I had a flu bug, and it didn't get too much worse than that. I only felt like that for a couple of days, but I still wasn't about to take any chances around Doreen. Since the weather was nice outside, I decided to spend as much time out there as possible and Doreen kept her distance while we were out there.

I took advantage of the unplanned time and worked outside on Doreen's garden design. Once the bushes and overgrown shrubs were pulled out with the skid steer and hauled away, I put the landscape fabric down where the deck would eventually go and brought the gravel in and dumped it. I also had to bring up dirt from the back pasture to fill in the holes that the bushes left. Once that was all prepped, Doreen would place the flowers where they needed to go so they could be planted.

Prior to COVID, that might have been a two-day job for us. But now it took us around ten days or more to finish it. And before we even finished, we were lucky to have dodged a bullet. Doreen came through that scare unharmed. That was too close for comfort. COVID had forced us on this new path and even controlled the pace we could go. Working together on our landscaping project had proved that. We learned to go slow and steady and don't push too hard. It would get done eventually. The house is a prime example of our new path. We're still gradually working on it.

That new gradual path has been a slower, more challenging and much larger adjustment for Doreen than for me. That's putting it mildly to say the least. I know how much the long term COVID effects have played on my system, and my experience pales in comparison to what Doreen went through. Hers was ten-fold times ten and then some.

I have been fortunate enough to be able to adapt to my newfound physical limitations and adjust accordingly. I find myself running out of energy far quicker than before, and my physical strength has weakened more than I care to admit. The work I used to be able to do around the farm, and elsewhere, had notably decreased along with the increased amount of time it takes to accomplish my tasks. Some people say it's because I'm getting older and it's a normal stage everyone goes through. That's true to some extent.

But I know what I was capable of before, and how my body was physically able to handle it. With the very noticeable decline in my stamina and the much larger recovery time to recuperate, that tells me it's not just from age. It's just like the acceleration labs the scientists use for experiments to speed up time to get their results. I feel like I've aged eight to ten years in those two short months of being sick.

I have come along way physically from that rock bottom period, but I must admit, I think I peaked in my recovery for well over two years now, and the natural gradual decline has been at work ever since. I only mention that in hopes people might get a clearer picture of what kind of toll COVID had taken on my system. I have thanked God so many times though that He still allows me to do what I do. Now keep that reference in mind as I share a portion of the new path Doreen must travel. Remember this saying? "Ready or not… Life changes"

Doreen's New Path

I'm not sure how Doreen could have possibly prepared herself for the complete upheaval that she has had to endure. Her life has been completely turned upside down, and every day she is completely reminded of that. There are no remnants left of her previous normal physical life of non-stop activity. She never liked to sit still and always needed to be "doing something" or "going somewhere". She loved to work, and never was afraid of hard work no matter what it was. Although she could not physically outwork me, she would run circles around me with every other aspect of any project. Her determination and will to get something done was far superior to mine, and she would do that tirelessly.

And then one day, a tiny invisible bug changed everything, especially physically. Her previous, mostly unlimited life would now have very distinct physical "limitations". That was not a word Doreen had ever been accustomed to. But reality has a way of expressing itself whether you like it or not.

The biggest and most obvious cause of these life altering limitations comes from her lungs. At this point in time, her lungs are at fifty-nine percent of capacity which obviously has a huge impact on the rest of her body. It doesn't take too much activity to deplete her levels physically, and it takes much, much longer to recuperate. As hard as she tries not to let that slow her down, it's like trying to run the one-hundred-yard dash with a ball and chain tied around your ankle. In Doreen's case, she has one tied around each ankle.

That's another part where she has had issues with, her muscles. She had lost so much muscle tissue while she was motionless in bed in the hospitals, and still has farther to go to get that back. More than likely it will be limited.

I remember the first time I saw her legs when the nurse pulled the bed sheet back so they could turn her. I looked down started to cry because they were just skin and bones. She hardly had any calve muscles, and they looked more sticks with feet attached. I wasn't expecting to see that back then, but it explains why she still is not completely steady on her feet when she walks. She can only handle a very limited amount of walking before she needs to sit and rest, mainly because of her oxygen levels, and her right foot.

Then there's the occasion where she pushes herself a little too much, and she will start to cough and breathe harder. That's not just from physical exertion either. She finds herself coughing even when she is just talking normal. She coughs all the time, and she can't help it. Those are just a few of the constant issues she now must deal with every day. She too encounters the normal decline that comes from aging, but with all the obvious major changes in her physical condition, along with the numerous annoying little changes since getting sick, her results during that short time have been extreme.

There is definitely one area which has not been affected from her illness or declined due to aging. It's her determination and her positive outlook. I believe her faith in God has been the pillar which reinforces her will to move forward. She has told me numerous times that she has accepted this new path she is on, and oddly enough, she is at peace with it. She has said "This is where God has placed me at this point in my life, so I can feel sorry for myself and look for pity, or I can make the best of it and move forward. I think God wants me to move forward. I believe that's why I'm still here." With everything she has gone through, that's an amazing attitude! It's not hard to figure out why I love her so much!

I mentioned how she's not afraid of hard work which includes her drive to improve. Her new routines demonstrate her fearless efforts to continue her rehabilitation journey. She has far surpassed the insurance companies allowable pulmonary rehab sessions, but the hospital in Mendota has a generous reduced rate for those who want to continue with rehab. Doreen goes on Tuesdays and Thursdays every week for an hour session.

I went with once to watch her, and they had her use four machines that time, and kept an eye on her stats while she worked them. With her continued "program", she has been able to increase the resistance, distance and the time on the various machines. I believe her continual rehabilitation program has helped her beyond measure. I dread to think where

Tragedy...or Blessing?

she would be physically if she didn't pursue that, and didn't continue to push herself to do it. She also goes occasionally for acupuncture and massage therapy to help improve her condition as well.

She also has her home routines which keep her busy throughout the week, like laundry which is the most physical chore. There are only two of us, so it's only three to four loads a week, but that chore can be a full day for her. She spends some time each week on her passions, Diamond Dotz ®, scrapbooking, and watching her bees to mention a few. She's done well with knowing what her body is telling her and has had to learn how to sit down to relax (she previously didn't know how to that) before she physically exerts herself too far. That doesn't mean I don't constantly voice my opinion about her pushing herself too far, which she now calls me her "helicopter husband". That's okay. I'm fine with that title.

I am also impressed at the strict regiment she follows taking her medications and supplements, and with keeping track of her oxygen and her blood sugar levels. She has also done a phenomenal job watching her daily diet. I think part of that comes from her hospital stays where they insisted that she had to be a diabetic. She will do everything in her power not to let that happen probably because she has had enough needles stuck in her during those few short months.

Over-all, she manages to keep herself busy every day and has made me laugh many times when she questions how she ever got everything done before when she worked full time. I've heard retired people say that many times over the years.

I've also heard it said many times "S**t happens". In our case, follow that saying with "and plans change". Nobody ever expects their life to literally change in a blink of an eye, but ours did. And I thank God constantly that Doreen is still here to even blink her eyes.

In the grand scheme of things with the time I have left on this earth, having her by my side is all I really want, and I will enjoy every single moment of that time together. As long as we're together and keep God at the helm, we will handle whatever comes our way. If you don't believe that, just look at the devastating nightmare we just came through. I can't begin to imagine what the outcome would have looked like if we didn't have our faith to lean on.

We are now past the extreme physical hell Doreen had to endure and have come to a completely new way of life. It's a new life of many adjustments which will still take some time to get acclimated with. The most obvious to see is Doreen's physical challenges, but there's also the mental and emotional challenges having to deal with all the drastic changes we now must navigate on this new path.

And then, of course, is the financial portion of that equation. It's all intertwined. After Doreen got home and was feeling a little better, I knew at some point we would have to come to grips with our situation and have a heart-to-heart conversation on what our financial future might hold. Doreen had already been thinking about it but hadn't said anything to me. She didn't have to because I already knew it had been bothering her. How were we possibly going to be able to handle things if we would be down to only one paycheck?

I did my best to reassure her we would be okay and told her "I can't believe that God has brought us this far only to leave us hanging at this point and tell us we're now on our own." I believed that then, now, and for the rest of my life. He will never abandon us or leave us, ever. That doesn't mean though I can call Him up for financial advice.

We were going to have to make some tough decisions moving forward, and even many concessions in our lifestyle.

Tragedy...or Blessing?

It had been easier for me to cope with this new financial predicament than it was for Doreen. I was able to think about it for all those months that she was in the hospital. She, on the other hand, had walked out the door one day somewhat healthy only to wake up months later in a strange new world, not even being able to move on her own. It was inevitable. We wouldn't be able to live the same way we were used to just six months before, and we had to figure out a new plan.

I had already started that process with the help of our kids while she was still in the hospital. We originally had a Disney trip set up with Kirstyn's family in April 2022, but it was obvious that mom would not be able to handle a vacation like that, so we canceled that trip without her knowing until much later when she was awake and coherent.

Then there was our fortieth anniversary trip in July 2022 with all nineteen of us going to Tennessee. We had rented a cabin in the Smoky Mountains for five days which could sleep thirty people, and even had an indoor pool on the lowest level. It looked incredible, and we knew we were going to have a blast on that trip. Doreen was home to help finalize that sad decision to cancel, but the reality of her circumstances and her new physical condition left us no choice. Besides, would she even be able to handle the thin mountain air? The easy unanimous decision was mom's health and having her home was most important.

Another decision I made before she woke up was the number of mouths to take care of around our little farm. Part of that decision came from my own physical challenges of not being able to handle the load, but primarily because of the elevated expenses of taking care of the cows. The biggest costs come from buying feed and the high cost of hay that had skyrocketed. So, I sold most of the cows and all of the calves to cut down on the costs as well as my workload. I had sold all the chickens prior to that. The feed cost for them had also gone up and they were just too much for me to handle. I knew back then money was going to be tight in the near future, but I also knew I was physically struggling just to do the daily chores.

I didn't want to make those choices, and I wasn't sure how Doreen would handle my decisions, but I knew they needed to be done. Our conversations now were about what to do financially moving forward and how we would be able to manage them. There were a lot of things we had to cut back on or revise, or even cancel as we went down our list. Some things were easy, and some were not.

The one item on the list I had dreaded the most was our Disney Vacation Club® membership. That was really our only "luxury" item, and it was a real expensive one. That was one of Doreen's most prized possessions because of all the memories we had made with our kids and grand kids since 2005. We had even used our points several times for trips with just the two of us as well. But once the grand kids came along, we would go with one family each year for a week or so, which always resulted in a great time with lots of pictures for the scrapbooks.

Those precious moments were priceless, and now we had to decide if we could really afford to continue or not. It was an easy decision for me because I was becoming disappointed with Disney's new cultural direction instead of sticking with Walt's original themes and ideas. That's just my opinion though. Besides, we really couldn't afford it anymore.

I was really expecting Doreen to challenge my suggestion, but she agreed almost instantly without much debate. Her response confirmed what I suspected, but didn't really want to submit to. Whether she knew it consciously, or somehow understood sub-consciously, the life she knew and loved was history and would never be the same again. My heart broke as we confirmed the decision to sell our points because I knew just how much she loved and cherished those trips with the kids.

But life changes and we had to adapt. Doreen handled the phone calls and the paperwork and in a relatively short period of time, our membership was gone. We did surprisingly well financially and were able to catch up on some bills and even held some money back to put towards a 2002 John Deere Gator for Doreen. She found it on an auction and was able to buy it for a really good price, and it looked almost brand new.

She was hesitant with spending money on a yard vehicle, but I knew she would need assistance in moving around in the yard, and I was concerned with her mobility and steadiness on uneven ground. The bonus of that purchase was mine. I could save some footsteps going out to the back pasture. It was a win/win purchase, and I consider it a blessing from God because of the way everything just came together.

We are still making adjustments and compromises, and I imagine that will never cease. Especially with the unpredictable wildcard: inflation. Between fuel and food, I'm not sure which one is more frustrating. Well, maybe it's the food. I am dumbfounded and shocked every time we go to the grocery store. It's only the two of us. We don't buy any meat and very little soda and our bill ranges between two hundred dollars on light trips, and up to three hundred and fifty dollars on trips that require extra's like laundry detergent and healthcare products.

I am always shocked when I see the total amount and look at what's in the cart, and it's not even to the top. It's tough on us, but I can't begin to imagine how much pressure and stress it must be on young families. And I keep hearing in the news how much everything is improving. Really? Where? Certainly not in our neighborhood. But, even with all that said, Doreen and I are still very grateful for all the blessings we do have.

Sure, it's true, money clearly has a role to play in our daily lives. But the abundance of, or the lack of, doesn't factor into the bond and love we share, even on this new path. I won't lie though; it has been tough getting used to only one income when we've been so accustomed to two. I've heard some say to look on the bright side: "At least Doreen is retired."

Retirement sounds great, doesn't it? You would think so, unless you're forced into it. Doreen loved to work and enjoyed her job and her paycheck. I believe if she had the physical stamina and ability, she would go back to work. But she doesn't and probably never will, and the hardest part has been that she feels like she's not contributing. I tell her she still is, just in a different role. She still wants to do more, but the reality is that her lungs just can't handle it. Common sense would support that, which the majority of people could understand. Take away over forty percent of your oxygen and you're guaranteed to have substantial physical limitations.

I completely understood that reality long before she even got home. The vast array of medical professionals I encountered had all talked about that inevitable outcome almost from the very beginning. I can't count how many times I had those conversations throughout her progression through those facilities. Every one of those professionals who saw how much damage had been done to her lungs all expressed the same concerns about her future oxygen capacity, and the effects it would have on her and her abilities, or should we say disabilities.

I had been told numerous times that Doreen was one of the extreme COVID cases, and the best thing I could do for her at the time was to pray and take it one day at a time. Having lived through that experience, it was obvious to me that our previous life was a closed chapter. We were in un-chartered territory, and we were going to have to adapt to a new way of life at some point once she got home.

Doreen's Missing Paycheck

After we finally got past the first couple of months of Doreen being home and was making great progress, all things considered, that was when we addressed our new financial shortage. At that time, Doreen still had great hope that she would improve enough to handle going back to work. I was very skeptical, but I didn't want to discourage her in any way. She had a long road in front of her and I wanted her to keep her head up so she would push forward.

We decided to have her file for Social Security Disability after talking with a few family members and friends who had some experience with that. That was in March 2022, and in true government fashion, it took several weeks just to get the ball rolling. She found out all the requirements of what was needed to file her case. She had recently gone through a Pulmonary Function Test which they surprisingly would allow to count towards the requirements. She also needed a mental health evaluation as well as having to see an Internist from their approved list.

After having all of that done over the next several months, she filed all the paperwork. Then, of course, it was hurry up and wait. After a few more months had gone by, she finally got the notice. She had been denied, but she could appeal her case. Based on everything she had gone through, we thought for-sure she would have been accepted. Go figure.

- Ready or not...Life changes -

So, we had to start the process all over again. Months and months of jumping through all those hoops again. Wait a minute…let's stop right here. At this very point, I began writing on a Friday night when a storm arose and was getting more intense as it got closer. Just an hour before it hit, I was on a roll. I was ranting about how our government was making us go through an agonizing, snail-paced process to try and get some financial assistance we obviously needed just to sustain ourselves.

I even had examples from a Dr. Phil show where he talked about some of the things our government actually spends our money on. I wrote down just a very small list of ridiculous items where our entrusted politicians have wasted millions of our taxpayer's dollars on such outrageous and asinine projects. My blood was boiling at the thought of such blatant carelessness and lack of concern for their "employers", "*We the people…*"

On that night, I had typed more in that one hour than I had at any other time while writing this. Then the lights flickered on and off and I could hear the wind outside. It picked up suddenly and was getting louder as the minutes rolled by. I learned once before during this process to constantly hit the save button any time I paused, just so I wouldn't lose what I had just wrote. I hit the save button at least ten times or more in that hour. There were very few times I paused to contemplate my next sentence, and the keyboard didn't get any rest.

After hitting the save button one more time, just as I was finishing my thoughts and shutting down for the night because of the intensifying storm, the power went completely out. I panicked at first, but I knew I had saved it numerous times before everything went black, so I wasn't too worried about my prized review I had just described, was safe and complete.

Tragedy...or Blessing?

The power was back on in the morning, and I grabbed my coffee and fired the system back up to make sure my captured message was still there. As soon as I opened this chapter back up and scrolled down, my heart sank. Everything I wrote the night before was all gone...except for my anger. But now it was also magnified by the loss of my writing. I said a string of choice words as I banged on the keys to shut it down again.

How could that have happened? I saved it over and over. I was very upset because I really liked what I had typed. I'm not a writer. I knew I would not be able to duplicate exactly what I had written the night before. I walked away feeling defeated.

I needed a distraction. Since it was Saturday and everything outside was soaked from the storm the night before, it sounded like a good idea to do a spring cleaning inside, even though it was summer. Besides, the house kind of needed it because I had been a little lax on the cleaning chores. Doreen physically can't handle those tasks, even though she wants to help. I won't let her because it makes me a nervous wreck. Her body doesn't need that kind of strain or exertion put on it.

She constantly apologizes to me for not being able to help me out more, but there's absolutely no reason to. It was still very fresh in my mind of what life was like around here when she wasn't home. I don't ever want to go through that experience ever again, so I will do absolutely everything by myself if that's what it takes to keep her safe and healthy. Well, as healthy as she can be at this stage in her life.

Along with the cleaning duties that day, there were also a few shelving units she wanted moved around so she could have more room for her finished scrap books. While I did the heavier duties, she used her time to organize her craft room and scrap books. We both got a lot done that day. After showers and dinner, she asked if I was going to type or not. I was still very upset and told her I didn't want to, so she asked if I wanted to watch a movie instead. We sat down on the couch, both of us exhausted, and turned the movie on.

It was a unique Hallmark movie because it had a very moving story of faith in God. The main character was able to bring people back to God by getting them to think about the blessings God has given them. When the movie was over, Doreen and I looked at each other, smiled and said how much we both really enjoyed watching that. You don't see things like that on TV very often anymore. I have to say, it was very gratifying. My day had started in anger but ended completely at peace.

During the day on Sunday, Doreen asked me again if I was going to type. I was a bit conflicted on how to continue where I had left off before the storm, when Doreen said to me "Maybe God didn't want you to write what you did." I was rather stunned by what she had just said. That never crossed my mind before she said that. Then she said, "What is your story all about?" I looked at her and told her she knows it's about the journey *we* went through. She asked me the question again. I was still puzzled. Then she looked at me once again and said, "It's in your title…Tragedy or *What?*" At that moment, I knew what she meant…Blessing. She finished up by saying "Maybe God wants you to focus on His Blessings." Once again, it's easy to see why I love her so much.

So, here's where I pick up where I left off on the night of that storm. Doreen's second round in her quest of Social Security Disability was almost a mirror image of the first round, including the months and months of processing and waiting. She was turned down the second time. All of her healthcare professionals, including the doctors, and all of our family and friends were completely dumbfounded as to why she was turned down again because she, as some described, was the "Poster Child" of what long-term COVID disability looks like.

Our final recourse was to hire an attorney who specializes in disability cases to pursue it farther. As you might guess, that costs a lot of money, but we had no choice. Without Doreen's income, we're going in the wrong direction quicker than what we thought we would.

Fifteen months after she started the process, she finally had her day in court in front of a judge. Fortunately, it was a virtual appearance between Doreen, the attorney, someone from the disability department, and the judge. Otherwise, we would have had to drive over two hours to the north side of Chicago to appear. I won't admit how many times in my earlier years where I had to appear before a traffic judge, but it is nerve-wracking. That was her first time in front of a judge, so I know she was stressed out.

Finally, after the judge reviewed her case and asked her a lot of questions, including the comments from the lady that was the government's occupational specialist (not sure of her actual title) who voiced, in her opinion, Doreen should be able to go back to work. The judge said he had made his decision and ruled in favor of Doreen to receive full benefits. Hallelujah, that part of the process was over…finally. In true government fashion though, it still took a few more months before she saw her first dime. It finally came through, and that was a blessing.

That's Life

Life is constantly changing, and always will, ready or not. Even when we think we have it all under control, the truth is, we really have no control. I think the best we can do is to manage our attitude, adjust our focus, and then humble ourselves to whatever the given circumstances and outcomes are. But the most important part in that equation is to have faith and trust in God.

Doreen and I learned that very quickly firsthand. Our lifestyle, and the life we were so accustomed to, had literally been changed overnight back in August 2021. It came so fast and so hard it shook our family to the core and altered many other lives in its wake as well. Enough time has now passed that most of those collateral adjusted lives have gone back to normal with just a few faint memories of how they had been affected from *our* life-altering storm. For Doreen and I, and our family, the memories from that experience are as fresh as yesterday, and the scars it left behind will be a constant reminder…every day. And that's okay.

It is said there are always two sides to every story. Our story is no exception. On one hand, there are the charred remains from a raging fire that swept through our lives much like a wildfire through a forest. The devastation from the wildfire is in plain site and tugs at your heart. You see so much loss. Doreen and I have witnessed that very example on our trips through Yellowstone.

But the other side of that same story is the potential for growth and new life. The clutter that covered and shaded so much untapped beauty has been removed. At first glance, you don't see it. But when you look really close, you can see the rebirth expanding right before your very eyes. Over time, when you stand back and view that very same landscape, you'll witness a whole new scene full of beauty and abundance, which also includes some remnants of the past. That's God's grace at work. Our trips to Yellowstone have blessed us with that site as well. Maybe that's why one of Doreen's favorite places to go is Yellowstone. We are planning on going back sometime in the future, and I have a feeling we will have a new-found appreciation for God's majesty.

So, has our life been changed? It absolutely has. Were we ready for it? No, we absolutely were not. The wildfire that blazed through and devastated our previous lifestyle has brought us to a place of re-growth and new beauty on the horizon. We have chosen (key word) to let our roots be anchored in the rich abundant soil of our Lord Jesus Christ. If you plant your life in that soil, His unending love, grace and blessings will produce a breath-taking beauty beyond compare. So, which side of this story would *you* choose?

- Ready or not…Life changes -

> [8] Let the morning bring me word of your unfailing love, for I have put my trust in you. Show me the way I should go, for to you I lift up my soul. [10] Teach me to do your will, for you are my God; may your good Spirit lead me on level ground.
>
> Psalm 143:8, 10 (NIV)

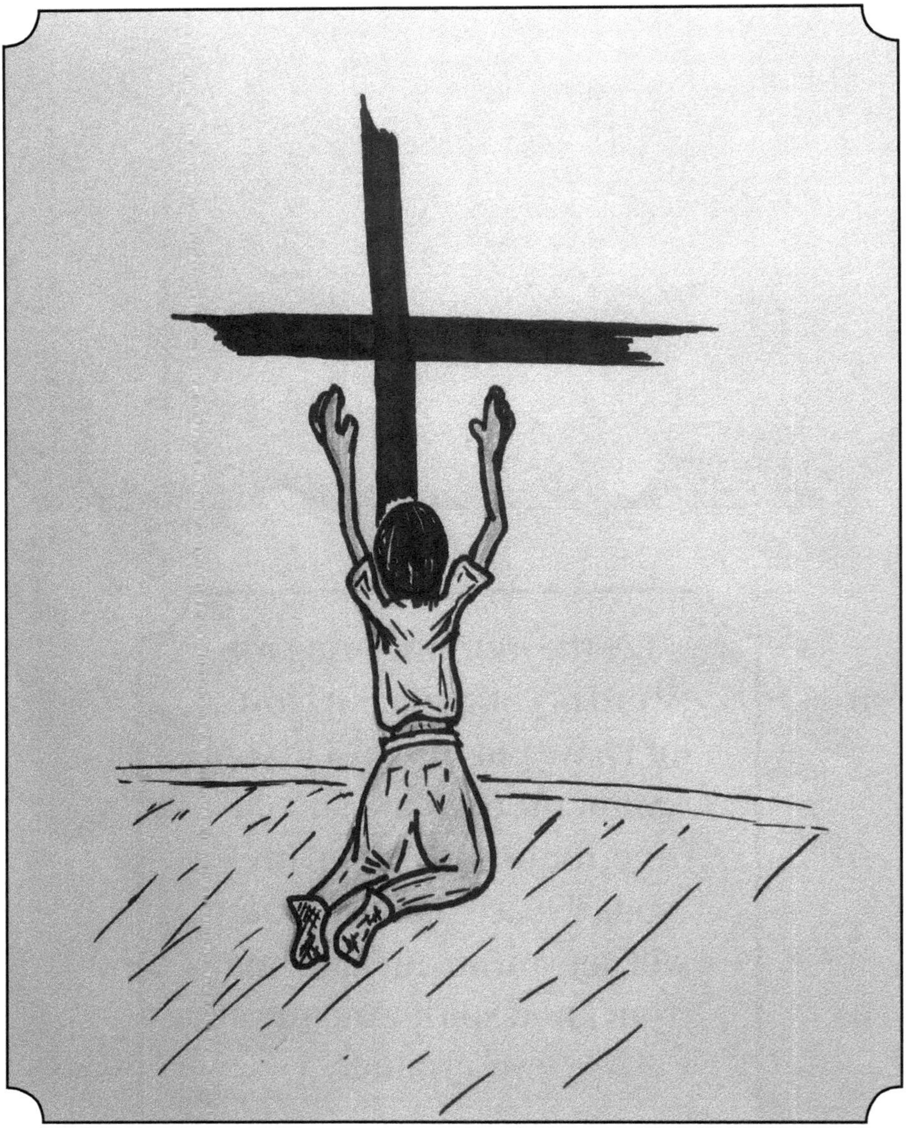

Chapter Seven: Blessings Found

- Don't Look Too Far -

God has given Doreen and I a second chance for our love story to continue. A new direction and appreciation for the bond we share, and for the love that has grown far deeper into our souls which makes us one. Not just one with each other, but also one with God. That's the second most important blessing God has given us, each other. The number one blessing above all blessings is of course: Jesus.

> *"For God so loved the world that He gave His one and only Son, that whoever believes in Him shall not perish but have eternal life."* (John 3:16 NIV)

There's no way it could get any better than that! If we keep our priorities focused on that truth, and it is His will, His Amazing Grace will let us continue our journey together. So, does that mean if we stay perfectly focused on Jesus our new path will always be smooth and easy? No, it certainly doesn't. That's because we can't even come close to perfection, and because we live in a sinful world. But, because of Jesus and *His story*, when our journey together is done on this earth, we will be together in eternity because "Our Love is Forever" (we bought a shirt with that saying on our honeymoon and still have it). It's Jesus who gives us that confidence and peace.

And that blessing is easy and open to all. You just need to believe in *Who* it comes from.

In today's world, there are many who believe those so-called blessings are self induced. That would be an illusion of self-control. Our world today has been pushing God farther and farther away and focusing on a self-serving gratification. It's like using a lifestyle credit card which can be used to "buy" what feels good now without having to wait, and not having to be accountable to anyone or any thing. Those self created blessings couldn't be farther from the truth because there is only One who can create blessings; The Creator Himself. Too many in this world have not learned that truth yet, and sadly we know enough of them. We pray they discover Him before their time on this earth is done. I need you <u>all</u> to get this:

The road to Heaven <u>only</u> goes through Jesus!

In John 14:6 (NIV), Jesus tells us in His own words:

> *"I am the Way and the Truth and the Life. No one comes to the Father except through Me."* Amen.

Speaking of learning, this educational period in my life was nothing like I and my family had ever experienced before. There wouldn't be any essays to write or any quizzes to take. There would, however, be tests. Not the traditional tests that you take to pass or fail, but core tests of our very being, of our hearts and souls. We were all put in the same circumstance with Doreen's tragedy, but each of our tests would be uniquely individual to *our* experience. Each came with their own individual trials and challenges that would have to be dealt with one way or another. The level of struggle and stress also was vast and unequaled. The end results though would all be the same; Growth. We experienced growth in our faith in God, growth in our own character, growth in our compassion for others, growth in our love for each other. That was a blessing grand-slam.

Think about it. All that growth came out of a tragic event that pushed our family far beyond anything we had ever experienced before. For me, it took me to the absolute rock bottom where I surrendered the very essence of my being. On that specific night, it felt like an eternity, yet it was only a brief moment. Unbeknownst to me at the time, those precious few seconds gave me the boost my soul needed, not only for me to continue, but to grow so far beyond anything I thought I was ever capable of.

We are coming up on three years from the beginning of our dark tragic voyage, but as of this very minute, I continue to see and feel the growth and expansion of my heart and soul. And that my friends, is a phenomenal blessing. What I <u>didn't</u> have to learn was all the blessings I discovered on our journey were completely un-derserved because of all my transgressions. But I did have to <u>re-learn</u> that it was Jesus' righteousness that cleaned my slate and made me whole again to the Father. His *Amazing Grace* (have you guessed that's my favorite hymn yet?) and His abundant blessings had carried us through that raging storm. *"Lord save me!"* and He did…again.

I'm not sure I will ever be able to look at another roller coaster without having a flash-back of the panic and desperation we lived in slow motion as that storm battered our family's foundation. Roller coasters today come in a wide range of experiences. From the mild coasters for little kids all the way to the insane death-defying plunges that take your breath away. I'm not exactly sure how many ways in this story

I described our roller coaster experience, but I know none of those descriptions could fully portray what it truly felt like. It was like the full fury of hell had been unleashed while we stood paralyzed in fear. Our ride truly was life or death. Yet, even in those very moments, God still planted His blessings which took hindsight to see and realize. This is just one example of those hidden blessings in plain site, but it takes faith to see:

September 30th, 2021 to October 5th, 2021

It was the perfect storm. She had been totally unconscious for the last four weeks. Her body was slowly deteriorating every day from the lack of movement. She was extremely weak, and her body was not healing properly. She had been physically turned by the nurses at the hospitals every two hours to prevent bed sores. And then, she was moved from a bed to a gurney, got to ride in an ambulance on some of Illinois' finest roads, and then moved into another bed. Since her system was so weak and was healing slower than a snail's pace, it's no wonder why there was a leak from the PEG tube incision in her stomach lining. She ended up in the emergency room at another hospital within minutes after leaving the acute rehab center just to keep her alive. And I didn't know… (And there's the blessing.) If I had known what happened that night and where she was, I would have taken off in the car in the middle of the night to try and get there as fast as I could. Who knows what might have happened under those desperate circumstances. Instead, God used that same exact time on that agonizing night to reach me in the depths of my soul and point out what I needed to do, that night and the rest of my life. That unnoticed blessing ended up saving my life. And I'm not just talking about my physical life.

I have a question for you: "Was God's plan that night a blessing? Or was it a miracle? Or was it both?" I believe it was actually both. God so generously blessed my soul that night while at the same time performed a miracle by extending Doreen's life. I will never forget those moments and will be grateful for all of eternity for His love and mercy He gave to us that night. But it wasn't just that night. There had been a multitude of God's miracles throughout our story. I mentioned before that I've known about God performing miracles very early in my life. But now, witnessing those orchestrated miracles using the right people, in the right place, at the right time left me humbled and in awe.

In the Lord's Prayer, we say, "... *Thy will be done, on earth as it is in heaven...*" I am so thankful that His will had included the doctors and nurses and all of Doreen's caretakers throughout our journey. I'm obviously very biased, but most of the people who took care of Doreen during her life altering journey had formed a special connection with her. Their genuine compassion for her was real. I witnessed it over and over again. That compassion didn't only apply to Doreen. There were countless times, especially in the beginning, where I was told not to get too far ahead and should focus on the immediate minutes and hours in front of Doreen.

At that time, there was the real possibility of Doreen not pulling through and they were truly concerned for me and my family. They were afraid of us getting our hopes up too high. It took some time until my hopes were certainly high, eventually all the way to heaven. So, each time Doreen would make some unexpected improvement, and I would hear one of them say "It's a miracle", it reinforced the place where I put my hope in: Jesus.

It's true, there were so many times when things turned and went in the wrong direction, which is why those miracles meant so much more when things turned back around and moved forward. Time and time again I witnessed what I could only describe as miracles. I saw with my own eyes Doreen's miracles progress in her physical and mental capabilities which blossomed out of that cautious and skeptical landscape. Based on her stats and condition from the beginning, I heard numerous times that there was a "*Strong possibility of permanent brain damage*" and "*She may never be able to…again.*" Honestly, there were occasions where my faith and hope had been shaken to the point of extinction, but those timed miracles were precisely performed according to God's plan which reinforced what my soul needed most, exactly in those moments.

So, do I believe in God's miracles? That's a silly question. When you go through an experience like we did, and truly humble and submit yourself to the heavenly Father's will, those miracles can and do happen. You just have to believe in *Who* they come from. I think a lot of times people can only see the obvious and glaring miracles that are in plain sight for all to see. Something like the birth of a child, or a cancer-free remission for example. Many today would not consider sending a text message as a miracle. But when Doreen sent out her first update and you consider everything she had been through over those past four months, yep, that was a miracle in my book. I personally witnessed so many of those "little" miracles throughout our journey, too many to count. I have just one question though: "Is there such a thing as a "little" miracle?"

Blessings on the other hand though are in the eyes of the beholder. What one considers a blessing, another may not. God's blessings are whatever *you* choose to acknowledge, big or small or anywhere in between. Blessings can be recognized instantly or be disguised and go un-noticed over a period of time, maybe even a long time. Whatever the case may be, once acknowledged and claimed, we need to make sure to finish in gratitude to the One from whom all blessings flow. I think sometimes we forget that last part. I still occasionally forget even though God's over-whelming grace during the last three years has been beyond abundant. There are times when I sit in absolute awe when I reflect on the events and the results that brought Doreen and I to this point in our lives.

The tragedy that clearly plagued our lives for months in hindsight has been dwarfed by the multitude of blessings God has bestowed upon us. For instance, the extreme hailstorm that hit just six hours after Doreen was put on the vent. My heart had been crushed from the devastating uncertainty that morning only to have a storm total my car and cause extensive damage to our house and property. At that moment of course, I could care less about anything other than Doreen. But eventually it had to be dealt with. It ended up being a blessing in disguise because it eliminated a car payment which helped our reduced cash-flow, and it allowed us to get a new roof and new windows, as well as upgrade the front of our house. Those things all needed to be done sooner than later, but we had been putting them off because of the costs. A tragedy turned into a blessing. I wouldn't recommend to anyone the route we had to take, but a blessing received regardless.

That tragedy also brought to the forefront another blessing, one that lay dormant and unacknowledged for a long time. I've known for many years that I've worked for a great family-owned company. Our tragedy revealed to me how blessed I have been to work for such a unique company, one that has more compassion and concern for the well-being of their people, verses the sole focus of the company's bottom line.

They know how to prioritize what's truly important in this life and that's rare in today's business world. I will always be grateful for their love and support, and especially for all their prayers.

Prayers are powerful, but they're not a guarantee. They are though a direct line from you to God. That connection is like no other found on this earth. You are speaking straight to the source of all creation, and He will listen. He desires a relationship with us through that communication, but totally leaves it up to us. If that doesn't humble you, I'm not sure anything could. And, by the way, He answers our prayers. I know, because I witnessed the power of prayer firsthand, over and over and over again. It only took a few phone calls and a social media post or two for that power of prayer to be unleashed which streamed straight to heaven. Doreen needed prayers immediately, and they started with my kids and their network of relationships which spread quickly in our local area. At the same exact time, our extended Hasse family and life-long family friends were there in what seemed like a blink of an eye to show their love and support and offer their prayers for us as well.

It didn't stop there. The people that Doreen and I worked with continually prayed and spread out even to some of the customers through work. Doreen even had a group of Nuns in Texas regularly praying for her throughout this experience. She had people praying to God on her behalf from the Northern border to the Southern border, and from the East coast to the West coast and everywhere in between. From family and friends to acquaintances and even total strangers, there were so many praying for Doreen. That show of love and compassion humbled me and even at times had overwhelmed my heart. Talk about a blessing that made *my cup overflow*. The amount of people who cared and their prayers proved to do just that. We will be forever grateful to all those who united in prayer in our time of need. May God bless them, each and every one, with the same grace and mercy that He has given to Doreen & I.

Prayers are also unique and personal. There was one time in the very beginning right after I became aware of the severity of Doreen's circumstances. While I was sitting alone in silence trying to comprehend what was happening, I strangely started to think about an old movie I watched as a kid. There were some angels listening to people pray for someone who was lost, and they sent some help. So, I thought it would be a good idea if I could get enough people praying at the same time, maybe God would send some help for Doreen. I don't know how the social media group chat works, but a number of people came together for it. I didn't participate, but I did see a prayer later that my son Bryan posted. He wrote:

"Since I couldn't speak on the group chat, I tried but could not produce any sound…every time I formed words in my head, I just could not provide them to you all. Maybe we could all bow our heads to pray":

"Dear Lord Heavenly Father, may You please guide the Doctors and Nurses involved to be able to provide the right comfort and care for Doreen/Mom. We trust that You have her in Your arms and will provide what she needs in this moment. May You hear our collection of prayers and thoughts. Please give strength to Steve/Dad and give him comfort that he is doing the absolute best for her. Please wash a wave of peace on everyone and allow us to remember and trust in Your works here, though we may not understand why. Please Lord, we beg You to bring

Doreen/Mom through this so we can all spend more time with her. We all feel as though she is not done here. We love you Lord and trust in Your will. Amen"

God heard that beautiful prayer, and many just like it over the months following. I know He felt the genuine love and compassion of each one of those prayers. Do you want to know how I know that? He answered them according to His will. Do I believe in the power of prayer? Absolutely!

Throughout this trial, I found myself at times praying specifically to one of the Holy Trinity. Most of the times though, it was all inclusive: God. I must admit, Three in One had kind of been a difficult concept for me to understand all these years. I'm sure it is for a lot of people. So just by coincidence we went to church at First Lutheran in Princeton one Sunday because we really enjoy Pastor Bill's sermons. That Sunday though, it was the children's sermon that clarified the Three in One concept for me. Pastor Bill used a simple apple, which he cut in half and showed it to the children. He pointed out the outer skin which completely covers and protects the whole apple, then the nourishing flesh inside the apple, and then the seeds that were in the center of the apple, which can grow. He showed us there were three distinct parts, yet it was still one apple. That was so profound to me. So basically, God encompasses everything all at the same time. Pastor Bill's explanation simplified the Holy Trinity so a child could understand, including me. I finally got it after all these years, which of course, I count as another blessing.

With that new awareness, I looked back at those painful months of despair and realized that God never left my side. He was there every moment of every day, especially those times when my mind would not stop asking endless loop questions which had no definitive human answers. But occasionally, some of those questions would have an immediate answer. I would hear a response in my mind which made me stop and wonder "Where did that came from?" I was usually puzzled or confused on those occasions, but it broke the pattern of questions I was asking and made me focus on the answer I just "found". Here are some very distinct results which came from a couple of those profound moments, which again, were some of the many blessings I will be thankful for the rest of my life.

At some point in time, every family experiences a situation where one member inflicts pain on another member, whether intentional or not. It may not be during a tragedy, but in our case it was. Both were deeply hurt, and neither wanted to concede. I was in the middle, but my total focus was on Doreen, so I really didn't want to be in that position.

I heard both versions which hurt both ways. It wasn't the normal "He said, she said", but more like "He said, she heard; She said, he heard." My initial response was "I don't care if you don't like each other or even speak to each other ever again. But (I emphasized that word), I expect both of you to be civil to each other around your mother." That was the best fatherly advice I could muster at that point. It continued to bother me, and it was on my mind for a quite awhile.

Then one night while I listened to the kitchen clock as my mind refused to stop, the Lord's Prayer out of nowhere popped into my mind, specifically the part "...*Forgive us our trespasses as we forgive those who trespass against us...*" That was it! That was the answer. The next time I spoke to each of them, I asked them both this one question: "If you can't forgive your sibling, which one of *your* sins does God not have to forgive *you* for?" I recited the Lord's Prayer as a reminder. Did they truly forgive? That's between them and God. I thought God would give me a gold star for that one.

Not so fast. I found myself in a confrontation with Josh one night. We disagreed on several things with neither one of us giving in. The discussion had escalated into a heated quarrel which ended up with words that were later regretted. I hung up the phone in anger and only looked at my side of the issue. That night when I went to bed in silence, I sat in my recliner with the pups on my lap. My mind was in a frenzy over the discussion that night. Out of nowhere, that quiet voice in my mind said "*You* handled that all wrong. *You* need to apologize." I obviously must have been losing my mind, because I certainly wouldn't have told myself that. He should apologize to me. A little later that night, those words came back, and I felt the level of tension subside. That voice (one of the Holy Trinity maybe?) was right.

The next night when I called Josh with the day's update on mom, I started off by apologizing which completely changed the whole conversation that night, and our relationship. Josh and I have had a pretty good relationship over the years, but we just weren't very close because his interests were not mine, and my interests were not his. But since that encounter, we both agree, we enjoy our relationship more now than all the previous years combined. Forgiveness, when expressed and accepted, is a two-way blessing. God gets a "gold star" for that one; well actually... He gets all the gold stars.

From this spiritual expedition, I've found it takes those quiet moments when you are by yourself, with your own thoughts and a truly open heart. That's when you can be the closest to God and *feel* His presence. It worked for me anyway. The Gospel also talks about the many times Jesus secluded Himself in a quiet place throughout His ministries so He could talk with His Father. We need those quiet moments so we can hear without distractions. Unfortunately, this world is filled with noise and distractions.

For the past two years now, I found a Christian radio station called "Family Radio" (I recommend checking out their app at FamilyRadio.org). I spend two hours a day driving back and forth to work, which a portion of that time before was spent being irritated from people's driving habits. There may have even been a foul word or two or ten spoken during those encounters. But now, listening to the awesome music and hearing the different Bible passages read, it's hard to be angry when you're listening, and occasionally singing along, to God's word and praise.

One day on my way home, I had my windows rolled down. The noise from outside was very loud, so I turned my radio up so I could hear it. As I drove out of the traffic congestion, I had a thought that made me smile and even chuckle a little. When the noise from outside world gets too loud, just turn the volume up on Jesus and those distractions will fade away. I know though, I will have to keep adjusting that volume for the rest of my life to keep my focus on my Redeemer.

I know in this sinful world that we all live in, there's a spiritual warfare going on with the prince of darkness. Knowing that fact, I think I'm going to stick close to the Cross of Christ. Even with that being said, I know I will continue to stumble and make mistakes which I will have to account for some day. So, here's a suggestion for all of you who will be behind me in line waiting to get into heaven. Bring a good book or two with to read, because I will be holding up the line for quite a while as I confess all *my* sins.

I thought I did well for the previous sixty years. I checked off a lot of boxes on the Christian scorecard. I tried (another word would be attempted) to be a nice guy to others and help out when I could (more like when convenient). I totally loved my wife, my kids and grand kids, my extended family and friends...well, most of the time. Come on, I think everyone would have to admit that one. I went to church occasionally, which most of the time included the big three: Christmas, Good Friday (my favorite) and Easter. That sounds pretty good, maybe even above average by today's standard I would guess. Life was going well so I must have been doing things "right". After all, God gave me my own "free-will" to make my own decisions, and to make the best of what I possibly could.

Sure, there were some trials and tribulations, but nothing too radical I couldn't handle or that a little time couldn't fix. I fell into the rut of complacency and comfort which allowed me to coast and take too many things for granted. I've made many mistakes, but taking things for granted was high on the list. We all do it. I think that is a part of human nature but there's no real good reason for that practice, or habit, or whatever you want to call it.

Time is a very common item we all take for granted. I mentioned many times throughout this story about how time seems to move fast or slow depending on the circumstance I was going through at that time. What I had learned is just how precious time truly is. Time is short, but *Eternity* is long. So, taking things for granted, whether it's a simple or complex task, an activity or event, a place, time or even your own health, but taking the people in your life for granted is totally inexcusable. And, the absolute worst of all, would be taking God for granted. Trust me, I know because I did *all* the above.

August 21st, 2021 changed everything. Or at least started me in a new direction and awareness, and most importantly, a new appreciation for everything I took for granted, especially God. I learned and figured out what is most important in this life, and it's not wealth and status or any other material "things". Those earthly treasures and power we strive and stress so hard to accumulate in life are only a temporary mirage of a fictitious happiness. Don't believe me? Look around at all the examples of people who are completely miserable, and yet by appearance have everything we believe it takes to make one happy. We're confused at their emptiness because they "have it all". But sometimes it takes a tragedy to clear away the cluster and noise from this earthly focus that is constantly instilled from every direction.

I figured out, for me anyway, the most important part of this life we've been entrusted with is the love and connection we share with others, and with God. Without those blessed connections, does life really have any true meaning? Those relationships, those special bonds we create externally with others and internally with our Heavenly Father are what bring the *authentic* happiness and joy to our hearts and souls. That is the *true* priceless treasure in our lives here on this earth.

I have done more than my fair share of chasing after those worldly possessions which I presumed was the right target for a great life. So, the harder you work, the more successful you become, which in turn equals a greater reward. That was the equation I had used to pursue "happiness" for all those years up until our life-altering event. And then my focus turned on a dime. I completely forgot about all those insatiable trinkets that consumed so much of my life. Those "things" instantly lost all their value. Every ounce of me was now focused on something this material world could not give: The love of my life. Doreen has always been such an immense part of my heart and soul and always will be. This tragedy had her life in the balance, and all I could do was to hold onto the bond we shared and rely on my feeble unchallenged faith.

It's been said that "God doesn't give you more than you can handle." I questioned that phrase many, many times throughout this experience. I never, ever had to deal with anything that had been as traumatic as this before. Loosing both my parents was extremely difficult, but I always had

Doreen to shore me up to get me through. But this time, because it was Doreen, I felt a crushing desperation that paralyzed my very existence. How could God possibly think I could handle that?

Sure, my faith had been tested in the past, but this time it was off the charts. It's said that hindsight is always twenty/twenty, but the problem with that saying was it didn't give me the length of time needed for that clarity. It took a lot of patience, which I believe complimented my faith. Eventually, with honesty and humility, it became clear, and I realized what needed to be experienced so I would grow in a way like never before.

Change: It's inevitable. The uncertainty it brings can scare the hell out of you, especially if you are in a forced situation. Our dark COVID circumstances certainly were forced and unwelcome. The upheaval in our life was instant, and it changed our lives forever. Doreen's "new life" doesn't resemble anything she was capable of before. She has had more than her fair share of struggles, but her attitude and adaptations have been amazing to watch. With a role model like Doreen, you would think I would be able to follow her example.

I had heard hundreds of times from the medical professionals that no two people are alike and no two COVID cases were alike. That holds true on the recovery side as well, and I've noticed a few issues where changes altered my previous condition and not for the better. Physically my eyesight and hearing are getting worse, which some say it's because of age, but it is at a much faster pace than prior to getting sick. Then there's my mental state where my focus has shortened and my CRS (can't remember s**t) is accelerating. Also, my emotions are more intense and can be triggered by a mere thought. There are many times where I try to talk about these past few years where I get choked up and no words form, and I am unable to speak. These changes are unwanted, yet here to stay.

But change can also stimulate growth. In our case, these imposed changes had an astounding positive impact on my spiritual growth. My faith needed some work, okay, maybe a lot of work. I found myself talking to God more during this time, more than I had done previously in my lifetime combined, but I knew it didn't guarantee the outcome I yearned for. But having those conversations only strengthened my faith in God, which in turn, gave me Hope in God's Grace, which in turn, blessed me so far beyond my comprehension which humbled my heart, which ultimately has given me peace. I wouldn't trade that blessing for anything.

As my faith expanded, His blessings became more apparent as I surrendered *my* will to His. I heard this story back in the early 1990's on one of my many motivational cassettes I used to listen to, and this one story stuck with me all those years. This story in a way illustrates my point. I'm probably not saying it one hundred percent correctly, but this is what I remember:

A man was standing on his front porch as the flood waters rose to the steps. A boat came by and asked the man to climb in and they would take him to safety. He replied "No, God will save me." The heavy rains continued, and he climbed up on the porch roof, and another boat came by and asked him to get in. He again replied "No, God will save me." The flood waters continued to rise, and the man had to climb out on to the second-floor roof which was the only place left to go. A helicopter flew over head and called down for the man to grab onto the ladder so they could take him to safety. He yelled yet again "No, God will save me." You guessed it, the man died. When he got to heaven, he asked God "I told everyone You would save me. Why did you let me die?" God simply replied "I sent you two boats and a helicopter. All *you* had to do was grab on."

The man had his faith, but he blindly used it. Through our tragedy I learned it's one thing to *have* your faith: it's another to *live* your faith. I can now live by my faith because I believe and trust in the wisdom and strength of God which far surpasses all human understanding. The great part for me is that I don't have to try and understand. I only have to believe and trust. That I understand.

With that clarity and certainty now instilled, any life changes that now come along won't be so terrifying, no matter the circumstance. Guaranteed there will be changes, and not just for me. Doreen has endured some very radical changes, especially physically, throughout her journey. She continues to astonish me with what she has overcome, and with what she still tries to accomplish. True, her body has been permanently weakened, but I believe her heart and soul has been strengthened. Up until now I have spoken on her behalf, so here she is with her own words…

> "This is Doreen. I wanted to put a little of my thoughts and input into this book Steve has written. One saying I found that so relates to me is:
>
> *The road I've traveled hasn't been easy, but I'm still here. The only reason I'm here today is because God was walking that road with me every step of the way. Amen!*
>
> I will always remember the day I "woke up" and saw my right foot and said "That's one ugly foot. Wait, that's my foot. What the heck happened? Where am I?"

The road to recovery for me had begun and as Steve explained, it has been a long, ongoing one. I am not where I would like to be, but I am where I am meant to be. I will do all in my power and strength to continue to get better, but if where I am now is how I am to be, I am fine with that. I can and have adapted.

I finally, at the two-year mark, sat down and read what Steve had written. I had a fear of reading it and somehow having it flaring up the unknown feelings for me of what my body had gone through. It did not. However, it really brought everything my family has told me about what I went through into context. I bawled reading what my body went through, but also bawled and had a better understanding at a deeper level of what Steve and my family and friends went through on their journey with me. I am forever grateful and blessed to have so many awesome people surrounding me, and *especially* for God keeping me in His hands throughout this journey. **Let go and let God!** What an awesome five words! We all need to say those words every day!

God has us. God will do for us. God will protect us and keep us safe. He knows our future and has before we were even a speck of a thought. We just need to remind ourselves that He is Our God and is here for us!

You cannot break a person
Who gets their strength from God

I'm not broken, just readjusted. I am a survivor and a miracle of God and will cherish that knowledge for the rest of my days on this earth.

Love, Doreen "

Now do you finally understand why I love her so much and why I feel so blessed? God could not have blessed me with a better partner for my life than Doreen! I will be forever grateful to God for the love Doreen & I have been so blessed to share together!

So why did I want to write this and re-live all that pain, suffering and anguish? There was a real good reason. I made a promise that I had to keep, a promise I could not break. It came about one night after Doreen's surgery. I had a little extra time before bed, so I grabbed my daily devotional book to try and catch up some more. Honestly, I hadn't spent a lot of time focusing on that.

I was only up to mid-September, and I should have been caught up already. I turned to the next page which was September 16th, and I started to read. The story was from the fifth chapter of Mark about the healing of a demon-possessed man and how Jesus drove the evil out and healed him. With everything we had been through, that Bible verse struck my heart.

> 18 *As Jesus was getting into the boat, the man who had been demon-possessed begged to go with him.* 19 *Jesus did not let him, but said, "Go home to your family and tell them how much the Lord has done for you, and how he has had mercy on you."*

(Mark 5:18-19 NIV)

As soon as I finished that sentence, I stopped, looked up and said out loud, "God, I can do that! Please help Doreen get better and I *will* tell everyone I can."

God answered my prayer that night, so here we are now with my promise. It took me a long time to figure out how I was going to be able to keep my word with Him. But I finally concluded that telling our whole story to whoever wanted to hear, sharing it through these pages, would be the best way for me to proclaim God's mercy and amazing grace.

I must admit though, there were many times when I wasn't sure if I could continue writing, and the tears and raw emotion consumed those moments. After a few deep breaths, my mind usually came to the question "God why…?" Throughout this whole journey I never asked the question: *God why did You let this happen?* Instead, my question to Him was always: "God *why* have You blessed me so much?" That question helped get me through all those months, and I used that same question again to help me get through writing this story. I never questioned His intentions. Remember this: God has *never* used the word "oops".

I thought I had always trusted God. I heard and read about how you should "trust God" for years and years. I was baptized and had gone from kindergarten to eighth grade at St. Peter Lutheran Church & School, got married and baptized my children at the same church, and had gone to a few different Lutheran churches up until now. I even read my daily devotional book. There were consistent reminders to trust God every step of the way.

Throughout all those years, I had become so accustomed to trusting God that I should be an expert, or at least a knowledgeable believer. But the words became so familiar that: 1) I got complacent and didn't pay attention to what the actual true meaning was to trust God, and 2) There were no actions on my part showing my trust in God. There were many times over the years where Doreen and I, or just me, really needed God's help for one reason or another, and my timing to trust Him then was very convenient for me. And, for the most part, things pretty much always worked out okay. Maybe not exactly the timing I wanted, or the exact outcome I wanted, but we/I were able to get through whatever the situation was at the time.

That worked for over sixty years, so I had to be trusting God in the "right" way, right? Well…it's not that there is really a wrong way to trust God, unless you don't believe, and then it doesn't really matter for you.

For me, the real test of my faith and trust started on August 21st, 2021. This time though, unlike all the others, I had to reach down to the depths of my very soul to learn that invaluable lesson. That is the part of your soul where you are completely vulnerable and humble, and where you are the closest to God. The reason I believe that comes from this saying that touched me years ago, which continues to keep me centered of who I really am. Once again, I heard this on one of those cassettes a long time ago, and I remember it going something like this:

> We are not *Human Beings* here on this earth having a spiritual experience. Rather, we are *Spiritual Beings* here on this earth having a human experience.

I believe those two sentences sum up who we really are. Our journey, this human experience we just went through, has only strengthened that belief because we truly are spiritual beings. That is where God communicates to us, through our soul. He certainly touched mine. You see, up until that moment when I was sitting on the couch and cried out "I got nothing left," I had been trusting God through my human prism or what I thought trusting God meant. It took me a while to grasp the meaning of those two words on that night, because it felt different in my heart like never before. His plan continued. He touched my soul with a deeper meaning, calling my faith to submit to: *Trust God's timing. Trust God's delays.* I later discovered those six words (to me at least) are at the very core of trusting God. God's timing for literally everything *is* perfect, and God's delays *are* always placed perfectly, even if we don't understand them. The bottom line is: **God is perfect.** That truth is where *all* our trust in Him should come from.

****

I will leave you with this final thought.

****

We are all unique individuals who experience life in infinite different ways. Since we all live in this sinful world, you never know what might lie just around the corner. It may be something great or maybe something tragic. Tragedies can come in all forms, sizes and circumstances. Whatever the intensity, one thing is for certain; You will have to deal with it. From our life altering experience, I can only offer anyone this advice:

Don't wait until a tragedy comes into your life before you look for, or hope to find, God's love and blessings. His **endless love** and His **amazing grace** are already here…and <u>always</u> have been.

Trust God!

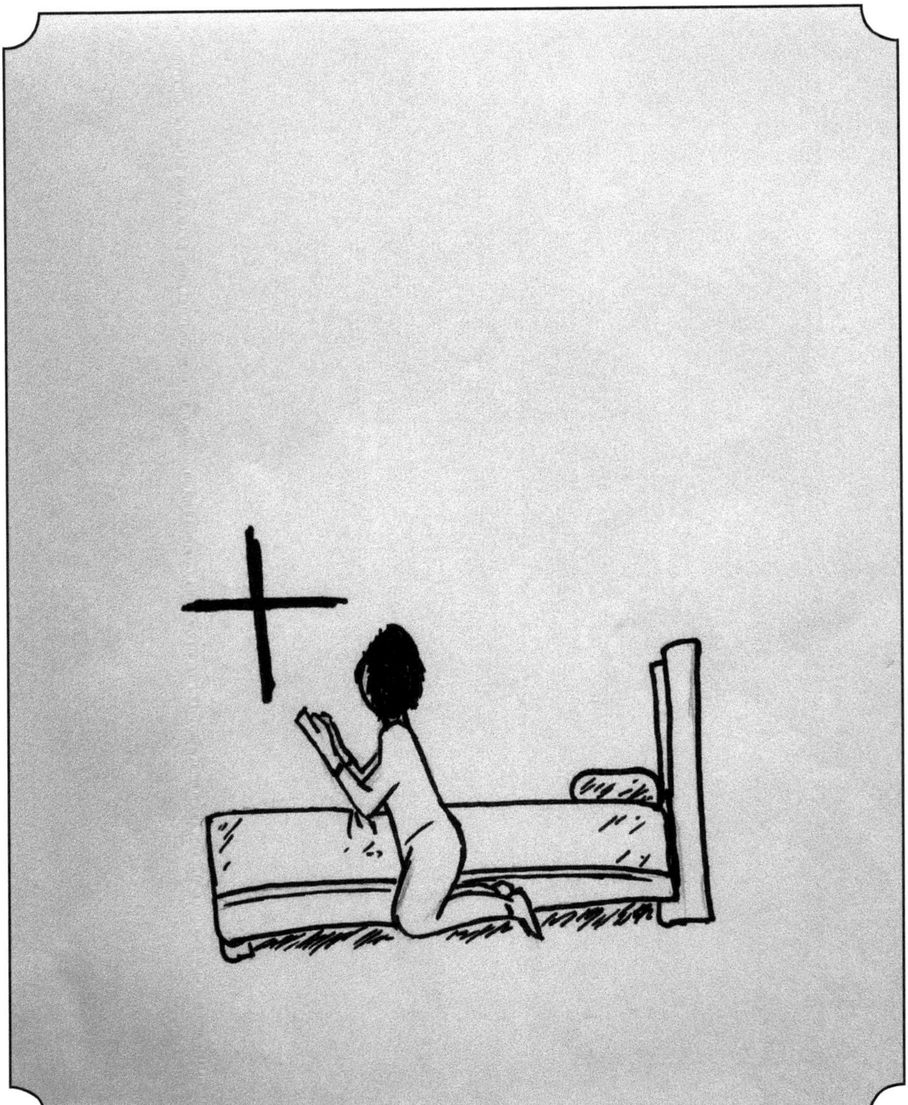

The Closing

My humble prayer…

"**Hey God, it's** me again. Where do I begin to truly express my gratitude which comes from being so blessed beyond my comprehension? Maybe I should start by saying thank You from the bottom of my heart and soul for letting Doreen and I continue again on our path together towards You. May Your love, grace and mercy continue to carry us through the rest of our days on this earth. Although we were on different paths during this same journey, we ended in the same Light where we humbled and submitted our wills to Yours. It was **Your will** and **Your plan** that was perfectly executed, which put the *right people, in the right place, at the right time.* **Everything** happened **exactly** the way it was **supposed** to. We know that to be true because of what *You* have done in our faith. We ask You to bless, keep and let Your face shine upon every soul that helped and participated throughout our journey. Most of all, thank You for sending Your Son Jesus who is *the only key* to Your kingdom. I know this wasn't really about *our* story, but *His*. If it is Your will God, I ask that You use the words in this book to touch the minds and hearts of whoever reads them and use it to draw those souls closer to You. I'm sorry it took me over sixty years to express them. So, whatever the future holds, I trust in *You* Lord. Thank You, Thank You, Thank You for being our awesome God, and especially for Doreen's Miracle! Amen."

This Blessing will be missed...
In Loving Memory of
Smokey

August 6, 2020 – December 28, 2023

Dogs are a unique blessing from God. They are living examples of what unconditional love and devotion look like. They bring a special joy and comfort that can truly touch your heart and soul like few things can. God's plan included placing Smokey and Bandit in our life with the distinct purpose of helping Doreen and I get through the darkest journey of our lives. I know His plan was perfect, and yet I still don't understand it all. Those two were not only my "prayer pups", but they also brought pure joy and motivation to Doreen. I can still hear her say "My puppies" as I watched her physically perk up every time I showed her their pictures. That was an amazing blessing to witness, and we will never forget how our "Smokey-Doodle" touched our lives. His soft gentle soul could be felt every time we looked into his eyes. We will miss him greatly, but we know we will see him again some day. Yes, we believe all good dogs go to Heaven. We love you Smokey!